neuman
8/09

Hallmark

For Liz, whose love has changed my whole life.

'Life is a mystery to be lived! Not a problem to be solved!

– Popplewell after Kierkegaard

HALLMARK

A Judge's Life at Oxford

Oliver Popplewell

I.B. TAURIS

LONDON · NEW YORK

Published in 2009 by I.B.Tauris & Co. Ltd
6 Salem Road, London W2 4BU
175 Fifth Avenue, New York NY 10010
www.ibtauris.com

Distributed in the United States and Canada Exclusively by Palgrave Macmillan,
175 Fifth Avenue, New York NY 10010

ISBN: 978 1 84511 781 8

A full CIP record for this book is available from the British Library
A full CIP record for this book is available from the Library of Congress
Library of Congress catalog card: available

Typeset in New Baskerville by Dexter Haven Associates Ltd, London
Printed and bound in Great Britain by CPI Antony Rowe, Chippenham

FSC
Mixed Sources
Product group from well-managed
forests and other controlled sources

Cert no. SGS-COC-2953
www.fsc.org
© 1996 Forest Stewardship Council

CONTENTS

ILLUSTRATIONS

FOREWORD

Stephen Fry

They say the world is getting old. What might be regarded as a self-evident truth by the rest of us seems to have arrived with something of the force of a revelation to marketing men and women. What they mean by an aging world is of course an aging consumer: the silver surfer, the *Saga Magazine* subscriber with money in his or her pocket and a renewed appetite for life, sensation and self-improvement. In the late 1940s and early 50s the teenager was the great marketing discovery. Well, now that same bobby-soxer or that bobby-soxer's boyfriend is past the age of retirement and looking to do something more than mow the lawn and hang around shopping centres in elastic-waisted trousers getting all cross about apostrophes.

If the British senior has a poster child, a hero, a role model, a glittering silver icon, then surely it should be Oliver Popplewell. The story in these pages of how he swapped his judicial robes for an undergraduate's gown will surely stand as an inspiration to all of those who, newly arrived at or fast approaching retirement, need to know that life has not yet yielded up its secrets.

Combining the hectic and amusingly far from glamorous life of chaperone to a movie star granddaughter with that of Oxford fresher, our spry hero chronicles his life with an irresistible blend of shrewd observation, puzzled innocence, self-deprecating candour and comic resignation. But we cannot be fooled: only an individual equipped with a strong, strong will, phenomenal powers of concentration and a formidable brain would be capable of achieving what Oliver has achieved. His reward? The journey itself, undoubtedly, but happily for him, romance too.

It may not be given to many to fulfil their retirement dreams with a success as spectacular as his, but he has shown the way. The requisite qualities of modesty, charm and openness to experience which won him his treasured prizes also make him the perfect companion along the way. Having known Oliver all my life I can only say that when I grow up I would like to be just like him.

1

Judicial Senility

On 15 August 2002, when I reached the age of seventy-five, I became judicially senile. On 14 August I could have tried any case involving millions of pounds and dealt with the worst sort of murders. On 15 August I would not have been allowed to try even a careless driving case. What then to do?

I had always been interested in by-elections, so, as my previous book *Benchmark* (an autobiography subtitled *Life, Laughter and the Law*) was in the publishers' hands, I thought it would be amusing to write another book about by-elections. To start with I decided that I would select three or four of the best-known by-elections before the Second World War, which were St George's, Westminster, East Fulham and Oxford. Having written those three chapters, I would then turn to by-elections during the war and by-elections such as Orpington, post-war. To begin my research it seemed sensible to go to the newspapers of the day.

To that end I sought out the Inner Temple librarian to secure access to *The Times* newspapers of the 1930s. They were housed in a basement and I caused considerable problems because somebody from the library had to go and open up the basement and then lock it up after me. However, it was necessary in order to start the research and so I persisted. I spent about four or five painstaking weeks on this exercise and was optimistic about putting something sensible to paper. I also acquired a considerable library of politicians' reminiscences and political biographies. In one of the political biographies I came across the bibliography which revealed that Professor Butler at Nuffield College, and his team from there, had already written a book about British by-elections. They were, of course, the experts in this field. I obtained a copy of the book and realised that it covered almost all the by-elections with which I would want to deal, certainly up to the 1950s. The book had obviously been carefully researched, and was full of detailed commentary about the consequences of the result. It seemed to me that if I were to produce a similar volume, albeit dealing with some by-elections after the 1950s, I would be covering much of the same ground. It would not have the scholarship of Professor Butler's book, and, even if ever produced, would be unlikely to have much of a sale. Accordingly that project fell to the ground.

In September 2002 I was asked if I would take Fred, one of my grandsons, to Australia. Fred was taking part in *Peter Pan*, a film being made south of Brisbane in which he had the part of Michael Darling. He had no previous acting experience and he came to get the part in a rather curious way. His older sister, Anna, had been in a number of films including Daphne du Maurier's *Frenchman's Creek*, and Nancy Mitford's *Love in a Cold Climate.* She was invited along to an audition to play Wendy in *Peter Pan* and Fred was sent along with her, because there was no-one to look after him at home. He was told to keep out of the way and not to be a bother. Anna was regarded as too sophisticated to be Wendy but the producer then asked Fred whether he would be interested in being auditioned. Fred's experience of acting at that stage was nil and he was somewhat indifferent about the whole idea. Anyway, they auditioned him for the part, which they then offered him.

It was necessary for there to be a chaperone, not only to take him out to Australia but also to accompany him on the set. Neither of his parents was able to get away from work and accordingly I flew out with Fred to Surfer's Paradise, about forty miles south of Brisbane on the Gold Coast. Here the film was going to be shot. Fred was then aged seven and his mother had equipped him, because he was a very keen sportsman, with all that was necessary for him to play cricket – helmet, bat, batting gloves, white flannels, box, pads and boots – so that if he were to play any cricket in Australia he would be fully equipped. The film people were enormously friendly and looked after Fred and the other children marvellously well. One weekend they arranged to have a barbeque on the beach which would include some surfing and, as they said, a possibility of some beach cricket. At about 7 am on the Sunday when this entertainment had been arranged, Fred came into my hotel room. He was wearing his helmet, batting gloves, pads, box, boots and white flannels and was all ready to play. I explained as tactfully as I could that it was unlikely that the other children would be so equipped and that, if he wore that kit on the beach, it might well get damaged. Somewhat reluctantly, therefore, he shed his gear. We had a splendid day on the beach. There was in fact no cricket but Fred was proudly able to use his gear when he joined a local club and played proper cricket with some under-nine-year-old Australians.

On my return to England I began to consider what I was now going to do. I needed something that would occupy my mind, be interesting and would involve seeing people. Having been left a widower for some two years, I regarded these things as essential in order to make life bearable. I was grumbling to myself about not being able to write my book on by-elections and thinking about the politics involved, when it occurred to me that I might go and read politics at Oxford University. PPE, or Politics, Philosophy and Economics, is a course which does not, as far as I know, have an equivalent elsewhere. When I had been at Cambridge reading law I had often gone with John Vaizey, later Lord Vaizey and a distinguished economist, to economics lectures which I had much enjoyed – not least because there was no exam that had to be taken at the end of them. They were given by Professor Joan Robinson who was well known for her radical views. The lectures were fraught with danger, because she had the habit of suddenly pointing at a student and asking him or her a singularly difficult question. Not being in the Economics Faculty, I dreaded lest my ignorance should be displayed.

I therefore rang up the Admissions Office at Oxford to find out whether I, as a some-time graduate from Cambridge, could take a postgraduate course. I was told that there was no postgraduate PPE but that I could apply as a 'mature student'. Mature students seemed to encompass those who had had a previous degree, or who had been doing a job, and now wanted some further education. They would be doing the same course as undergraduates who were 'not mature'. There was, however, a certain urgency about this application, because according to the information provided by the Admissions Office, applications for entry had to be in within ten days.

I talked with the Admissions people about where I should apply. The form left it up to me to decide, although it was also possible to leave it to the Admissions organisation. Harris Manchester, of which I have to confess I had never heard, was one of two colleges which took mature students. Originally called Manchester College, it had arrived at Oxford from Manchester in the late nineteenth century as a religious college. It had successively become a Hall of Residence and then, in the 1990s, part of the University. Lord Harris, the carpet magnate, had generously contributed to the college in memory of his son and his name was joined to that of the college. I was constantly reproved by the Admissions people for referring to the entrance as postgraduate entrance when mature student was the magic phrase. It seemed to me that while there were other well known and distinguished colleges, it was with other mature students that I would want to associate. I did not wish to find myself sitting at dinner in Hall with young people who were scarcely older than my grandchildren! Accordingly, I selected Harris Manchester as my first choice, and left the choice of other colleges to the Admissions people.

My application for admission required me to provide a fee of £10 and also a document setting out my previous degrees at Cambridge. In addition, I was required to provide three references to speak about my intellectual capacity. As all my tutors were now long dead and gone, this was not a very easy request to fulfil but Lord Justice Schieman and Sir Philip Otton, who had known me both at the Bar and on the Bench, were kind enough to write confidential reports, as indeed did the Hon. Michael Beloff QC who was Master of Trinity. It seemed to me that having the support of the head of a college would do no harm. Their references were provided in a sealed envelope marked 'Private and Confidential' and the contents were therefore withheld from me, although I was intrigued to know what they had written.

In addition, I was required to provide two pieces of written work in English of 2000 words each, written within the last few years. I doubted whether any of my judgements would qualify for this or indeed would be sufficiently appropriate for the subject I was taking. As it happened, I had comparatively recently given the Tom Olsen Lecture at St Bride's Church, the title of which was 'The Arrogance of Power'. In it I gave particular examples of power exercised by politicians, the media and lawyers, limiting the ambit of the lecture so as not to include contemporary examples, as I had had no wish to end up back in court, at the wrong end of a defamation action, and as a litigant rather than as judge.

This lecture was readily reducible into two parts of written work of some 2000 words each and while it did not deal very much with economics, it certainly dealt with politics and philosophy. I was further required to set out the reasons why I wished to come to Oxford and to read PPE. I explained about my interest in politics and that, when at Cambridge, I had gone with John Vaizey to a number of economics lectures which had interested me. I also mentioned that, in the course of my classical education, I had read a number of works of philosophy in Greek and Latin – but not that this was all so long ago that I could hardly remember the names of the works involved or who had written them. It all sounded very vague and airy-fairy and I envied those of my grandchildren who had classes at school to coach them in the art of composing personal statements, but I sent off all the material nonetheless, and sat back, waiting to see what would happen. A few weeks later I received a note from the college saying that they had now completed their preliminary assessment of my application and were pleased to confirm that I was invited to attend for an interview at Oxford. I was given a time for the interview with a dire warning about the disadvantages of arriving late. They indicated that I would be set a written exam and they kindly included a specimen of a previous exam. I duly attended at the college. I was taken in tow by one of the students who explained to me what university life was like. I didn't really have the heart to explain to him that I had been through this before, but he was very helpful and I was grateful to have something to take my mind off the forthcoming exam and interviews.

Mid-morning I was ushered into a room where there were twenty or thirty other students, not all of whom were reading PPE. After some preliminary guidance, the exam papers were handed out. We were allowed fifteen minutes' reading and then we were off. I had always been quite good at taking exams but I had certainly not done one for well over fifty years and viewed the whole process with considerable apprehension. However, I managed to complete the exam within the time allowed and felt I had not made too bad a shy at it.

I was then sent off to have lunch, after which I was to meet up with the three tutors and be interviewed by them. Before the interview I was to be provided with a sheet of paper on which some question was written and I was required at the interview to argue both sides of the case. This did not have any very great qualms for me, as I had spent my life doing precisely that. The subject of the argument was whether top-up fees were a good thing or not. I was not sure whether my tutors would think that it was very important that Oxford University should remain elitist and that places should go to those with the highest qualifications. Or perhaps they still had traces of the 1960s' philosophy and would think that Oxford should be available to all and sundry and that there should be discrimination in favour of those whose education had been rather modestly provided by the state.

There then followed the interview itself in which the three tutors sat on one side of the room in three separate chairs and I sat in a single chair on the other side. It was rather like *Mastermind* – except that I knew very little about any of my 'specialist subjects'. First of all I had to argue both points of view on top-up fees, which I did without getting a hint from the tutors as to which argument they preferred. This was somewhat disconcerting. They then each respectively proceeded to ask me questions about their particular subject. This was not a dialogue. I answered the question asked, whereupon they each wrote down something on a piece of paper and looked at each other meaningfully, but made no comment. One tutor having finished his particular questioning, I was passed over to the next one. They all seemed terribly clever and very young. I don't know whether they were more frightened of me than I was of them, but it was a nerve-wracking experience and I began to understand what it must be like to be in the witness box.

The next port of call was to see the Principal of Harris Manchester, the Reverend Dr Ralph Waller, who appeared to be in his late forties and therefore much the same age as my own children. However, he put me very much at ease and we had an interesting discussion about life in general and university education in particular, and then he asked me a good number of questions about myself. At the end of this interview he observed that, while I had the same chance as all the other applicants, I had to understand that the philosophy of Harris Manchester was to send their pupils out into the world so that they could usefully contribute to the general weal of society. I wanted to comment that, when I left Harris Manchester, I should be something like seventy-nine years old and I rather felt that I had made my contribution to society over the previous fifty years. However, luckily I forbore to make that observation and left, having being told that I should get the results some time before Christmas.

Thereafter I rushed down to the post every morning to see whether there was a brown envelope. Finally on 19 December, a large brown envelope arrived. The thickness of the envelope led me to believe that it was an acceptance, which indeed it was. The papers included all sorts of interesting information, including regulations against harassment and against keeping any firearm, ammunition or other offensive weapons. Additionally there was a good deal of documentation about the necessity of providing guarantees for payment of the fees and a suggestion that it would be prudent to apply for a Local Authority Grant. The Chairman of the Local Council was a personal friend of mine and I thought it would cause some considerable disquiet if I made the application. In any event, the County Council were only offering loans.

My acceptance at Oxford University caused a good deal of hilarity among my children, who asked what I was going to do in my gap year, whether I was going to go to the Freshers Ball and whether I would like them to come and take me out at weekends. They also opened a book in which I was 40–1 against being President of the Student Union, 80–1 against being President of the Union and 1000–1 against getting another Cricket Blue. I riposted that I was going to take out a student loan, repayable in fifty years' time.

When my colleagues and friends heard of it, their reactions were mixed. Some thought it the most astonishing thing, others were full of praise and yet others said they thought I was very brave. I remembered *Yes, Minister* in which Sir Humphrey Appleby was always saying to his Minister, 'That was a brave decision' – which would cause the Minister to turn white and have serious second thoughts.

Meanwhile, I was invited by my son and daughter-in-law to accompany my granddaughter Anna to Luxembourg where she was taking part in the film of the novel *The Girl with the Pearl Earring*. Although I had taken her brother Fred out to Australia to film in the previous autumn without any difficulty, I was told I needed to apply for a licence to act as a chaperone. This gave rise to a good deal of bureaucratic nonsense which caused me to write to *The Times*. My letter read:

One of my grandchildren has a small part in a film. My son and daughter-in-law, who are busy working, have asked me to chaperone her on location abroad.

It might be thought that their consent would be sufficient. That would be too simple. This is Government-directed. I have to apply for a licence from the County Council, fill in forms and attend at the offices of the Children's Education Welfare Department for an interview. I have to identify on a form two referees and they each have to fill in their own forms. I have to explain on my form my experience of children. Having had five children and 12 grandchildren I believe I can surmount this hurdle.

Identity is more difficult; a simple passport photo is not enough. I must also produce my passport. Is that enough? No, remember this is a nanny state. I also have to produce my driving licence. Is that enough? Of course not. I am now required to attend at the offices again, armed with a bank statement or similar to prove I am who I say I am. These are merely the preliminaries to police approval.

Part of the form requires me to give my mother's maiden name. She died over 20 years ago aged nearly 90. They have not yet asked for her birth certificate, but I wouldn't bet against it.

On 17 November 2002 the *Sunday Telegraph* published an article about it all with the headline 'Judge is told he needs licence to take grandchild on trip abroad'. My letter occasioned a good deal of merriment among my friends and also gave rise to a number of letters from carping correspondents, which judges often receive in the course of their judicial duties. They ended up in the waste paper basket. But, despite my ridiculing of the red-tape process, the Council finally gave me a licence and off I went to Luxembourg to chaperone Anna.

The next step in my progress towards being a student was an introductory day provided by the college to enable those unfamiliar with academic life to meet with the dons and their fellow students, and to acclimatise themselves to the atmosphere of university life. We were told that if we felt in any way nervous about this procedure we could bring either a friend or a parent to help reduce the anxiety about coming up. My children helpfully offered to come with me but I thought this would be more of a hindrance than a help.

Meanwhile I pursued the quest of attempting to get my book *Benchmark* sold. Lord's, the famous cricket ground, has a very good bookshop and it was willing to sell as many books as I could provide and also to allow me to have a signing session. The authorities at Lord's were also entirely willing to make an announcement over the tannoy that there would be signed books in the bookshop although I was in somewhat stiff competition with Michael Atherton, the former English captain.

Unfortunately, for some reason which I could never fathom, the bookshop only received three or four copies of my book from my publishers, and so the idea of my having a signing was hopeless. This sadly happened on a number of occasions and so a great opportunity for marketing the book was lost. When I went to the bookshop I saw a young lady looking through my book. I couldn't make up my mind whether to say anything, and see whether she bought it, or to wait and see whether she put it back on the shelf. In the end, I told her that I was the author, that it was a very good book and that she ought to buy it, but I still suspect she put it back on the shelf. Like all authors in bookshops, I found that the place where my books were being exhibited did not command the first-class position that I considered my literary efforts justified. However, I also discovered that with very little effort on my part, a rather elderly book about Botham could easily be moved into my space and my book could occupy his space. Whether this had any marked effect on sales I have never found out.

But I was much encouraged when I received a kind invitation from Richard Ingrams, the editor of *The Oldie* magazine, to attend a literary lunch. *The Oldie*, as its name implies, is aimed at fifty-plus-year-olds and other young people. It has a literary lunch once a month when three authors are invited to attend, sign books and sing for their supper. My companions included Claire Tomalin, who had written a definitive book on Pepys (*Samuel Pepys: The Unequalled Self*) with which she won the Whitbread Prize. This was somewhere way above the scholastic quality of *Benchmark* but it seemed to me that my appearing on the scorecard with her would attract an audience who might otherwise have never heard of *Benchmark*. The other author was John Michel who had just written an autobiography.

Accordingly I went along at 12 o'clock to Simpson's where, after a number of drinks, the three of us authors sat down behind a wooden table with our books on display behind. If somebody wanted to buy a book, he or she went to one corner of the room where helpful literary-looking ladies could sell the chosen book to them; he or she then presented it to the particular author to get it signed. Claire Tomalin had already signed about seventy of her books before the first purchaser of mine came along. I had begun to feel rather neglected. However, when this purchaser presented his book for me to sign, I asked him, as I always did, what he would like me to write. He said that his name was 'John

Johnson'. So I was about to sign 'with best wishes to John Johnson' when he said, 'You don't remember me do you?' There then ensued the following conversation. 'No, I don't, I'm sorry to say, remind me.' 'I appeared in front of you some years ago.' 'Really, what was that about?' I asked. 'I was suing the Stock Exchange.' 'Did you win?' I said. 'No,' he replied. So I then asked him how he would like me to inscribe his book. He said, 'To John Johnson. Sorry.' I put a couple of exclamation marks after the word 'sorry' in case he thought I was being serious, and might rush off to the Court of Appeal. We had an exceedingly good lunch and I think it did something for the sales. The following month *The Oldie* was kind enough to say how much they had enjoyed having us all.

I attended a number of functions where I spoke and talked very boringly about the book and people were good enough to say that they had enjoyed reading it. I'm not sure that that enjoyment was necessarily reflected in the sales. Indeed my ardour was somewhat dimmed when I went to Blackwell's in Oxford, which had been very kind in promoting my books, and found that it had a good number in stock, some of which had not been signed. I asked the lady in charge whether she would like me to autograph some more and she went to find out how many there were. She came back and said, 'Well, don't autograph more than three or four, in case we have to send the remainder back.' It was only after she had said this, and seen the look on my face, that she realised quite what she had said and was sweetly apologetic. I went into Waterstone's to see if the same had occurred there. They were, I'm afraid, rather stuffy and although they looked up the name of my book on their computer, they purported never to have heard of it and declined to answer any further enquiries about it.

2

Golden Summer and Oxford

The summer of 2003 was one of those golden summers when the sun never stopped shining, when I seemed perpetually on holiday and when any idea of work seemed very remote. I fell in love with a woman over twenty years younger than me, who, somewhat to my surprise, appeared to think that the whole idea was a very good thing. Television and radio stations were keen to interview me, despite what some might have thought were the antiquated and stereotypical nature of the views of a retired High Court judge. Life as a seventy-six year old (surely not, really) was self-indulgent and heady.

Off I went to the opera at Garsington and Glyndebourne, to the mockery of my children, who knew that the New Seekers were much more my cup of cultural tea than Richard Strauss or Wolfgang Amadeus. It was my first visit to Glyndebourne, invited by my new friend, Liz Gloster QC, whose attentions, luckily for me, did not seem to be wholly directed at the musical entertainment. The opera was *The Marriage of Figaro*, which seemed a bit near the bone, but I did not think that it was perhaps for me to voice that particular connection. I spent several days at Lord's, including one splendid day with all the grandchildren in a box. Three of the granddaughters arrived with the latest Harry Potter book, which had just been published that morning. They sat in the front row obsessively devouring it, while the boys devoted themselves to the cricket. I thought, perhaps rather uncharitably, that the next year the girls might not get invited.

I went with Andrew (my second son and a QC) and his doctor wife, Debs, to Madrid for a weekend. There we saw some lovely pictures, ate extremely well and discovered that a whole bottle of sherry between three of us caused no pain, particularly if accompanied by a good deal of ice. Andrew and Debs were somewhat mystified by my recurrent trips to the lavatory at the Prado and the Thyssen galleries, until, as Debs subsequently told me many months later, she overheard me bellowing sweet nothings down my mobile phone to Liz. But Debs, discreetly, said nothing at the time, although she was agog to know who was the recipient of this surprising (for me) display of affection.

I then spent a lovely week staying with Liz and her then husband, Stanley Brodie (also a successful QC) at a villa she had taken at Porto Ercole, on the Monte Argentario, in Tuscany which was pure lotus eating. Liz was one of the outstanding advocates of her generation, very pretty and full of charm. More of her anon. There was a swimming pool, food prepared by staff, a yacht with a crew and an engaging group of people who came and went. The only decisions to be made were whether to have red or white wine at lunch and that problem was readily solved by having both. Another guest, Willie Goodhart QC (a Liberal Democrat peer and an authority on Constitutional Law), attempted to keep our minds in gear by eliciting our (albeit, in my case, crustacean) views on the proposed Judicial Appointments Commission and I received delectable invitations to stay from two attractive widows who had castles in Ayrshire. We were joined by Christopher Chataway and his wife, Carola. He was a great athlete in his youth and was one of Roger Bannister's pacers when the latter ran the four-minute mile. He put us all to shame by running great distances early every morning and being enormously fit. I didn't somehow think that I was going to be emulating his septuagenarian athletic prowess when I went up to Oxford.

Then I went on to have somewhat of a more bracing holiday in Norfolk, with number four son, Ed and his wife Clare, and their three children, teaching them to sail. Unbeknownst to me, this set of children were also monitoring my frequent mobile phone calls. Months later Clare told me that, when I left my phone charging in the kitchen, they would secretly scroll down my dialled calls to see whether I was ringing the unknown recipient, 'Liz' yet again. I also holidayed in Normandy with my eldest son, Nigel, his wife, Inge, and their three children, where we discovered that our Enterprise, 14-foot fibre-glass sailing dinghy, which had lain idle for six or seven years, was still perfectly serviceable. These grandchildren also began to learn to sail, but their instantly acquired self-reliance quickly enabled them to reject the didactic bellows of their grandfather.

I then went to stay with my friends, the Burbages, in their house at Cap Ferret, in Bordeaux. David and his wife Sandra (but always known

1   Harris Manchester College

as S) I had first met when he was High Sheriff of the West Midlands and we had become firm friends. Apart from running a very successful firm making kitchen furniture, he was heavily involved with the Cathedral at Coventry and with the RSC at Stratford. He was deservedly awarded an OBE for his services to the community. I got to the right part of France without too much difficulty but found myself hopelessly lost trying to find their house and had to be rescued. SatNav had not yet arrived on my horizon. Their house, whose garden stretched down to the Arcachon Bassin, had the most idyllic view. The house was extremely comfortable and they provided generous hospitality. They had always taken a holiday house there, but had seen this particular house – an old shooting lodge – some years before, liked it, and spent a year doing it up, traditionally, but quite beautifully. David and I went over to Lynch Bages to look around the châteaux and to buy some wine. Driving through the vineyards of Bordeaux is a remarkable experience, and we saw the grapes, starting to be picked because it was a very early year. It is easy to forget how close to each other these distinguished vineyards are, so that the Lafites and Latours of this world lie side by side with lesser vineyards whose products do not command the same attention. We sailed and drank and picnicked and enjoyed the September sunshine. It was only years later that S ticked me off for spending too much time on my mobile phone to an unknown Liz and not attending sufficiently to her house guests.

Back in England I was down to earth with a huge bump. Suddenly I had to prepare for my new life as a student (no longer realistically known as 'undergraduate') at Oxford. One lot of my children decided for my birthday to provide me with a whole series of small presents, which, when I opened them, revealed a pencil sharpener, a bar of soap, some Alka Seltzer, an alarm clock, a sewing kit, and other items necessary for an incipient undergraduate. One of the other children enquired whether the package had included some condoms. It did not.

Thus it was all set at the beginning of October for me to go to Oxford. I decided, because I had had so much hospitality from friends, that I ought to have a party. So I organised what I thought was a rather smartly named drinks party 'to celebrate the end of my gap year'. Everyone was very encouraging and wished me luck. On Tuesday 7 October I drove to Oxford to start my three-year study of PPE at Harris Manchester. I had had one rather shattering experience. Anne Ballard, who had been a student at Harris Manchester for two years, and who had just come down, had agreed to sell me her gown and mortar board. She lived locally. When I went to collect them from her she showed me *The Times Higher Education Supplement* with a front-page article about the so-called 'near bankruptcy' of Harris Manchester. There was also a full-length feature article in the middle of the paper, suggesting that Lord Harris had not come up with the requisite funds, that the college had totally mismanaged its financial affairs, and that the college might well be on the verge of bankruptcy. To say that this caused me some alarm would be an understatement. However when I wrote to Dr Lesley Smith, my senior tutor, to ask for leave of absence to go and conduct an arbitration at the end of October, I mentioned this. She wrote back to say that this was all old hat, that most of it was untrue, that the college had prepared a press release which she enclosed but which they had not put out, and that the situation was firmly under control. I breathed a sigh of relief.

When I arrive at college, I am allowed – with a special sticker – to park the car outside in order to unload. Parking in Oxford is otherwise an absolute nightmare, as is driving into the city. Luckily the Brunnings, who are the in-laws of my third son, Alexander, live in Summertown and kindly agreed to let me park my car there. This was a tremendous boon because otherwise I was not sure how I would get home to Buckinghamshire whenever I wanted to. I am shown to my room by the wife of the Principal. (This was a special privilege, which makes me feel cherished – but nonetheless old.) I realise immediately that this is not Trinity or Christchurch. I have a small room about 8 foot x 15 foot with a chest of drawers, wash basin, bed, writing table and a cupboard. There will be no question of my entertaining guests to sherry in my room as I did in Cambridge or more importantly of sitting up through the night with fellow students and putting the world to rights. Perhaps the latter is a bonus, because at my age I have to accept that my seeking to put the world to rights is a purposeless exercise. I meet up with the other students in Hall where the food is perfectly agreeable, although nothing very fancy. I suspect that there is no question of ever having a meal served in my room by the college butlers or ordering a drink from the Buttery.

We are provided with an induction programme which starts on the Wednesday and goes on for the whole of the first week. On Wednesday almost every moment of our day is organised. First, we meet the senior tutor, nice Dr Lesley Smith, who tells us what is expected of us. Then we meet the Dean and the Junior Dean, the academic Bursar, the Finance Officer, the Office Manager and the Housekeeper. We are all adjured to keep our doors firmly locked because of theft and, above all, not to smoke in our rooms. It's a bit different from my Cambridge days, when we only sported the oak when we wanted to be private. Otherwise we always left the door open. There was also a good deal of smoking – albeit of tobacco, rather than of anything more heinous.

Another difference between Oxford now, and Cambridge then, is the reliance on the computer. Julian, who is employed by the college for this purpose, is assigned to look at our laptops to make sure we haven't either got a virus or, more importantly, imported a virus into college. The technical knowledge of most of my fellow students is much to be admired. Apparently all the lectures are on the website now, which is an advantage over the good old days at Cambridge when you had to go to even the most boring of lectures in order to pick up the handout notes. My laptop, for some unknown reason, does not work very quickly, and is, therefore, taken off me and put into quarantine. We are then invited, in a sweet old-fashioned way, to take tea with our dons. I am again reminded how young they all are and how obviously fearfully clever. This is followed by a service in the Chapel which is poorly attended, followed by a full college meeting presided over by the Principal.

I discover that there are four of us in college reading PPE in my year. They are John White, a retired senior partner from the city firm of solicitors, Cameron McKenna, a young German student called Janis Finsberg, and Hannan Maayan from Israel. All the freshers are required to attend a meeting in one of the rooms in college where we are addressed by the Principal and the Senior Tutor, followed by the President of the Junior Common Room (JCR). The last of these was aged about eighteen or nineteen and extolled the virtues of the JCR Bar. The object of his address was to educate us about what life would be really like in the college. At the end he invited questions and I enquired about keeping terms. In my time at Cambridge, we not only had to go up to the University on day one and go back home on day sixty or so, but, if we spent a day away from the University (for which we had to have permission), we had to spend another day at the University. It transpired that there is nothing like that in present university life. The rule which existed in our day that girls had to be out of the room by 10 pm, has long since been abolished. Provided the student arrives on day one and leaves on day sixty, and attends the tutorials armed with an essay, he can, as far as I can make out, spend all term time in the Bahamas. That's not actually what I intend to do but it is an interesting insight into the change which has overtaken university life.

The subject of the college's financial position was much discussed. I was somewhat anxious that I should not make any payment of the fees until the position had been settled. The Principal dealt with this quite easily and pointed out that the article related to matters which had occurred some time before and that there was no question of the college not being able to meet its obligations. Indeed, he pointed out, the college was in a very healthy financial state. I was prompted to ask why, if that were the case, the college fees were not reduced, but refrained from doing so. In the room next to me, which I am told is one of the better rooms in college, is John White, marginally younger than me but from the same sort of generation.

The next morning, Thursday, we meet up with our tutors and get given our marching orders. The list of books to read is formidable, the subjects are very frightening, the exams, which are prelims, occur next term so there is not very much time to read and understand. It is also the time when we hand over our cheques to the college and to the University. I begin to understand how great the problem of finance is for most of the students. I am happily in a position to pay, but the college fees and the University fees are enormous and, even with a student loan, it is not easy for a lot of them. There are various grants available, but I suspect that a number of them will find it very difficult to make ends meet. The idea of fees being put up in 2006 is a horrendous one. I go and see Julian about my computer but it's still not ready. I cannot understand why my limited computer activity appears so seriously to have corrupted it. It is not as though I have been free-surfing around unsuitable websites, although my self-concocted spreadsheets for my wine collection may have spawned a few offending cookies that are not compatible with the Harris Manchester intra-net. On the Thursday night, Liz comes up from London to take me out to dinner. I have a good deal to drink and find that the steps back into the college seem to move surprisingly rapidly. But at least we did not have to climb back into the college over the high, wrought iron gates, as we would have had to have done at Cambridge.

On Friday I go to the Freshers Fair. It was not enough to take your student card (absolutely vital if you want to go anywhere in Oxford, and which provides a discount at certain shops); it was also necessary to have some other pass, which I didn't have, and so, like a naughty schoolboy, I was denied entry and sent back to obtain the formal piece of paper.

2 Working in the library

The Freshers Fair is like an Indian bazaar with three or four hundred gaily coloured stalls, each representing some different organisation. It was very crowded and badly displayed, but I ferreted out the bumph about the Oxford University Law Society and the University Rugby Club. I have to say that I passed on the Bullingdon Club and the Oxford University Labour Club. The Cambridge equivalent of the latter I had joined back in 1948, in a misguided attempt to save the world, and I was not sure that my undoubtedly sophisticated, albeit mature, social skills were quite what the young bloods of the Bullingdon were after. But the University Rugby Club was much more up my street.

As a member of the Hawks' Club, the Cambridge Sporting Club, I was already able, when visiting Oxford, to use the facilities of Vincent's, the Oxford Sporting Club. Upon my arrival in Oxford, I had written to the secretary of the latter to suggest that, as I was going to be a more or less permanent resident in Oxford, I quite appreciated that the reciprocal arrangements which governed the occasional visit of a Cantab. Hawk were perhaps not wholly appropriate for someone in my position. I therefore offered to pay some sort of subscription. I eventually received a reply that the matter was going to be considered by the committee. I await the result with some interest, because it would be very convenient to make use of the facilities at Vincent's. But, apart from the convenience, my vanity would be very much tickled by becoming an Honorary Member, which would enable me to wear what I regard as the best club tie in the business. I also mean to join the Food and Drink Society, which seems to be the right sort of society for a 'mature' student, but could not find its stall at the Fair. Perhaps I will make some further effort at a later date to join, if I have time from writing essays. I spent a busy weekend going to the High Sheriff Service at Milton Keynes, and then went to dine on high table with Robin Butler, the Master of University College. This was a most agreeable C.P. Snow type of occasion, if somewhat out of keeping with my humble undergraduate status.

On Monday, I begin work in real earnest. Rousseau and Mill are the two subjects with which we have to grapple. I find both of them exceedingly difficult. Writing essays on philosophical topics seems to be much harder work than anything I did on the Bench or at the Bar. The first tutorial on Wednesday with Lesley Smith was worthwhile. I go with the Israeli student, Hannan, who is articulate and knowledgeable, and it is a pleasure to listen to him. I am not sure whether he could say the same

19

about me. The pattern which Lesley Smith adopts is that one of us reads his essay, and then we both discuss it. Luckily, it was Hannan who had to read his essay this first week, which we then discussed, whereas I simply had to hand mine in on time. From time to time Lesley Smith turned to me and asked me a series of probing questions, some of which I could answer and some of which I couldn't. I slightly felt that I hadn't read my papers properly, which reminded me of those early days at the Bar when an unsympathetic judge looked at me and no doubt thought to himself, 'Why hasn't this chap read his brief?' Meanwhile we are all chasing the same books from the library, which is slightly tiresome. The cost of new books is quite prohibitive. The libraries are very good, but everybody is after the same books and the loan from the Faculty libraries is only for a short period. The catalogues are now on computer and, unless you can work the system, it takes hours to find what you want. The college librarian, Sue, could not be kinder in helping me locate things, but I still look in the old-fashioned hard-copy catalogue which for me is a much easier way of finding books. Meanwhile Julian has sorted out my laptop and very kindly spent an hour putting it all together. I then discovered that when I send a composite email message to 'the boys' (my four sons) it now goes to numerous other people in my electronic address book, but that is a small hiccough.

One or two of the lectures are exceedingly boring. The Economics course is particularly disappointing. I was really looking forward to it on the basis that we would discuss topics like the money supply, and what caused unemployment and interest rates to rise and fall. But these topics do not seem to be on the syllabus. This term we are studying micro-economics, which consists of analysing very tedious mathematical formulae. The college tutor is excellent but the lecturer is hopeless. I have therefore skipped his lectures, as has John White. I have got all the books and I shall just have to put a wet towel around my head and swot. My best supervisor at Cambridge always told me that the most important decision in one's first year is to identify which lectures one would be better missing for the sake of one's intellectual development, and spending the extra hour one was thereby afforded in bed with a good book.

I join the Oxford University Law Society and find that one of the meetings is at Trinity College, where Michael Beloff QC and barristers from Blackstone Chambers are going to tell us all about life at the Bar.

Not much, I fear, that I don't know about already. Later on Jonathan Aitken is coming down to talk. This may be quite an amusing meeting, since he appeared in front of me in his famous libel trial against the *Guardian* and I shall certainly go if I can. I am joining the University Rugby Club. They seem to have a good fixture list and the home games are mostly in the evening. John Prodger, whom I have known for a long time, is the Oxford Representative on the RFU and it will be agreeable to go with him to some of the matches. But I don't somehow see myself being trialled for the University side.

I have not brought my television set here yet, partly because I am not quite sure whether it will work, and partly because there simply hasn't been time to watch television. However, as the Rugby World Cup is on, it may be that my resolve will fade and I will spend an evening or two quietly watching the box. I was a member of the Oxford University Real Tennis Club in Merton Street some while ago, before I came to the University, and I decide that that would be a good way of getting some exercise. So I have booked a court for next week to have a lesson and I hope, not only that I shall get a bit of exercise, but that I may meet one or two people of my own age against whom to play. It happened that, when I went to the court, I found Lesley Smith there, playing with a foursome who were both nearer my age and showing a similar lack of skill.

Meanwhile I have written to the editor of the *Oxford Mail* to see whether I could write a column for them. Liz suggested that I ought to write a weekly column. I have the feeling that she thinks I should syndicate my contribution to *Country Life*, if not the *New York Herald Tribune*. We shall see what that produces. I have also written to the Director of BBC Radio Oxford to see whether they will be interested in my views about contemporary life in Oxford. I suspect they will not. Anyway, as they say, 'Watch this space!'

There is an old joke of the young student asking his tutor what the rules at Oxford are. When he is told that there are no rules, he is very pleased. He is then told by the tutor that if he breaks any of them he will be sent down! Life at Oxford seems to bear this out. Everything is very free and easy. Christian names are de rigueur. Everybody communicates by email, and jackets and ties seem only to be worn on very high days and holidays. It is taking me a considerable time to identify my fellow students. They all greet me as 'Oliver' and I simply reply, 'Hi!'

One of the more idiotic Oxford occasions occurs on the third Saturday after we go up. This is what is called matriculation. It is explained to us that this is when we join the University. As we have been at the University now for some three weeks and have paid a considerable amount of money to the University for that privilege, it seems a bit bizarre. It is, however, compulsory, so, on a nice autumn Saturday morning, we all parade, dressed up in dark suits and white tie, gowns and a mortar board, for this strange ceremony. We go, as a college, to the Sheldonian where the freshers from other colleges are also assembled. We bring the whole of the traffic in Oxford to a grinding halt. Once assembled outside the Sheldonian we march in, to find an organ playing wildly inappropriate military music. After being seated, we are addressed by the Vice-Chancellor on how important it is to take advantage of whatever is on offer at Oxford. A part of this is conducted in Latin, which makes the ceremony even more bizarre. Having endured this charade for three-quarters of an hour, we return to college where we have to have a team photograph. There is no escaping this because everybody's name is on a card. I confess I look very sulky, which I felt, and I don't think the photograph will be one of my treasured possessions.

I am afraid I behaved very badly. When we were standing outside the Sheldonian, some nice young girl from another college asked me whether it wasn't the most exciting day of my life. She told me how much she was looking forward to the occasion and that her parents were coming up specially to see her. She couldn't wait to be photographed with the rest of her fellow students. Rather unkindly, I told her that I had better things to do on a lovely Saturday morning, and that watching paint dry was probably more amusing than what we were doing. I felt thoroughly ashamed of myself afterwards for spoiling what was for her a very important day. After the photographs, the college was awash with swooning parents and admiring grandparents. I don't often make comparisons between Oxford and Cambridge, but at Cambridge we didn't have anything quite so silly as this, the nearest being the degree ceremony after the final exams, which, at least, had some purpose and was not compulsory.

We have two supervisions a week and, by and large, two lectures a day. Because I tend to go home at weekends and don't do a lot of work then, my essay writing is confined to five days. It is really very hard work. My fellow students seem to be equally hard-working but also very clever and the tutors are very encouraging. One of them told us that the first essay that we had written was very good. I suspect he did this in order to encourage us. We don't get marked, but we get serious comments which are very penetrating and make one feel somewhat intellectually insecure. The subjects which I'm doing leave no room for waffling, as I did when reading law at Cambridge and, although none of the subjects could be described as an exact science, the questions required very detailed and considered answers.

I hear nothing from the *Oxford Mail* but I am rung up by Rachel Johnson, the sister of Boris Johnson, sometime editor of *The Spectator*, to enquire whether she could do an article about me. I agree to do this and she comes down and we have a most entertaining morning. She asks thoroughly sensible and intelligent questions, as one would expect. We go out and have an extremely good lunch. Two days later the article appears in *The Spectator*. It is enormously friendly, describing my reasons for being here, the life I am leading and giving a gentle plug for *Benchmark*. Her article spawns a whole lot of other articles. The *Independent*, the next day, produces an article without consulting me and gets some of it wrong. The *Sunday Times* also does an article which is really an excerpt from Rachel's. Then various local newspapers, like the *Oxford Student*, *Cherwell* and the *Oxford Mail*, also produce articles. This, not unnaturally, gives rise to a good deal of amusement among my fellow students but it is all good publicity for *Benchmark*.

The *Sunday Times* want me to write an article about life at university for an edition at Christmas, and so too do the *Daily Telegraph*. I plainly cannot write a diary of my first term for both. Accordingly I opt for the *Sunday Times*. But is my life interesting enough? These are soul-searching questions. I am also invited by *The Times* to do a piece for them. This consists of being provided with half a dozen selected questions from readers, chosen by *The Times*, which I answer. This goes on their website. I then get a call from Carlton Television who want to interview me for a programme going out after the 6 o'clock news. All these interviews seem to require the attendance of a photographer and I spend most of one morning being photographed all around the college. Liz is extremely critical that, in the pictures, my very ordinary blue blazer turns out to be an amazing purple. Sartorial presentation, apparently, is the key to building up one's public persona. The Carlton interview is very sympathetic and fun and, again, they are kind enough to show me reading *Benchmark* and to give it a plug. The Principal is naturally delighted that Harris Manchester is getting good publicity, but I think that I have now milked my boring story of the 'Oldest Fresher in Town' to its full extent. I then get a call from *Saga*, who wants to do a piece for its Christmas magazine. This entails being photographed, yet again, for the best part of two or three hours. I am not sure that my bone-structure is up to it. *Saga* too is going to commission an article by Rachel Johnson, so let us hope that, once again, it will be kindly and well written. I feel quite vulnerable.

I go to a meeting of the Oxford University Law Society, where barrister members of Blackstone Chambers come and address the audience. I hadn't realised quite how difficult it now is to get a pupillage in Chambers, let alone a tenancy, for which a first-class degree is apparently a pre-requisite. I am quite satisfied that, if the present system of selecting pupils had existed in my day, I would still be in the Navy! I just wonder whether a good second-class degree might not sometimes produce a better, because more understanding, advocate. I am approached by the College Law Society, which is run by the clever young law don, Louise Gullifer, to talk to them, which I do. I have an audience of about thirty or forty, including some law students from other parts of the University. I give them a potted version of *Benchmark*, which I plug unmercifully. They ask intelligent questions and I encourage them to go to the Bar.

I take odd nights off, when I go home. This means on my return, leaving the house at about 6 o'clock to avoid traffic going in to Oxford, and to get to breakfast before lectures. My friends think that I am confined to barracks during the week. It is almost true because of the amount of work which I have to do. However, I am able to go and see *The Girl with the Pearl Earring* in which my granddaughter, Anna, appears. It is a most delightful film and has been very well reviewed. I have to confess to some disappointment because, although pictorially it is very attractive and the film follows the book very closely, the two major players, Vermeer and Griet, seem to me to be played one-dimensionally and the film lacks pace. I hope I am wrong because they were talking about Oscars but I should be astonished if the film makes an impact on the American market. We shall see. Anna's part was not very large and she never had many lines, but she was clearly identifiable.

Next week I have two excitements. Jonathan Aitken is coming to talk to the University Law Society and I am to conduct a moot at Trinity as a sort of thanks to Michael Beloff for all the help which he has given me. These moots are always full of very difficult legal questions, the answers to which have never been judicially resolved. The students naturally regard anything coming from a judge, even an elderly retired judge, as being the definitive answer. As I suspect, I am slightly out of touch with the current law and I regard the whole exercise with a good deal of apprehension. I have little doubt that listening to Jonathan Aitken will be more amusing. Having become Vice-Principals of the University Rugby Club (which involves no more than contributing a substantial sum by way of down payment), John White and I decide to go and see the University play Major Stanley's XV. We have beer and sandwiches before the match and then watch a cracking good game, in which the University, without a fair number of its blues, run rings around Stanley's XV. It is fine entertainment but I am not at all sure where my loyalties are going to lie for the Varsity match.

I am constantly asked what difference I find between my life at Oxford now and my life at Cambridge as an undergraduate. I have to point out that we are not comparing like with like. When I went up to Cambridge in 1948, the war was recently over but we lived under the constant threat of Russian aggression and of nuclear war. The Berlin air lift and the Korean war took place during my three years there. There was never a time when there wasn't constant anxiety about the future. Food continued to be rationed. Everything was in short supply and it was a time of considerable austerity. Because a lot of people had just come back from the war and were anxious to get on with life, it was, I suspect, a more serious community and more worldly wise.

Our tutors were, with some exceptions, much more elderly than they are today. There was an old joke that one of the history dons had gone over to America with the *Mayflower* and had now returned to teach American History in the college. I suspect that the quality of lectures was not much different but it is a great advantage to the indolent student that most of the lectures these days can be found on a website.

And in our day at Cambridge there were a lot of rules – gowns to be worn in the town, girls to be out of college rooms by 10 pm (as I've said); undergraduates to be in by 10 pm, and any staying out late or staying away for the night required special leave from the tutor. Whereas climbing in to college at Cambridge after 10 pm was common practice, it is quite unnecessary at Oxford. I have already mentioned the differences regarding security and smoking. Of course Harris Manchester is slightly different from the other colleges in that the students here are more mature and it may not be fair to compare life at Harris Manchester with our life at Cambridge.

Certainly the standard of games at Cambridge, because of everybody being that much older, was very much higher. Whereas in my University cricket side I was lucky to play with six or seven Internationals, now Cambridge are combined with a local college of learning – and Oxford with Oxford Brookes. The three-day Varsity match no longer takes place at Lord's. It must be a very long time since either of the universities really put up much of a show against the first-class counties. What is true in cricket is true in rugby and in athletics. There is more of a problem about the Boat Race. The universities allow Olympic oarsmen to take part in the Boat Race, seeking yet another bauble, instead of making it a race between genuine undergraduates. I have always felt that the Boat Race should be strictly an undergraduate race. It doesn't need graduates, as happens in football or rugby or cricket to enable the University to compete with visiting sides, because Oxford and Cambridge are simply rowing against each other. However, this particular view does not seem to have much support from the rowing hearties at Vincent's and I conclude that it might be better to keep my opinion on this particular topic to myself in the future.

3

Settling Down

After the first fortnight or so of term, I settle into a gentle routine. I get up about 7.30 am. Breakfast is at 8, and lectures start at 10 o'clock. I go back for lunch in college and then I work in the afternoon or sometimes play real tennis. Dinner is at 6.45 and then I return to the books. The day-to-day food is good, but not haute cuisine. It is always well served and we are marvellously well looked after by the college steward, David, who is a legend in his lifetime and seems to remember everybody's name, visiting dignitary and student alike. Amazingly he has not yet been head-hunted by a grander college. On Tuesdays we have a cooked breakfast and on Mondays and Wednesdays there is a formal dinner where we wear gowns. The reader may think these details unimportant, but, like Napoleon's army, undergraduates march on their stomachs. Nobody misses Tuesday breakfast. On guest nights and formal occasions, the food ratchets up a gastronomic notch, or two, and is very good indeed. When I get invited to dine at other colleges on high table, I find that there can be a tendency for dons from some of the older colleges to be somewhat snooty about Harris Manchester as arriviste. On these occasions, I tend to swirl the wine in my glass dismissively, look disparagingly at the offering on the crested college plate in front of me, and comment that, while there is, of course, a difference between a very old college with a Royal foundation and Harris Manchester with its tasteful, pale green carpets, nonetheless the latter did manage to serve a rather charming old Cos the other night... That usually diverts the conversation to a more agreeable channel.

I soon sort out what lectures are worth going to and what are not, and in any event I should be able to extract most of them from the website. Very gradually I become more proficient at my computer, although I am by no means totally literate. My tutors complain that my handwriting is so awful that I ought to type my essays. My typing is equally dismal. However, a kind Scottish friend, Caroline Lorimer, tells me about a bit of kit called 'Dragon Speak'. This software, when loaded into my computer, enables me to dictate what I want to say, which is then reproduced on the screen. Although by no means 100 per cent perfect – no doubt because my diction is not sufficiently Transatlantic classless to be immediately recognisable – it magically enables me to write an essay by dictation. It has totally saved my life and averted the midnight typing crisis. But it does throw up some wonderful mistakes and has the disadvantage that, if somebody comes into the room or the telephone goes when the microphone is switched on, a whole lot of gobbledy gook appears on the screen. (I hope that, like the Bond films, I will get some huge commission for mentioning this brand, but I have to say that, so far, my publishers have not been astute enough to realise the great commercial potential in this respect.)

We go to two supervisions a week, distributed among the three subjects, which we are studying. This term, for Politics, I am paired with Hannan, the Israeli student. What is challenging for me is that he thinks and articulates in a lateral way, which is wholly different from the way in which my contemporaries would approach some of the concepts we are studying. I cannot, therefore, simply trot out my established views, or prejudices, which might be acceptable, or even amusing, at a Buckinghamshire dinner party or at the Garrick. I have to reassess whether a long-held view on a political issue is indeed defensible, and, if so, counter-attack to support it. There is no mileage in the Old Boy school of discussion. While with Lesley Smith we take turns in reading out our essays, with the other tutors we hand them in the night before, get them back at the tutorial, and discuss them. The tutors are, so far as I am concerned, very long-suffering. Their chief criticism is that I don't address the question. I confess that I find the Oxford approach to essays rather narrow in outlook. One is required to dissect – if not parse – every word in the question and then provide a reasoned response, almost literally to each word. Any attempt to demonstrate one's general knowledge about the subject seems actively to be discouraged. I have no doubt that, gradually, I shall get used to this approach. It is particularly true in Politics, where I tend to show off my general knowledge, only to be constantly reminded that it is political theory, and not political history, which is the syllabus for this year.

At the end of term we all have to go to our tutors for what are called 'collections'. These are, in fact, the fancy Oxford name for the giving out of reports. Again, the three tutors are in a circle with the student in the dentist's chair. The reports are handed out. The student is given an opportunity to look at them and make any comment that he likes. Mine are very much as I anticipated, namely, 'Can do better, must answer the question, but is enjoying life'. Well, thank God for that, at least. One wonders what they might have said if they thought I was having a miserable time. Perhaps 'Oliver should get out on the games field more often and be more of a team player in the JCR bar'. Needless to say, I am not assertive enough to make any contra comments. I have always enjoyed reading the children's and the grandchildren's reports and so I thought it only fair that they should have an opportunity of reading mine. So at Christmas the children and grandchildren had a good laugh about grandfather's academic progress. Or lack of.

In January, I rejoined the real tennis club and I play once a week. I am so out of touch, partly I think because my eyesight isn't as good as it was and partly because my right knee is playing up. I enjoy it immensely, and I hope, with a bit of practice, to improve – which wouldn't be difficult. It is a good way of getting some exercise, because the hockey and rugby field are out of bounds and squash is too dangerous for someone of my age. I need both my eyes. But real tennis is quite intellectual. As a young man, one never imagined that there would come a time when one wouldn't be a superhero at sport. As a middle-aged man, I adequately deceived myself. But now the realities of even the most well-performing of artificial hips dictates recognition of inadequacy. Nonetheless, I can still beat Liz triumphantly on the tennis court at home at the weekends. Which is not saying much as she – having had two front teeth knocked out by a backhand at tennis doubles at prep. school – is about as sporty as a Meissen tea cup.

Meanwhile on the publicity front, I am constantly approached by various journalists and by the media in general. The article I am commissioned to write for the *Sunday Times* runs into some trouble. When they asked me to write the article, I had already been approached by a number of national newspapers and by local papers. I asked the *Sunday Times* if it were in order for me to write for these other people. Quite properly they said they wanted my article to be an 'exclusive' and that, while they didn't mind my writing for local papers or magazines, they would not be happy my writing for a national newspaper. Accordingly, I declined the offer from the other national newspapers and wrote a series of rather boring articles for various Oxford journals and appeared on local television. I also took part in several interviews on the BBC. Even I, as the most rampant egotist, am slightly worried about personal over-exposure.

Among the articles I wrote locally was one for a local magazine called *Crucible* which had recently come out. I think it was their third edition. It was plainly a magazine that didn't have much financial backing and, accordingly, I did not charge them any fee for my writing about my life at Oxford. It was duly published and I heard no more. Meanwhile, I sent off my article to the *Sunday Times* and waited expectantly for it to be published. Shortly before publication, the *Sunday Times* rang me up in some distress saying that the article from the *Crucible* about my life at Oxford had been published that morning in the *Guardian* newspaper. I had not authorised the *Guardian* to publish it, and I was very anxious that this might interfere with the article the *Sunday Times* were shortly going to publish. I wrote a rather sharp letter to the *Crucible* and to the *Guardian*, expressing my dismay.

Happily the *Sunday Times* published a full-length article on the following Sunday, which had the most inappropriate picture of me, in my (now abandoned) red judicial robes and wig, towering over the spires of Oxford. I was slightly worried that someone from the Lord Chancellor's Department was going to ring up and threaten to sue me for taking the brand in vain. I waited with some interest to see what replies I got from the *Crucible* and the *Guardian*. I got a most apologetic letter from the *Crucible* saying how sorry they were, that they didn't realise that the copyright was in me, and that they had given permission to the *Guardian* without fee and were genuinely very contrite. I got no reply from the *Guardian* and, a little later sent off another letter threatening proceedings. I heard nothing more so I issued a summons in the County Court. However, when I got back to Oxford for the summer term I discovered an email on my laptop. My laptop would only receive emails when linked up to the Harris Manchester website. So the *Guardian*'s email had never reached me. The *Guardian* apologised, and offered to pay me for the article. I felt very embarrassed at having issued proceedings and sent off an email immediately cancelling them. The *Guardian* and I conducted a friendly correspondence and it all ended up with sweetness and light.

Indeed, I was asked by one of their journalists if I would write an article about the trial of Saddam Hussein. I declined. It was a subject about which I knew absolutely nothing and I thought that an elderly undergraduate's perspective would hardly illuminate the minds of *Guardian* readers. I was beginning to think that I was getting myself too much involved in journalism and in becoming a public figure. The story about my being the oldest undergraduate at Oxford clearly had a limited life span and all the juice had been squeezed out of that particular lemon. Equally I felt that I had done quite enough broadcasting and appearing on television and that it was time to go back to being a student and applying myself to my work.

Meanwhile the films in which my grandchildren had featured had their premieres. As well as Anna in *The Girl with the Pearl Earring*, I saw Lulu in *Love Actually*, the most amazing film for those that do ROMANCE, which, some complain, I don't, actually, and Fred in *Peter Pan* – financed by Mohammed Al Fayed, in memory of his dead son. The films all received a certain amount of acclaim. I have to admit that I basked in being their grandfather. At Bird and Fortune-type dinner parties, I was able to bang on about the grandchildren in a manner that has defeated the most intrepid of Hampstead wives. Liz tells me that one must never ask a woman 'And what do your children/grandchildren do?' as being a deeply sexist question. But I couldn't wait for someone to ask me, sexist or not. Having seen Fred and Anna on site, I suddenly appreciated the divide between the filming daily-drudge and the screen's so-called reality. For example, in Anna's film, I saw shots of Luxembourg (where I had been on chaperone duty) seamlessly combined with shots of Delft where I had not been. The *Daily Mail* had caught up with the fact that these three grandchildren were mine and published an article with photographs headed 'M'Lud's Bright Stars'. Ghastly; but it would be wrong not to admit that I was immensely proud of them all. The *Daily Mail* also, in a separate issue, published an item in its gossip column about my relationship with Liz, and the fact that she had left her husband. This was the first of a number of similar articles, the content of which was mainly rather spiteful tittle-tattle, which had only a marginal connection with the truth. But, although the articles distressed Liz, there was little or nothing one could do, short of a privacy suit which might have had dubious chances of success, given my previous exposure in the media. But one did wonder why on earth even *Daily Mail* readers should be interested in reading such stuff.

The Christmas vacation was spent visiting all the children, working on my PPE books, and collecting penalty points on my driving licence, while speeding to Norfolk. At the beginning of the Hilary term there are college exams, also called collections. The first Friday of term was spent in doing two sets of exams and, on the Saturday, we were allowed to do the third exam at home. The result was somewhat predictable, namely that I must address the question more closely. This is obviously a problem which I need to resolve and with which, so far, I have not come to terms. I watched the University rugby match in the vacation on the television. I realised where my real loyalties lay when Cambridge, having been well behind for most of the match, scored a last-minute try. I leapt out of my seat in the excitement. I shall certainly support Cambridge in the University cricket match, but the Boat Race is more difficult to call.

One of the effects of the publicity which I attract is the receipt of a great number of letters from people whom I have met in different walks of life over the years. I discovered that David Raeburn, who was the second scholar at Charterhouse with me, is teaching at New College and he kindly invited me to go and dine on high table there. I had a letter from a lady who was anxious to do much the same as me. She pointed out that I was merely a child compared with her; she had been born in 1922 and was proposing to graduate well into her eighties. Good for her; I hope she has as much fun as me. Other people wrote with reminiscences of seeing me in court or simply congratulating me on going back to university. I had an email from a fellow Old Carthusian who is a mature student at Christchurch. He has kindly invited me to go and dine with him there, on the basis that we are two 'oldies'. I enjoyed a marvellous evening on high table with the dons in attractive surroundings amid generous hospitality. I was also invited to go and dine at Oriel with a friend from Norfolk, and Vincent's Club have kindly asked me to their directors' dinner. I finally made contact with the secretary of Vincent's and have arranged to have lunch with him to sort out the subscription issue. Someone suggested that if I bought everybody in sight a drink, I would soon become a member. I have yet to see how this pans out!

Top-up fees are the great talking-point here. Indeed, on the day of the debate in Parliament, students occupied the examination schools, thus preventing us (quite conveniently!) from going to any lectures. I can understand the students' concern, because fees are very expensive and certainly many of the students at Harris Manchester, and, no doubt, throughout the University, do not come from privileged backgrounds.

Among the various activities to which I am looking forward is speaking at a debate at the Union. I have been invited to talk about the acceptance or refusal of honours, although, as yet, I am not sure which side of the motion I am meant to be supporting. Some excitement was generated at Christmas, before the New Year's honours list was published, by the leaking of confidential memoranda about how some people had been considered for honours and others rejected. An enquiry is to be set up as to the future of honours. A number of people came forward saying that they had refused honours and therefore it has a certain amount of topicality. Roger Toulson, who is a High Court judge and is Chairman of the Law Commission, was coming up to the Trinity Law Society to speak about proposals for law reform. Michael Beloff, the Master of Trinity, invited me to go and listen and then to have dinner with them all. When Roger was delayed, I was afraid that I might have to give an impromptu address on a subject upon which I certainly held some strong personal views, but had no current knowledge. Luckily Roger duly arrived and gave an informed and amusing talk. I find it entertaining to adopt the chameleon role of approaching such an evening as though I am indeed a new student, with no experience of issues such as the need for the reform of the law of homicide. Wisely, however, on this occasion I decided to keep my mouth firmly shut and let the keen Trinity law students ask all the questions.

One of the more idiotic things that we have to do this term is to spend a day being taught how to cope with statistics and data, in preparation for a compulsory exam in the summer term on the topic. The course, which was introduced a year ago, is sold on the basis that it will look good on people's CVs and be an advantage in job applications thereafter. None of this – hopefully – affects me. I didn't come to Oxford to read statistics or learn how to present statistical data with the assistance of computer-generated pie charts. I view the whole thing with considerable gloom. However, it has to be done, because passing this exam is a necessary qualification in order to enable me to take the second-year PPE course. I find it difficult enough coping with my core subjects, without having to do this ridiculous and superficial IT course in addition. My complaints fall on deaf ears, however. I doze through most of the course and bunk off home early, leaving the hard-working John White to collect all the handouts for me.

Having decided to adopt a somewhat low profile media-wise, my efforts are somewhat sabotaged by a big article in *Saga Magazine* about students at Harris Manchester, which included a two- or three-page article about me. It also included references to Liz, who was somewhat put out with the article's suggestion that she had fallen in love with me, rather than the other way around! I decided that this was probably the last article in which I was going to be involved and that I would now retire and become a private student.

However, I was lucky enough to generate some income to put towards my fees, by going to Lucerne to do an arbitration for CAS (Court of Arbitration for Sport). This concerned a dispute about the rules governing the marking of ice-skating, not exactly a sport with which I was intimately familiar. But the issues were the same as those that surface in many sports disputes – what do the rules mean in their context. As a judge or arbitrator it is always important to remember that, although many disputes may seem to be trivial, in fact for the parties they can have a life or death importance, in reputational or financial terms. I had an agreeable thirty-six hours and my colleagues, one of whom was Italian and the other Swiss, were charming and intelligent and we reached a unanimous decision without any difficulty. The Italian President then drafted an arbitration award, which he sent me. It seemed to me to be far too detailed and discursive, verging on the flowery in style, rather than addressing the issues in dispute. I diplomatically pointed out that I didn't agree with the format, although I agreed with the conclusion. I was then told that my corrections had to be in within two or three days! However, no doubt in the interests of Euro-comity, time was then extended and I was able to make what at least I considered to be some constructive criticisms to sharpen up the award.

Another source of income has been from *The Times Higher Educational Supplement* which asked me to review a number of books on the presumed basis of my knowing, or, at least, having once known, something about the law. And so I have written critiques of a number of books, whose subject matters range from incest in the fifteenth century (not as amusing as it sounds) to the loss of individual liberty in modern society and the state of our prisons. It is an interesting thing to do, not just because I get the handout of a free book, but also because it gives me the opportunity to exercise my decision-making functions. It is too easy, as one gets older, simply to regurgitate the views which one once held, perhaps sensibly at the time, in ever-increasingly polarised terms. The reality is that it becomes all the more important to revisit one's most fiercely held opinions and to test them, against the fabric of contemporary thought and in the light of current-day circumstances, to see whether they do indeed reflect the balanced conclusions of a mature and enlightened mind, as one has in a self-satisfied manner, previously supposed. But all too often, when pointing the laser beam, one realises that what in fact one has revealed are the pomposities of an intellectual dinosaur. Of course, writing book reviews does not pay nearly as well as spinning out one's life history in the more popular press, and the former involves a good deal more work. But beggars cannot be choosers and I am flattered even to be asked to write on intellectual topics.

I was also invited by one of the newspapers to write an article about a popular television programme, in which so-called celebrities go onto a desert island, and make total fools of themselves. They live rough, eat the most revolting items and eventually, by some arcane method of selection, one person emerges as the winner. In order to do this, I had to watch the programme. Apparently it has an audience of twelve million people. How intelligent people can watch this sort of rubbish, I simply do not know. I was asked to write 1000 words. All I could think was that it was totally naff, but happily, before I had put pen to paper, the paper decided that they didn't want the article, or at any rate that they didn't want an article written by me.

One of the great triumphs of the term, however, is that I am now a member of Vincent's. I met the President and the Secretary and gave them lunch and a drink. They told me that I could pay a subscription and join. I enquired whether that entitled me to wear the tie. They said it did. Accordingly, I immediately went out and bought one. I now sport a

Vincent's tie which I hope will gently irritate my Oxford friends who got Blues. Meanwhile I am invited to various colleges. Oriel Law Society has a dinner, after which Dame Elizabeth Butler-Sloss, President of the Family Division is to speak. Michael Wright, who was in Chambers with me and has now just retired from being a High Court judge, is also there. We have a very engaging evening, Elizabeth speaks very well about family law issues, and the students (not including me, who knows nothing about this area of the law) ask intelligent questions.

A heavy fall of snow brings Oxford to a total standstill. The Americans in the college are bemused beyond belief and cannot understand how pathetic we are when faced with this sort of drama, which to them is no more than a fall of gentle rain. As a result of now being a member of Vincent's, I am invited to a dinner at University College for the officials of the club and some of the dons. Robin Butler, Master of the college, makes a very gracious speech and Roger Bannister is also there looking terribly fit. They are to have a 50th anniversary of his four-minute mile later on in the year, although, somewhat disappointingly, he says that he is not actually going to run! However, one of Bannister's pacers, Christopher Chataway (now Chairman at Bletchley Park), runs regularly, and it would not surprise me if he were to take part. I discover that Vincent's has a dining room and so, in an attempt to introduce some Brideshead style into my student life, I arrange to have a dinner party there. The Butlers, David Raeburn and his wife, John White and his wife, and Liz and I go. I take my own wine and we are enormously well looked after. I suspect that I will repeat this exercise because I owe a number of people hospitality.

Soon afterwards, I am invited to Bletchley to a Rotary dinner by Kenneth King, who like me, is a trustee at Bletchley Park, to speak about my life. It's a good selling point for *Benchmark*. But it is an hour's drive and I get caught up in a horrendous traffic jam. However, the people are all very friendly though I know no-one. The dinner is somewhat modest and, because I am driving, I am not able to drink. There comes the moment when I am being introduced by Kenneth King. He is in the middle of his generous description of my credentials, when he collapses on the floor, having had a heart attack. This naturally brings proceedings to an abrupt end. He is taken into intensive care (where he makes good progress). I drive back for another hour, soberly reflecting on the dangers of after-dinner speaking. Subsequently, I am invited to Bletchley Park itself to give the same speech which this time goes off without any problem. As they do not provide me with any dinner on this occasion, I have to take sandwiches and eat them furtively in a corner before everyone arrives. I enjoy these occasions, not because of the egotistical buzz of talking about oneself (which I hope I no longer enjoy), but rather because of the questions I get asked and the wide variety of people I meet. One lady had been at school with my wife, Margaret, whom she remembered, as well as her sisters, so we had a long and friendly reminiscence. But realistically I think that I have probably now exhausted my enthusiasm for giving speeches about *Benchmark*, although it does have the effect of giving the book a bit of publicity and indeed, at Bletchley, there were a number of purchases.

Liz receives an invitation to go to Cambridge for the Squire Law Library Appeal, which involves listening to a speech by Harry Woolf, the Lord Chief Justice, followed by a dinner given by Cambridge law professors and dons. She invites me as her guest and I graciously accept. However, the next day I have a tutorial at Oxford, then have to be in London for a meeting of the XL Club (a cricket club for those over forty), and thereafter return for my speaking debut at the Oxford Union. I therefore realise that it will be quite impossible for me to get to the dinner in Cambridge and return the next day in time to fulfil all my

3   Oliver at the Oxford Union

obligations. To Liz none of this is any problem. When I explain to her that it is a three-hour car drive or train journey from Oxford to Cambridge, and the same by way of return, she pooh-poohs my concerns and says that it can be done in forty minutes. Given that she has many qualities, but map reading and geography are not among them, I am exceedingly sceptical. But it turns out that she has looked up helicopter flights, and engaged a helicopter to take us from Oxford Airport to Marshall Airport at Cambridge and to return. So she picks me up in her car and whisks me off to Oxford Airport, where we are airlifted across country and end up in Cambridge forty minutes later. I have been in a helicopter before but it is still a very exciting experience and, for Liz, it was the first time so she was particularly thrilled. We made ourselves comfortable at the Garden House Hotel and then went to the new Squire Law Library to hear Harry.

The Squire Law Library is part of an enormous and impressive complex. We arrive just in time and sit in the press box. Harry has a bad cold which affects his delivery, but what he has to say is dynamite. He refers to the Minister for Constitutional Affairs (Lord Chancellor as he

4 Judge's service at Buckingham

still is) as a 'Cheerful Chappie' and lays into the Government for its nonsensical ideas about reforming the House of Lords and the judicial system. We have a copy of his speech in front of us and next day the papers are full of Harry's attack. We get up early next morning in order to leave Cambridge at 8 am, only to find when we get to the airfield that there is low cloud at Cambridge and the same at Oxford. It is therefore impossible to take off immediately. We sit there for about an hour and a half, wondering how best to get back to Oxford and whether it would not be more sensible to go straight to London to my meeting. I was not sure how I was going to explain to my tutor that I was in Cambridge, on a frolic, when I should have been at a tutorial. Happily, the weather lifts, we scream back to Oxford, I get to my tutorial just in time. The helicopter pilot was pretty relaxed about the whole thing but pointed out that his life was also at risk and that, when flying at about 1000 feet as we were, low cloud is a very great hazard. He told us that, on one occasion, visibility had got so bad that he simply put down in the nearest field and waited for it to clear. Liz could not quite see why we didn't land in the quad at Harris Manchester. It would certainly have occasioned a good deal of excitement among my fellow students.

I rushed up to London to my meeting and then back to take part in the Union debate about the honours system. The leak about how honours have been distributed had aroused a good deal of passion among a number of people. The motion for debate was that if an honour were offered, it should be refused. This was to be proposed by a feisty young lady, who had been a big debater before she had gone down. I was to oppose the motion together with others. I duly arrived at the Union to be greeted by the President in a white tie and floral button-hole and the Secretary, Treasurer and committee. They all seemed incredibly young, somewhat naive, but, no doubt, justifiably, very pleased with themselves. It was an evening in which the candidates to be President also took part in the debate. It was thought that their speeches might influence the outcome of the election. This seemed to me to be a fairly strange procedure, because, once elected, the President doesn't speak. The debate itself was, I thought, pretty trivial. It was poorly attended. I made a joke about a camel, which – according to Liz – I managed to fluff. Such other points as I made also fell fairly flat. I felt my performance had been unimpressive, but I wasn't exactly bowled over by the brilliance of any of the other speakers either. I suppose that the Union was always somewhat trivial, although at Cambridge it generally seemed to be packed with distinguished speakers. I suspect that memory is enhanced by the passage of time and that the President and other officers were just as self-important in those days as the present generation.

The election for the President took place over the following days. After a good deal of shenanigans, Oswana Baffia was elected. The election of the President of the Union always seems to give rise to conflict. There are complicated rules against canvassing. In this case Oswana Baffia got the most votes. There were allegations made against her that she had been cheating. There were allegations by her that the others had been cheating. In the end she was cleared and the other two were banned for periods of time. It is difficult to take it at all seriously, although certainly, in the past, to be President of the Union at either Oxford or Cambridge was a passport to a political career.

Harry Woolf, the Lord Chief Justice, and Ann Raffety, the High Court judge sitting at Oxford, came down to the Crown Court to show the flag. They invited me to the judges' lodgings which are now in a lovely old house about six miles outside Oxford, towards Bicester. They compare favourably with the former lodgings at Shotover. Shotover had been John Miller's residence. He had been in charge of the Queen's carriage horses, and was a charming old gentleman. Shotover had become, sadly, a rather dilapidated house with a lot of uncomfortable rooms. The kitchen, when I had stayed there previously as a judge, was subject to some trenchant criticism, not limited to the density of its cockroach population. But John Miller was enormously gracious and moved out into a flat at the very top of the house when the judges arrived. The double-bed provided for the senior judge was about four-foot wide and had a distinct tilt into the middle. The rooms were full of lovely old mementos but, certainly when I was there in late spring, it was perishingly cold. I think that eventually the Lord Chancellor's Department decided that it was too expensive to maintain as lodgings.

Hilary term now came to an end with the usual meeting with the tutors in order to get our reports. Nothing had much changed so far as my intellectual efforts were concerned. The tutors were too kind to put their criticisms in the trenchant terms of a school report 'Must do better', but I guessed that that was their bottom line. I was still being told that I had to work out what was involved in the question, and confine my answer to that straitjacket. They were not impressed by my discursive, and, at times, reminiscent, style. The Easter vacation was totally blighted by the idiotic Statistics paper to which I have already referred. I suspect that the American company, whose brainchild it obviously was, had paid the University's Economics department a substantial sum of money to enable it to sell the software to luckless students. I reiterated my grumble to my tutors that, if I had wanted to do statistics, I could have fixed up to do a local authority adult education evening course in computer studies and not bothered to come up to Oxford at all. But the tutors remain resolute. John White and I, ever the aggressive macho lawyers, dream up an argument that the paper had been wished on us unilaterally, contrary to the published syllabus upon the basis of which we had signed up to do the course, and that we could perhaps challenge the department's insistence that we sit the paper by judicial review proceedings! But no such luck. My research showed that the Statistics paper was not only referred to in the prospectus but also found a place in the Regulations. As many as 17 per cent of students fail, but are allowed to resit it in September, thus fouling up their long vacation. If they fail again, that's an end of their university career. It's all very stupid because the paper has no bearing on PPE and it is simply a blight on everybody's time when they ought to be revising for proper exams. However, by hook or by crook, having wasted a fortnight of the vacation, I produce an attempt at a statistical analysis of the correlation between gender, race and socio-economic factors on the one hand, and educational achievements on the other. (I would rather have done a comparative review of some amusing cricket statistics, to demonstrate the superiority of Cambridge players (and wicket keepers in particular), but the mean-spirited programme providers did not see fit to provide access to that type of database.) Although I have sufficiently grasped the basics of the computer software, so that my pie charts appear in the most delectable rainbow hues and my data is presented in compelling and authoritative tables, the results of my statistical grind are utterly baffling. If the Ministry of Education is operating on the basis of similar conclusions to mine, no wonder successive governments have failed to present coherent educational policies. I just have a ghastly feeling that, maybe, somewhere along the way, I have misapplied a seductively simple mathematical formula. Still, I do not have world enough and time to go back and check my methodology. Whether my efforts will pass scrutiny, I have serious doubts, but, by this time, I am not sure that I care. I had a rather bad-tempered exchange with the department at having to sign a 'declaration of originality', on the basis, first, that it was not worth the paper it was written on and, secondly, that it reflected on one's honesty. I got the answer back that the requirement 'was in the Regulations'. I decided that the continued exchange of pleasantries along this line was not going to be very constructive and, indeed, that I might find myself being black-balled from submitting the paper at all.

The highlight of the vacation was a trip to Paris. Liz had bought, at a charity auction in aid of muscular dystrophy, a weekend for two in Paris. It was extremely good value as it enabled us to stay at the George V for three nights, to go out to dinner on two occasions and to lunch at a restaurant with three rosettes. The last was so *moderne*, both gastronomically and conceptually, that I felt we were part of some performing art troupe. The place itself was decorated with weirdly shaped tables and banquettes in pink and orange plush carpet: a sort of cross between Salvador Dali on a good day, and a high-class bordello, without the girls. There was no choice so far as the food was concerned: it was delicious, but served up in bite-size portions in hollowed out egg-shells, or nestled on china spoons, that left one absolutely gagging for a shepherd's pie. I also managed to get tickets for the England versus France rugby match. This last was the least successful part of the weekend because England were played out of sight and France won the Five Nations. That was not the only disaster of the weekend. Having taken my wallet out of my jacket as I was going down the steps to the Metro and having (or so I thought) then put it back, two or three minutes later I found that it had vanished. My pocket had obviously been picked. It was probably my own fault for opening my wallet in sight of other people, but with it firmly in my pocket, I am still astonished that the thieves were able to pinch it. We were not in a crowded train; we were on a staircase with nobody else, so far as I was concerned, about. But Liz noticed an extremely well-dressed couple, who, politely, indeed almost apologetically, stood back to let us pass down the stairs. I had to spend a lot of boring time getting in touch with the credit card companies. It was clear that the relevant call centre to which my *cri de coeur* was directed was in some far distant country. When I was asked where the theft had occurred, I had to keep re-iterating that it was in Paris WHICH WAS IN FRANCE, as though there was some other competing Paris, where unsuspecting tourists were more likely to get their cards pinched. Luckily the cards were not used, which brought to mind the joke about the husband whose wife's credit card got stolen and who explained that he was delighted because the thief had been spending so much less than his wife did.

4

Bits and Pieces

One of the things I do over the winter is to go shooting, four or five times a year. I belong to a small shoot near Beaconsfield, which is an unlikely place for a rural activity. It occurs on a farm of about 1500 acres with a wide variety of drives. It is a small friendly shoot, run by the son of friends of mine. I would judge the quality of the guns is quite high because we shoot a bird with roughly every three shots. As I only hit a bird once every 300 shots, it will be seen that the average of the other guns is very good. We have something like eight drives. We assemble at a pub at about 8.30 am and have a cup of coffee and some bacon sandwiches and then we do four or five drives before having a snack at the farm. We then have perhaps another two or three drives after that and then retire to the pub for a lunch/dinner at about 4.30. It's all very friendly. The average bag is about 200 birds so there is no question of wholesale slaughter. The drives vary from being in open country to being in a wood. I confess that I dislike being out in the open because it shows up my incompetence, about which the beaters are wisely silent. My best peg is to be in a wood where I am concealed from my fellow guns. Apart from one horrendous day when it never stopped raining, there has always been agreeable weather and lovely countryside. I find it a lot of fun.

Occasionally I get invited to other shoots and it's interesting to see how they are run. Some guns are incapable of taking their own birds but claim other people's. I have no such inclination partly because of the number of birds that I shoot is so limited and partly because I am indifferent to the ambitious self-glorification which seems to overcome some people in the shooting field, notwithstanding their well-brought up modesty in normal life.

Shortly before Christmas 2003, I am invited to Sir Paul Getty's shoot at Wormsley. I have been to Wormsley on a number of occasions for the cricket. Paul Getty created there a marvellous cricket pitch, similar to the Oval, where he entertained, very generously, the visiting clubs who played against his side. The cricket is of the highest quality. Recently retired professionals and current county players can be seen regularly. The tourists frequently appear. Paul invited some hundreds of people to enjoy lunch and tea with seemingly unlimited alcohol. Delicious home-made ice creams were brought round in a 'stop me and buy one'. His enthusiasm for cricket, encouraged by Gubby Allen and Mick Jagger (while all three were staying in a London clinic), is now a matter of history. His generosity to the game was enormous and frequently unsung. When he died in April 2003 there was an enormous memorial service at Westminster Cathedral to which the great and the good and many others went. The Archbishop of Westminster preached a singularly inappropriate sermon about rich men and needles and camels.

One of the problems I had faced when receiving generous hospitality from Paul and his wife, Victoria, was my inability to make any sort of return. However, at the reception after his memorial service, I suggested to Victoria that she might like to come out and have dinner one night with some other friends. Accordingly this was arranged. We went to the Garrick with Robin and Jo Peppiat and had an exceedingly agreeable evening.

At the Wormsley shoot, the first person I met was Jeremy Paxman, whom I had met on a number of occasions, both at Wormsley and while being interviewed. We drew adjoining pegs and he said to me 'I hope you are a poor shot, because I am.' When I said, honestly, in my case, that I was absolutely hopeless, he seemed pleased and off we went for the first drive. All the drives were out in the open so it was possible to see exactly what the other guns were doing. Jeremy had drawn number one peg on the first drive, on my right, and I was number two. We hadn't been standing there more than five minutes before 'bang, bang, bang' went his gun, and then out of the sky fell bird after bird, like manna from heaven. I felt duly chastened about his ability and 'bother you bloody Paxman', and we then moved onto the next drive. On this occasion again, we were out in the open, and I waved my gun rather aimlessly at a bird at about 30,000 feet, pulled the trigger, and down came the bird. Everybody saw this and there was a tremendous cheer. It was of course a totally lucky shot and not due in any way to my skills. However, I milked it for all it was worth during the rest of the day and observed to anybody who would listen that I was not taking any low birds but only high ones. As I scarcely hit another bird the entire day, this covered my deficiencies with some ease.

I don't think we were an impressive lot of guns because we fired some 900 shots and hit no more than about 150 birds. Curiously, the keeper was paid on the basis of birds actually shot, rather than on rounds fired. That seemed to me to be not much of an incentive to the keeper and reflected rather poorly on the guns. Incidentally, not far from our shoot at Beaconsfield was the shoot of Lord Burnham where, in 1913 the King and the Prince of Wales took down a party of some seven or eight guns, and, in the space of about five hours shot some 4000 birds with two loaders each. The story goes, that, on the way home, the King was heard to say to the Prince of Wales that he thought Burnham was slightly over the top. One might have thought that the party could have stopped at lunchtime, if not at the Royal elevenses.

I continue to be the subject of media interest. After *Saga Magazine* did a series of articles on mature students at Harris Manchester, *Director* magazine did a spread about people taking up a new career. All this was a lot of fun. When the grandchildren were all taking part in their premieres, I was asked to write an article about them and the family; I felt, however, that enough was probably enough and decided to decline invitations to go public about my life or the family. Truth to tell, the amount of material remaining was very limited. The *Oxford Student* wrote to me and wanted me to do eight articles during the term. I was not sure whether I really had the enthusiasm to write eight articles about life at Oxford from the elderly student's perspective. After all, I was not trying to pack my CV. I also took the mercenary view that, if I were going to do the job properly, which would take a certain amount of time, I would require to be paid. I am not the sort of chap who can dash off articles off the top of my head. However, the *Oxford Student* understandably said that it was a student magazine, and that it was short of cash; so the project fell by the wayside. It's interesting that people seem to think that anyone can write an article at the drop of a hat and that it requires no sort of effort or research. No doubt this is true of journalists, who can turn their hands quickly to anything, but for the rest of us, rather like making a speech, it requires a good deal of hard work and time, which I did not think that my tutors would think that I necessarily had available during the term.

My granddaughter, Anna meanwhile had auditioned for the major role of one of the children in C.S. Lewis's *The Lion, the Witch and the Wardrobe* and had been offered the part. To this end she goes off to New Zealand where the film is to be made for a period of some six months. Although she is about to take some GCSEs, the school very sensibly took the view that in her case they were comparatively unimportant and that to take the main part in a major film would be much better for her CV. So she went with their blessing. How times have changed at girls' schools. This generated some more media publicity and there was an article in the *Evening Standard* about the family and about grandfather. I was invited by the *Sunday Times* to express my view about the whole set up but this I declined for a number of reasons. The parents are keen to protect her privacy. The project is hers and not mine and although I am immensely proud of what she has done it didn't seem to me that an article by a doting grandfather would contribute much.

5

Exams

Summer, or Trinity, term is somewhat frenetic, with a few lectures and concentration on revision. Everybody goes about with rather a harassed look, except those in their second year who are exam free. As exams seem to take place at different times, it is quite impossible to tell how people are getting on. One of the quainter aspects of Oxford life is that the authorities require male undergraduates, undergoing perhaps the most traumatic moment of their lives, to dress up in a dark suit, white shirt, white bow tie, gown and mortar board in order to go to the exam. The girls are required to wear an equivalent outfit. Quite why this bizarre attire is compulsory is not easy to understand. Even less easy to understand is why, apparently, today's Nike clad generation of students have voted to retain the garb. Once inside the examination room, it is possible to strip down to something approaching normal. Given that the examination halls are not air-conditioned and the temperatures are very high, it seems a totally purposeless exercise to inflict this additional burden on the examinees.

I am invited to go to a meeting of the Canning Society which takes place in a room in Oriel. As its name implies, it is a political organisation, where one person is required to read a paper and, at the end of it, and even during the reading, questions are asked and then an informal discussion takes place. There were on this occasion some twenty or thirty highly intelligent students, and, although a good deal of drink was consumed, the level of debate was very high. Everyone was invited, if not required, to express a view. The subject on this occasion was China and whether it would dominate the world. I remember similar debates about Soviet Russia when at Cambridge; we feared that it would dominate our world. I pointed out the parallel between the break-up of the Soviet Union and the difficulties which the Chinese Government might face, because the peasant character is not always willing to be subject to monolithic power thousands of miles away. Thus it is possible to envisage parts of China with attitudes and customs very different from that of Beijing, where the rule of Beijing may not always be acceptable. Undergraduates at Cambridge tended to take these sort of discussions very seriously and somewhat pompously. But this was a very worthwhile evening, with the participants discussing an interesting topic with the right combination of wit and seriousness. When the young do express their views on political issues it can be very informative.

The European elections took place during term time. Because of my attitude towards Europe I voted for UKIP and was delighted at the large proportion of the votes which it obtained. Rather surprisingly, I find almost no support for our being in Europe among the undergraduates, even among those who come from other member states within the EU. In my view the Conservatives missed a trick, because if they had gone for a programme of coming out of Europe they would likely have swept the board. Their position of half in/half out is quite untenable – it is like being half pregnant! And the idea that by being in Europe we can in some way affect what happens I regard as a pipe-dream.

The good news is received early in the term that I have passed the dreaded Statistics paper, although unsurprisingly not, with brilliant marks. There is an acerbic comment from the examiner that I have misapplied one of the formulae, which goes some way to explaining the baffling conclusions of my analysis. But by this time I care not a jot that I have substituted x^2 for y^2 and go off to celebrate with John, who has also passed.

I take a day off to go to Lord's where I have a box for the family. I started this some four or five years ago, and now that the grandchildren are growing up they can manage a day's cricket. This was a day in one of the Test matches against New Zealand. It was a thrilling day's cricket which they all much enjoyed. To my delight, Harry Potter devotionals did not feature as part of the entertainment.

John White and I decided that we would go and see what Oxford cricket looks like. So we went up to the Parks to see Oxford University playing Somerset. Oxford University is a misnomer. The University team has amalgamated with the Oxford Brookes team, in order to provide a team to play the counties. I understand that Brookes contributes most of the players, though for the match between Oxford and Cambridge the players are all drawn from the original universities. Cambridge has the same problem. It is amalgamated with some other body and most of the players playing against the counties are not from the University. It's all very sad, and makes me realise just how lucky I was to be able to play first-class cricket for Cambridge University, against the counties, on more or less equal terms. The game against Somerset is an eye-opener. Oxford make 180 and Somerset are well on their way in a one-day game to reaching the target in under 20 overs, because they were going at 10 runs an over without any difficulty. What is appalling is the amount of chatter that goes on among the fielders. It is almost continuous. It reaches a crescendo when a ball is bowled which is not actually hit for four or six, with almost the entire team clapping or shouting. It serves absolutely no purpose. The chatter is such a continuous stream of advice that its aim cannot be that of encouragement. If its purpose is to indicate support or bonding, it is totally useless. It reminds me of what prep-school cricket used to be like, with everybody chattering like demented crows. If it raised the quality of the performance, it might have some purpose, but it plainly doesn't.

A few weeks later, Alan Dowding, who was three of my sons' housemaster at Radley, encouraged his contemporaries to come to a party at Oxford for the four-day Varsity match. Oxford and Cambridge now play each other at Lord's in the one-day game and the four-day game is played alternatively at the Parks and Fenners. Oxford is plainly a very much better side than Cambridge and totally outplayed Cambridge in both games. The gathering of contemporaries from Oxford and Cambridge was, however, very entertaining and a delightful opportunity to reminisce about life fifty years ago. I am sure that it was not only the passage of time that made us all agree that the quality of the modern generation suffers greatly by comparison with our sides of yesteryear! Some of our contemporaries had not aged very well, others were still sprightly and active, and old cricket talk is still one of the best ways of passing a day. I did not dare sport my new

Vincent's tie, but dug out an old, Hawks' Club number to display my continued solidarity.

Further invitations arrive to dine at high table, so I slough off my scruffy student gear and try and look dignified and grown up again. I dine at Somerville, which, to my surprise, is now a mixed college. From my (albeit limited) experience of Somerville undergraduates fifty years ago, I thought no man would ever be intellectually up to the mark to join such a sorority. But times have changed, and I am told that, today, all the brightest girls want to go to mixed colleges – and not just for superior architecture of some of the formerly men's colleges. Michael Sommer invites me to Christchurch and I go to Trinity from time to time. But the reality is that the summer term is about exams looming, not C.P. Snow high living. We are required to do essays under exam conditions for our tutorials. Not only do I have to learn to write neatly, but the maths for the Economics paper is proving a nightmare. The maths part of the paper counts for 20 marks out of a total of 100. When we started at the beginning of the year, the maths questions were not too difficult and did not seem to involve anything aggressively complex. Midway through the term, however, the department changed the syllabus. They have given us a sample paper, most of which is quite incomprehensible. John and I find it very difficult even though I got an A in Advanced Maths in School Certificate. However, the tutors are quite encouraging and point out that provided we get some answers right, it should not be too much of a problem. We shall see.

Exams in Oxford give rise to a number of problems. It is customary, at the end of exams, for friends of those taking part to assemble outside the examination school and empty bottles of champagne, flour and other unattractive substances over the examinee. Egg throwing has a particular popularity in certain disciplines. The rumour is that sales of purple dye have increased dramatically. This activity has apparently given rise to some complaint from the up-standing citizens of Oxford. The proctors and the police have put out a stern warning that anyone caught behaving like this will be severely punished. Exams go on for a good deal of the term and so there is this constant activity outside the examination schools. No-one seems to take the slightest notice of the directive from the authorities. Some of the people taking examinations very sensibly try to wear an old suit because they know what is in store for them, but there is much merriment after the exams with balloons and streamers, and it all seems to me to be fairly harmless.

Although I am doing exams, I still manage to lead a fairly social life. Liz and I manage to go to RAF Strike Command for a party, where jets dramatically fly past to salute the party goers. We are also invited to various dinners, firstly at the City of London School where they are raising money to pay for under-privileged students, then to Benchers night in the Inner Temple and subsequently to a dinner at the Hilton sponsored by De La Rue. The latter is a grand annual event for the members of the Diplomatic Corps as well as for the great and the good. Some months before, Patrick Wright (Lord Wright), who had been in charge of the Foreign Office and whom I had met on a number of occasions, rang me up and invited me to the dinner. I enthusiastically accepted, despite my loathing of having to struggle into white tie and evening dress, that had been purchased at a time when my dimensions were, if not exactly sylph like, at least a bit more sportif. To be truthful, I fancied the idea of the soulful, intellectual undergraduate rubbing shoulders with the glitterati of the Diplomatic Corps, even though the Dorchester ballroom was not quite the mirrored Hall at Versailles. Having secured my acceptance with consummate diplomatic cunning, Patrick then asked, by way of apparent, but charming, afterthought whether I would make the thank-you speech on behalf of the guests. I was, of course, trapped. I had no alternative but to accept. I then spent a great deal of time (when I should, no doubt, have been devoting myself to revision) wracking my brains about what I should say to these august representatives of the World's nations. That my speech had to be sophisticated and witty went without saying. But, puffed up with the perceived self-importance of my first entry onto the World's diplomatic stage, I felt that it was incumbent upon me to deliver a serious message, that they could all take home with them to their various states. I had crafted in my mind what I thought was a well-structured critique of the major defects in the constitution and operation of the European Union, which I was intending to spell out for the benefit of the representatives of the EU states and indeed those of the rest of the World. I was going to tell them that the young intelligentsia, with whom I was in daily contact at Oxford, were likewise unenamoured of the EU and that the UK needed a wider world perspective. In my mind's eye, I had almost been offered a UN ambassadorship on the delivery of this compelling work of rhetoric, when I suddenly had a realistic dose of extremely cold feet. I realised that I wasn't at all sure how well this would all go down after the chocolate souffle. I hurriedly began redrafting my speech so as to be less confrontational, only to find that it then deteriorated into a patter of tired old jokes. I was desperate. But, like many things in life, I needn't have worried. About a fortnight before the dinner, Patrick rang me up full of apologies. When I said that he had nothing to apologise for, he explained that the Minster of State at the Home Office, who had previously been invited and refused, had now decided that she would indeed like to come and deliver a serious message. Would I therefore be very upset if I were not able, after all, to make my speech? I explained to Patrick that nothing would give me greater pleasure than to come to a dinner where I didn't have to speak. So that's what I did. In the result, the Minister made an exceedingly boring speech, reading from her Home Office brief, while I was able to enjoy the evening in the knowledge that I (and perhaps also the Diplomatic Corps) had been spared what might have been one of my finest deliveries ever.

In June, Liz and I were invited to a party at the Chelsea Physic Garden in aid of the Haven Trust, a very worthwhile breast cancer charity. We much enjoyed the party but there was a terrible photograph of us which appeared in *Hello* magazine – I am glad to say our first and only appearance in that publication. It gave rise to a good deal of amusement among our friends. Liz bought, at an auction of promises, a special day out with the Tote at Ascot. Whether this will be an exciting afternoon we shall have to see. I also managed to fit in a mediation before term came to an end. The last weekend of term was spent frenetically revising and we did the exams on 21 and 22 June. The Politics paper was quite friendly and I feel satisfied that I shall have defeated the examiners. The Philosophy paper was more difficult and I keep my fingers crossed. The Economics paper was as awful as John White and I had expected, particularly so far as the maths questions were concerned. They bore no relation to the sample paper we had been given by the department. I believe I only attempted two of the maths questions and I am not sure that I got either of them right.

John had the idea, with which I agreed, of taking our tutors out to dinner in Oxford after the end of term, to thank them for all they had done for us. This we did towards the end of June. It was a jolly evening and we tried not to dwell on the horror of the exams. I like to think that the tutors enjoyed their evening as much as we did. There is now a period of two or three weeks before we hear the results.

In the summer vacation we spent a marvellous day on the river at Henley. I had bought, at an auction of promises, a day out on an old-fashioned wooden slipper launch, including a picnic lunch. The trip started at Hambledon. Luckily, it was a warm sunny day because it was an open boat. We motored down, six of us, through Henley, where they were practising for the Regatta, and through one of the locks. Full of champagne and smoked salmon sandwiches, we moored further down the river where we were provided with an enormously good lunch. We then meandered back again, modern day characters out of J.K. Jerome.

My right knee had been playing up for a number of months, and so earlier in the year I had been to see Justin Cobb who had previously operated on my hip, to see what should be done about it. Justin is a very distinguished orthopaedic surgeon and his wife Iona is a GP. When Andrew and Debs go skiing, they often go with the Cobbs, but so far have not needed to call on their professional skills on holiday. Justin gave me a full examination and took X-rays. It was decided that the most sensible course was to have the knee 'scraped' and for that purpose I booked an operation at the beginning of July. I was required to attend at 10 am which I duly did. I spent the morning being X-rayed, having blood tests, and having to spell out my medical history on numerous occasions. Otherwise I passed the time reading my newspaper and waiting for lunch. The operation was due to take place at about 3 pm in the afternoon.

Earlier, when I had told BUPA that I was having this operation, I had had a surprise. They wanted to know what sort of operation it was, so I sent them a copy of the hospital form which had some number on it. To BUPA this meant, not that I was having my knee scraped, but that my knee was going to be totally replaced! I had assumed that I was going in just for the afternoon and that I would be out either the same evening or the next morning, so it had rather shaken me when I was told that I was going to be in for a possible three- or four-day stint. At lunchtime on the day of the operation, Justin came to see me to discuss what was to happen. He asked how my knee was, and I said that, although I hadn't been playing tennis or sailing, it had given me no problems whatsoever recently. At this Justin sat up and asked me whether, if the knee were not giving any problem, it was sensible to have the operation at all. I said that was really his call, but as far as I was concerned, I was delighted to postpone it. I would then subject the knee to the rigours of sailing and tennis over the summer and see whether it reverted to its painful condition. Thus by 3 pm I had packed up and was on my way home. Poor Liz was rather miffed as she had very kindly arranged for flowers and mini bottles of champagne to be delivered to the hospital, and had returned some Glyndebourne tickets. Happily, we consumed the drink on another occasion.

In the middle of July came the dreaded news. I had passed Politics, I had passed Philosophy, and I had already passed the Statistics paper, but I had failed the Economics paper. So too, it transpired, had John, and we immediately got in touch with our tutors at Oxford to see what could be done about it. We both felt that we had been unfairly ambushed by the examiners by having been given a sample maths paper which bore no relation to the actual paper. We therefore appealed. We further discovered that the system of marking was, even by Oxford standards, somewhat bizarre. Apparently, in order to prevent students spending all their time doing the economics part of the paper, and to make them spend some time on the maths section, marks are actually deducted from the marks for economics, if the maths section is poorly done. Thus if the maths results were hopeless, it would be necessary, as we understood it, to get something like a good 2:1 on the economics section. We felt very cross that the department should introduce such a penal system.

Anyway, we did not succeed in our appeal. Mark Rogers, our splendid Economics tutor, who felt, not unreasonably, very upset at the failure of his students, came in during the summer, encouraged us to revise and kindly gave us extra tuition. It is really a long time since I have been so cross, particularly as I really enjoyed the Economics and felt very badly treated by the department. The department's reaction was predictable: that it was the same for everybody and that they were totally unwilling to interfere with the decision of the examiners. This naturally cast a blight over the whole of the summer vacation, because it was necessary for us to do the resit towards the end of September. For John this was doubly tiresome because he had arranged to go climbing in the Himalayas.

The summer was also fraught because August 7 would have been Margaret and my 50th wedding anniversary. It was the same day that Jennifer and Alan Dowding had got married and so had Richard and Penny Ling who were other friends who lived in Buckinghamshire. Naturally they both had parties to celebrate. I was invited and of course went. I am afraid I got very emotional, particularly when at one lunch there was the toast to absent friends. I did not distinguish myself.

We had otherwise quite a sociable summer. We went to the Buckingham Palace Garden Party. We went to the Lord Mayor's Dinner and we also went all the way down to Swansea to Elaine Ward's birthday party. Elaine and her husband Roger were old friends from Bucks. He had worked for GKN for most of his life and sadly died quite young. Liz and I then went to Ascot to take advantage of the day out with the Tote that Liz had purchased at a charity auction. We were invited to what was called the Tote's Box. This turned out to be a small room under the grandstand, with no view of the racing! Although our hosts did their best to make us very welcome, it was a rather dull occasion. We did, however get some tips from the owner of another racecourse, who was also a guest in the box, which made the afternoon more fun.

Our summer holiday started with us going to Norfolk with Alexander and his wife Sally. Alexander is my third son and worked, after leaving Cambridge, firstly at Warburgs and then at Mercury Asset Management. Sally had transformed our small cottage at Little Walsingham into a comfortable holiday house with great taste and they had acquired a large number of friends in smart Burnham Market. Some of their children started to learn to sail with great aptitude and it will not be long before Grandfather is being relegated to crew duties. On 7 August itself, I had planned a nostalgic visit to Ripon, which happily, coincided with two concerts of the National Children's Orchestra in which Hugo and Leo (Ed and Clare's older boys) were taking part, near Leeds. It was marvellous to see and hear them playing their cellos. Happily they have acquired their musical skills through Clare, the Popplewells being musically illiterate. My own musical ear is not highly attuned but I understand they played with distinction. It was fun to witness their enjoyment and, more particularly, to have family support on the eve of a rather emotional day.

Ripon has scarcely changed in fifty years. On our 40th wedding anniversary, Margaret and I had stayed at the hotel where we had had our reception. But this time I could not face it and simply went to the Cathedral where we had got married, said several prayers and had a good weep. I had forgotten just how beautiful Ripon Cathedral was and it brought back all sorts of wonderful memories. I cried most of the way back home in the car, but it was a good cathartic exercise.

6

More Bits and Pieces

One morning I find a message on my answer phone in college. A girl at the *Daily Mail* is asking me to ring her as a matter of urgency, because she wants to pick my brains on an important matter. By the time I pick up the message it is already forty-eight hours old and the purpose of it becomes clear the morning after that. The *Daily Mail* in their gossip column print a somewhat ill-informed and inaccurate article about Liz and me. It is clear that the telephone message was a device to get a quote from me about our relationship and had nothing whatever to do with 'picking my brains'. Such is the noble art of journalism. About every two or three months after this some article appears about us both. Sometimes they are only fairly accurate and, sometimes, not at all.

When I did libel work as a judge, I frequently had cases where the newspapers made very serious allegations against individuals which they maintained throughout a number of months, if not, years. Finally about a week before trial, they would suddenly throw their hand in and publish a most abject apology. This practice led me to be somewhat cynical about the reliability of allegations of this sort. When journalists' notebooks were eventually produced, sometimes they bore only the most marginal relation to the allegation. Sometimes the allegations were reinforced by 'a friend says'. The friend is, of course, never identified and one suspects that it is a device, as Gilbert & Sullivan would say, 'intended to give artistic verisimilitude to an otherwise bald and unconvincing narrative'.

What a sad life some of these rather grubby scribblers must have. A Pulitzer Prize is something which they will never achieve. It is not investigative journalism like Woodward's and Bernstein's. Fancy having to spend your life metaphorically trailing through the dustbins and seeing what you can find. I often feel really sorry for those who have to prostitute their somewhat limited talents in this way, for forty pieces of silver. The most sensible course for the recipient of this sort of rubbish is to remain silent. 'News' of this sort is ephemeral and while it gives a certain amount of amusement to one's friends and family, it is of only limited interest to the public.

The *Daily Mail* was the recipient of two public rebukes, many years ago. In 1918 Northcliffe, then the proprietor of the *Daily Mail*, gave Lloyd George an ultimatum about the terms of the Peace Treaty and the part, that he, Northcliffe, should play in the negotiations. Lloyd George rejected the idea that Northcliffe should play any part and, in a marvellous put-down in the House of Commons, gestured with his hand to his head indicating that Northcliffe had 'lost his marbles'.

The next proprietor, his brother, the hapless Rothermere, showed even less judgement. In 1923 when Mussolini sent a naval squadron to bombard Corfu, killing 16 refugees, Rothermere supported Mussolini.

The next public humiliation of the *Daily Mail* was by Baldwin in 1932. Beaverbrook, who owned the *Daily Express*, and Rothermere, sought to dictate to Baldwin policies about free trade. Baldwin's riposte about newspaper proprietors was 'that they exercise power without responsibility, the prerogative of the harlot throughout the ages', thus publicly condemning both the *Daily Mail* and the *Daily Express*. As I learnt from my politics lectures, the Government went on to win the St George's by-election and the newspaper proprietors were put to flight.

Nor was that the end of the Rothermere saga. In July 1933 with Hitler in power in Germany, Rothermere wrote a notorious leader in which he said 'any minor misdeeds of individual Nazis would be submerged by the massive benefits the new regime is already bestowing on Germany'. From then on he regularly corresponded with Hitler and sent him gifts. In 1934 he hosted a dinner for him at the Hotel Adler, where Ribbentrop, Goering and Goebbels were among the guests. Thereafter he was to be a regular visitor to Hitler. Lord Salisbury famously described the paper at its birth as 'by office boys for office boys'. How things have changed. It is now one of the most successful and influential papers.

None of these articles affected Liz's professional career because in April she was invited to become a High Court judge. She was particularly pleased because, although her practice had largely been in the Chancery Division with a good deal of commercial work, she was invited to sit in the Commercial Court, the first woman so to do. This was universally welcomed and we duly celebrated.

With the summer vacation came the necessity to retake the maths. John White and I were invited by Mark Rogers to go to have some extra coaching at the college and to concentrate on the economics, rather than on the maths. Unless there were a change of heart in relation to the syllabus, we were never going to do much good on the maths. After the coaching, at the end of August, and with various economics books, I am to fly to Bergen with Liz. We are booked to go for a fortnight on a Norwegian coastal trip, which involves three days at Bergen and then nine or ten days on the boat, going up to the northernmost part of Norway and back. What to wear is a matter of very great concern to Liz and we take what I regard as an excessive amount of baggage and she regards as inadequate.

Bergen itself is a lovely old town, and the Norwegians are very welcoming. However, it is very expensive. We chum up with a Welshman and his wife and go on a very exciting seventeen-mile rail journey through the mountains. We manage to pick up a *Sunday Times*, in which I have written a very boring article about the culture of compensation. It is full of most of my prejudices. As a result, I receive a dozen letters approving of what I have written. I am always astonished at how many people take the time and trouble to write, either in praise or condemnation, about anything that appears in the paper. As an example, I had a long and seemingly endless correspondence with a member of the MCC who thought I had libelled him in *Benchmark*. I hadn't. Letters of praise get filed; letters of condemnation end up in the waste paper basket.

After three days' sight-seeing in Bergen we go on the boat which is capable of holding 600 passengers but with only 190 on this trip it is not crowded. The dining room is enormous, and we have our own table for dinner. The food is fantastic, although after ten days we feel that we have got fins coming out of us, because we consume vast quantities of delicious fish. The ship is well appointed though it has not quite got the cachet of Swan Hellenic. There are many countries represented and the

5   Up the Norwegian fjords

spread of age is considerably lower than on Minerva, the well-known Swan Hellenic Cruise ship I decide on a routine of two hours' work a day. Sometimes I sit on deck in the sunshine as we sail through the fantastic fjords – which – is the object of the holiday. Sometimes I go to the quiet room, only to be disturbed by some noisy Americans who play bridge and insist on discussing every hand very loudly.

The small villages which nestle along the sides of the fjords are enchanting. We dock two or three times a day, sometimes for half an hour, sometimes for two or three hours, which enables us to get ashore, stretch our legs and see something of Norwegian life. The boat is one of the principal means of transport between towns for the Norwegians, and it delivers a lot of cargo and mail as it goes up the coast. The fjords are quite breathtaking and they all seem to be different. We learn of a very unhappy period in Norwegian life. When the Germans retreated from Norway at the end of the war they took to burning down whole villages – either out of bloody-mindedness, or because they were anxious about the Russians coming in from the north. Sometimes, they left just the church. They subjected the citizens to enormous hardship. Given what we now know about Nazi atrocities and their concentration camps, this should have come as no surprise, but it does. When we talk to some of the older shopkeepers whom we meet, there is still enormous resentment, even some sixty years on.

We go on numerous expeditions which are well organised with good guides, and there are plenty of interesting things to see. Wines and spirits are extremely expensive. We go to the local liquor shop where a

6   A Norwegian fjord

bottle of gin costs us £31. It isn't that I get rolling drunk every night, but somehow economic theories are always easier to understand after a drink or two! Liz is very good at testing me and I gradually get to learn the most important part of the economics, which I really enjoy. However, I am still resentful about the prospect of being confronted by the idiotic maths. But, it has to be.

We come to the halfway stage of the voyage at Kirkeness, which is a bitterly cold, unattractive town but it has one very good shoe shop. Here Liz indulges her predilection for shoes, by buying a very smart pair of red boots at little cost. In one town where we stopped off, the local cinema was advertising *Peter Pan* in which Fred had appeared. The poster naturally was in Norwegian and we thought it would be rather fun if we could take it back and give it to Fred. Unfortunately, the cinema itself was closed and nobody seemed to know where we could get the poster so we had to abandon the attempt. We visited the Lofoten Islands, which as a schoolboy I remember being the scene of one of the first raids by commandos, on German-held territory. They looked, and were, formidable. Liz took lots of photographs of some remarkable scenery, of which the sunsets were often quite outstanding.

Once back from this delightful holiday, we took ourselves off to France where the Wheelers and Rougiers came to stay. The Wheelers have been close neighbours in Bucks for over forty years and John Wheeler is a great wine buff. Richard Rougier was a contemporary of mine at the Bar and then became a High Court judge. As befits the son of the novelist Georgette Heyer, he has a marvellous command of the English language and it was always a joy to listen to him presenting a difficult case in Court in the most felicitous language. He was also a fine bridge player. Once at Lincoln, after we had settled a case in which we appeared as barristers against each other, we had a very liquid dinner and decided to play a few hands of bridge. Being something of a novice, I agreed to play provided that I had Richard as my partner. We found two other members of the Bar who agreed to make up a four. I managed so to call as to allow Richard to play the majority of our hands. All went swimmingly until the last hand by which time it was about 3 am and a good deal of drink had flowed. I picked up a hand to die for. I called six no trumps. We were vulnerable. We were doubled. I redoubled. I played the hand and made just four tricks. It was not a very happy way to end the evening. Richard was not pleased and has not ventured to play with me again!

In France, after the Rougiers had left us, we took the Wheelers for a day's outing to Brittany. We spent the night at Mont St Michel where Margaret and I had first had the idea of buying our cottage in France. We arrived late in the evening. This is a very good idea because by this hour the hoards of visitors have vanished and one is able to walk through the narrow and ancient streets, undisturbed. Mont St Michel at night is a fantastic sight. We had a very good dinner and were able next morning to visit the whole of the Mount without being overwhelmed by coach parties. At about 7 o'clock in the evening, the tide came in, and it is compulsive viewing. The theory that it rolls in faster than a man can run, or than a horse can gallop across the sand, may be just a myth, but, as one watches, one believes it has to be true. We then went on to St Malo, with its marvellous old town, and thence back home. Normally we tend to take our visitors to the various local châteaux, to the cathedral at Coutances, to the tapestry at Bayeux and to the Normandy beaches, so this was a new and exciting expedition.

Economics retake necessitates my returning to England. Again I have to dress up in a white tie, gown and so on. The economics part of the paper is not too bad but the maths is just as bad as it was previously, and I dread to think what the result will be. The thought of being sent down is too awful to contemplate. Several rather fraught weeks pass. No-one knows when the results will be out. John and I both agree that it has been a fairly traumatic experience. We have not heard the result of our appeal to the 'powers that be', but as we had to do the resit, clearly it has failed. Shortly before term starts, however, we hear the good news, via an email. We have both got through. Sighs of relief all round. Thus we return for the winter term with heads held high and our enthusiasm in no way diminished.

7

Second Year at Oxford

We all come back fully refreshed from the summer holidays and much relieved about the exam results. The new students wander around like headless chickens, not knowing where they are to go or what they are to do, and looking totally lost. I am sure we were the same. The rest of us put on an air of superiority but try and help the newcomers. Last year we had a whole lot of rather brash, noisy Americans. This year we seem to have fewer of them and many more students from other parts of the world. I don't know what the statistics are but I suspect that Harris Manchester has more than 50 per cent of its students from overseas. This is, no doubt, good for the finances of the college because they can be charged the full fee while the ordinary English student cannot. The breadth of geographical background also enriches our conversation in Hall. The subject of top-up fees is still high on the agenda. How anyone, after three years at university, can start out on life with a debt of £25,000 I do not know.

My generation was very lucky in that the grateful Government paid for our tuition and accommodation. At Queens' College, Cambridge we had quite a good social life. The various club dinners, such as the Boat Club, the Rugby Club and the Cricket Club, were the highlights of college entertainment. Outside college there were a good number of dances at the Dorothy Café, for which black tie was compulsory. They were not very expensive but wonderfully sociable. In smarter colleges, it was customary to entertain royally in your rooms. While it was possible at Queens' to send to the Buttery for a bottle or two, mostly we drank South African sherry, which in those days we were able to do without criticism.

We now have the choice of giving up one of the subjects in PPE. Last year, rather pompously, I said that I had come to Oxford to be educated and that there was no point giving up one subject. However, pride goes before a fall and having been told that the maths for second-year Economics was even worse than for the first year, I decided rather reluctantly to discard Economics. It is all very sad, because although it might sound surprising I really enjoyed questions on inflation, balance of payments, Keynes's theory and unemployment, and was much looking forward to pursuing them in greater depth. However, it was pointed out that if I did all three subjects, the choice of exams was much more limited. I was particularly keen to do, as one of my core subjects, a thesis on a political issue, and so, Economics has to go.

John and I no longer go together to Lesley Smith's tutorials on politics. This term I have as my colleague a young American girl called Erin, whose knowledge of English political life is enormously limited. I find these tutorials somewhat frustrating, because a good deal of the time has to be spent, by both Lesley and me, explaining to her the basic elements of English political life. Nor does she appear to be able to produce a coherent essay. (I subsequently learn that she got a first in her finals, which merely goes to show how poor my judgement is!) John and I continue Philosophy with our tutor Bill Mander. This term we do Locke and Berkeley. Having found Descartes not very easy, I have to say that Locke and Berkeley make him read like Jeffrey Archer! I am sure that I will get the hang of Philosophy sooner or later. It is very good going to tutorials with John, because he is very hard-working (I call him a swot), very articulate and very entertaining.

Ann Rafferty, who is now a High Court judge, comes to Oxford to sit at what used to be called the Assizes and I am invited by the High Sheriff, whom I know, to go to her church service at Christchurch. Here I find old friends from the Oxford circuit, Harold Wilson and James Irvine. The High Sheriffs are traditionally looked after by the Under Sheriff. The Under Sheriffs have almost always been solicitors and usually from the same firm, going back for generations. The Under Sheriff, because of his knowledge, is of immense value to a new High Sheriff, telling him (or her) about the nature of the duties involved, giving advice about official invitations and generally offering guidance about the office.

One of the functions of the Under Sheriff is to enforce debts and, if necessary, to put in the bailiffs, whom he employs. For some reason the Government decided that this was not a function that they should continue to exercise – even though they had done it perfectly successfully for hundreds of years. I suspect that the responsibility will be given to some quango which will have no such expertise and it will almost certainly, involve vastly increased expense. Why can't the Government stop interfering in matters of which they are totally ignorant? The raison d'être for Under Sheriffs having been withdrawn, the result has been that some of them now see no reason for continuing to assist the High Sheriffs. At Oxford, Harold Wilson, who has now retired from being a circuit judge, has taken on the role of Under Sheriff to assist the High Sheriff. In some other counties, the Under Sheriffs have happily continued to do their job.

The church service was impressively conducted and made more memorable by the presence of numerous Heads of Colleges, decked out in their various gowns and mortarboards. It reminded me of some of the cathedral services to which I had been when I was a judge. At Stafford the judge's procession from the lodgings to the church had been somewhat less than impressive because some of the crowd along the route proceeded to heckle us, thinking we were part of the University Rag. I also remember that particular service, because the High Sheriff's chaplain optimistically thought that speaking of mercy and compassion would make a good subject for his sermon. As he droned on, my thoughts turned to the first criminal case with which I was going to have to deal. When I had first read the papers, I had taken the preliminary view that the offence called for a sentence of either fourteen or sixteen years' imprisonment. The chaplain, who was by now fully launched into compassion and mercy was clearly going to get quite a shock when he came to sit in court and hear my passing sentence.

There was also the story, which I believe to true, of three judges going off to a church service in the official car, dressed up in their full-bottomed wigs and ceremonial robes. One of them noticed that the senior judge was not wearing his patent shoes with buckles, but, by mistake, was still in his bedroom slippers. It was now too late to return to the lodgings to change. The senior judge observed that no-one would probably notice, but that if they did, they would assume that it was now a tradition on that circuit for the senior judge to be so dressed.

I manage to lead quite a social life, both in Oxford and in London. We have amity dinners with other Inns, we have Benchers nights at the Inner Temple (which are for Benchers to take their wives or partners), and we have guest nights when one can invite a guest to a dinner. Although the general public wrongly insist that judges and barristers so spend their time wining and dining with each other, nonetheless such occasions are a very agreeable way of keeping up with one's friends and, perhaps more importantly, a useful way of keeping up to date with current legal issues.

Meanwhile, as President of the XL Club, I have to arrange speakers for our annual dinner in October. The XL Club is a splendid cricket club and, as the name suggests, is for those over the age of forty. There are still those in their sixties or seventies who are playing cricket. (Apart from the odd game of beach cricket, I have alas, hung up my gloves.) We play a great number of games against schools and clubs. We have a particular role in playing against schools, because we seek to set a high standard of cricket and behaviour. We tour quite extensively and have around 3000 members. I have now been President for some five or six years. My most important duty is to arrange for the four speakers at our annual dinner. One of the speakers is always, by tradition, the President of the MCC but getting three other speakers is never very easy. They are limited to ten minutes each and they need to be amusing speakers who also have some cricket connection. However, many years ago, the well-known solicitor David Napley, managed to propose the health of 'cricket' for twelve minutes without ever mentioning the word.

My task at the dinner is to introduce the speakers and to keep the thing moving. I also present the Henry Grierson trophy to the school which, in our opinion, has excelled itself in the matches against us. We take into account both cricketing skills and the school's attitude to the spirit of cricket. This time the award was won by one of the Scottish schools, whose captain of cricket is of Indian extraction. He made a very witty and entertaining speech and we all thought he would go far. There is a tape made of the speeches which members can buy, but it is a fact of life that listening to speeches in the cold light of day does not give the same pleasure as hearing them at the time.

Meanwhile, back at Oxford, John and I joined the University Rugby Club again as Vice-Presidents and we go and watch from time to time. This term, the University side seems to be exceedingly good, with a lot of very powerful backs who are well led by the captain in the scrum. The talk is that Cambridge are good, but will need to be very good to beat this immensely talented Oxford side. They have been suffering from a number of injuries, but still seem to have splendid substitutes, playing in a variety of different positions. The match against Major Stanley's XV is as exciting as it always was, although his team no longer contains any internationals. The visiting club sides, who now consist mainly of young professionals, no longer contain the great names like their predecessors.

David Burbage has become Master of the Furniture Makers and invites me to go and speak at one of his guest nights. His invitation was made some eighteen months ago, so there is no way of avoiding it. The Furniture Makers are a comparatively new livery company and their members, unlike members of some other livery companies, are all involved in the trade. We were given a very good evening and David spoke very well. My rather boring speech seemed to be quite well received. Next day we went and stayed the night with a fellow member of the Bar at his house at Bampton, in Oxfordshire. He had been Master of the Gardeners' Company and his garden was a tribute to his expertise. There was then a slight problem because we were due to visit Ed and Clare and watch their sons play some rugby. Although Liz had brought two or three cases of clothes, she had not packed anything suitable for a wet and cold rugby match. We therefore went into Bampton to find her some suitable jeans. I thought, as an undergraduate, that I ought also to have some. I therefore bought some very expensive and rather smart jeans which were somewhat superior to the normal student's dress code.

Liz meanwhile has been sent off to Birmingham to try some criminal cases. Having spent her years at the Bar in the Chancery Division and in the Commercial Court, she is somewhat inexperienced in crime, other than the experience which she managed to glean sitting as a judge in the Courts of Appeal in Jersey and Guernsey and prosecuting in the celebrated Guinness cases. Not surprisingly, she is somewhat nervous and anxious. However, she has, at Birmingham, some other experienced judges sitting with her and a very helpful local Bar to nurse her through her initiation as a criminal judge. Although it was something of a baptism of fire, she gets through it with flying colours and is reported by the local Bar as having done excellent work. Her Chambers give her a dinner at Lincoln's Inn to celebrate. She has to make a speech which she does with great aplomb and everyone is delighted that she has been appointed. I go to Birmingham from time to time to have dinner in the lodgings with her and meet a lot of old friends. It is now well-run, under a new regime.

The University match which I managed to watch on television is a very exciting affair and Oxford, in the end, won. I now find that my loyalties, so far as the University rugby match is concerned, are equally divided. I think this is due to the fact that I can identify with the Oxford side, from having watched it, whereas this isn't the case for the Boat Race or the cricket match. Indeed, I cannot believe that I could ever support Oxford in the University cricket match. Old habits die hard.

I have dinner one evening with Brian and Annie Wedlake. He used to do *The World at One* and she is the mother of Mark Nicholas who captained Hampshire at cricket and now is a well-known commentator on Channel 4. By chance, in the middle of dinner, I get a call from him from Australia, because Channel 4 is going to be excluded in the future from broadcasting cricket on television. The suggestion is that Sky will do it all. I have a long conversation with him and assure him that I will do my best to help, but I doubt that there is anything very useful that I can do. However, I write a letter to the *Telegraph*. I thought *The Times* would be unlikely to publish, also being owned by Murdoch. In the event the *Telegraph* don't publish it either. The ECB (England and Wales Cricket Board) has, in fact, already decided that the large sums offered by Sky 1 are required for cricket and that that is more important than preserving the very high quality of Channel 4 broadcasting. It's a very sad example of commercial pressures, but cricket just needs the money. Channel 4 cricket has brought a new approach to broadcasting and Mark Nicholas and Richie Benaud are two particular stars. It will be a tragedy to see them replaced.

We go and stay with the Rougiers down in Somerset and have a marvellous day driving across Exmoor. When we stop for lunch, we fall in with Boris Johnson's father who is apparently a candidate to be an MP. Meanwhile, in the run-up to Christmas, I do a bit of shooting, not with any great success and I also go to the mediators' lunch for the City Disputes Panel. I would like to do a lot more mediation and arbitration but I suspect that, getting to the age I am, and being out of the general swim, it is much less easy. We also go and see a great production at the National Theatre of Alan Bennett's *The History Boys*. It is slightly too long but very well acted, and like everything else that he writes, marvellously well structured.

I have found the work this term much more interesting and, so far as politics were concerned, there was much less theory. Thus I get a good report from Lesley, in particular for the way in which I helped Erin but Bill is still somewhat critical. His report suggests that common sense (which apparently I display) and philosophy are not very good bedfellows. I am misguided if I think that there are obvious answers to the questions that philosophy poses. I shall just have to change my ways. Next term I am to do British Politics from 1880 to the Modern Day with Professor Bogdanor, which I am sure will be very challenging. He is a constitutional expert who has written many books and articles on political subjects. I shall go to him on a one-to-one basis so it will really put me on my mettle. I shall find the change from theory a great bonus. At least I shall be very familiar with a large part of the syllabus, having lived through many of the events.

During my time at Cambridge, the highlight of the social scene was undoubtedly May Week, which in typical nonsensical Cantab way in fact started in June. As I was playing cricket for most of that time, I missed out on quite a number of parties but it was the May Week Balls, which were the main attraction. They were always enormous fun. They were well organised, with good cabarets from London. The food was always delicious and there was plenty of drink. As far as my recollection goes, they were not unduly expensive. The difficulty with playing cricket, however, was that to leave a May Ball at 6 o'clock in the morning and play cricket at 11 o'clock with only an hour's sleep, and then perhaps fielding for an entire day, was quite a strain on the constitution. I remember on one occasion one of our players coming directly from the Ball, going out to bat and walking straight past the stumps. He ended up in the stands at the far end of the ground. Cambridge in May Week was awash with beautiful girls, most of whom had come up from London for the parties. They all seemed to be most elegantly dressed and to be having a great party time. Oxford these days, by contrast, can scarcely be described as elegant. Dresses in general seem to be totally out of fashion, being replaced by short T-shirts which leave a great gap of flesh between the bottom of the shirt and the top of the hipster trousers. These are all the rage and are exceedingly unattractive.

The river was very much in evidence at Cambridge during the summer term, with noisy punting all along the backs. If this is the same at Oxford, it is marvellously well concealed; the river seems to play a comparitively unimportant part in Oxford life. I get the impression that Oxford is very much a winter city, with the colleges looking outstanding when there is thick snow but in the spring and summer Cambridge really has nothing to beat it. May Week was clearly definable and the May Balls on three successive nights readily accessible. May Balls at Cambridge played a very much more important part in social life than 'Commem' Balls at Oxford seem to now.

I am still being asked about the difference I find between Queens' then and Harris Manchester now. It is in fact very difficult to make a comparison between them, because, although at Cambridge we were a lot older than the ordinary undergraduates due to service in the forces, nevertheless the average age difference at Harris Manchester is quite considerable. I suppose the average age at Harris Manchester is somewhere between thirty and forty; at Queens' it was probably twenty-two or twenty-three. There is a great deal of beer drinking here, as I suspect there was at Cambridge. All those years back there was not much problem of town against gown. More particularly, we had to wear gowns in the town after dark in order that we could be identified, and failure to do so resulted in a fine by the proctors.

There seem to be no sort of restrictions on the students here. I find that my fellow students are generally well behaved. Curiously they seem, if not totally indifferent to politics, disinclined to engage in any meaningful conversation about political matters. The political clubs, which were such a feature of Cambridge life, seem somewhat dormant at Oxford. Because Harris Manchester is a very small college, the games' clubs do not exist in the same way as in other colleges. Another difference is that the students seem to be very much more hard-working than my contemporaries at Cambridge and probably more intelligent. Certainly a good number of my Cambridge friends would never get into Oxford or Cambridge today. Despite getting a 2:1 at Cambridge I don't remember working as hard there as I do here at Oxford. In particular, at Cambridge, I spent the entire summer term, before exams, playing cricket at Fenners. It is true that I was able to take my books down to the cricket ground and, as Cambridge had a strong batting side, quite often I could have a full day revising, sitting on the top of the pavilion. But it is not a form of revision which I would recommend. The word 'essay crisis' is something which did not exist for me at Cambridge.

There is a relaxed feeling this year because of the absence of exams, although college collections at the beginning of each term remind us that some application is required. I keep my hand in with the law by judging some moots, and also by doing some arbitration and mediation. Happily they can be fitted in with my studies. As at Cambridge, one soon sorted out the lectures which were worth going to. But the handouts here are appreciably better than those which we got at Cambridge and, as I've said, are on the website. Not being completely computer literate, I find the use of email as the only source of communication extremely tiresome. When my laptop does go wrong, it always seems to take weeks to put right and the problem is often caused by the most trivial problem, which I am unable to sort myself. In the meantime I am flooded with directives from tutors and others of which I am totally unaware and which therefore go unanswered. This naturally gives rise to a certain amount of angst.

Come Christmas we do the usual round of exchanging Christmas presents throughout the family and go to Andrew and Debs for Christmas and Boxing Day. Anna is back from New Zealand where she has been filming *The Lion, the Witch and the Wardrobe*. On Boxing Day we go to see Arsenal play Fulham. Arsenal are still unbeaten and they manage to win this particular game without too much difficulty. It's a very good-natured crowd and the game is free of some of the dramas endemic in matches against some other clubs.

We leave the game slightly early because we are booked to go to South Africa, to stay in Cape Town and to see the Test match in the New Year. I had to persuade Liz that four suitcases may be one too many, but she knows her way around the British Airways system and we get through check-in without having to pay any penalty. I first came to South Africa with Margaret, when I was President of the MCC, and then again two years ago, when I came out for the World Cup and stayed with my brother-in-law Robin and his wife Celia. Robin had been married to Margaret's younger sister Rosemary and after her death had married an old friend, now a widow. Liz has never been and it is very exciting for her. Because we booked rather late, in Cape Town we have to stay at three separate hotels, which is somewhat tiresome. We arrive at Cape Town Airport and I pick up the car which we have hired. Although I must have done it a great number of times, I manage to lose my way to the Vineyard where we are staying. We spend an hour or so driving around parts of Cape Town to which I had never been before, and eventually arrive hot and sweaty.

After settling in, we find Doug Insole and his partner Norma Palmer sitting beside the pool. He was my captain at Cambridge and played many times for England. After the first Test match, which we win, the English cricket establishment moves into the Vineyard. We have a most engaging evening listening to Geoffrey Boycott. He is now much more relaxed and affable than he ever was, although he still has strong views about other people's feelings in cricket. We also meet up with Philip Hodgson, whom I have known since MCC committee days. He has a box at the Newlands Ground, to which he invites us, and we spend a most engaging day there. Neil Durden-Smith and Judith Chalmers, meanwhile, invite us to their New Year's party at a house which they have taken in Constantia. It is some house. Not only does it have its own swimming pool and tennis court, but also a cricket net. We find ourselves among more cricketers from the establishment, and have a really good evening. Neil and Judith thank us enormously for some bottles of champagne which they believed we had given them. We hadn't, but it was impossible after the profuse thanks to confess the mistake.

The cricket at Newlands is slightly depressing because England bat and bowl like a lot of idiots and Kallis bats as though it's a ten-day Test. We move from the Vineyard to a hotel up on the Point, which is totally without character, and then finally to a lovely place with its own private wine estate, called Constantia Uitsig. The food there is to die for. We entertain a number of friends, including the Alliotts, whom we had met on the plane coming out, and who, on their return journey, called in for a glass of beer. John Alliott was a fellow Old Carthusian, though younger than me, and we had been at the Bar together and then became fellow judges. Some years ago we were in lodgings together at Maidstone and his wife, Patsy, was also there. John, as befits a retired Guards officer, was always very well turned out. However, at breakfast one morning, Patsy turned to John and made some critical comment about his attire. She then added, 'Oliver, on the other hand, is a very snappy dresser.' As I have always been regarded as rather shambolic, I persuaded Patsy to give me a certificate to the same effect which I could show proudly to my critics. They fell about in disbelief.

We also enjoy a good deal of hospitality from other friends. David Davies, who is an MCC member and a distinguished businessman, has the most lovely house at Hoots Bay to which we are invited. Food and drink are in abundance, and again we are among fellow cricketers. We also have a drink with the daughter and son-in-law of our Norfolk friends, the Sankeys. The children had actually spent the first night of their marriage in our cottage in France, thereby causing one of the rooms thereafter to be called 'The Honeymoon Suite'. We had breakfast in the gardens at Kirstenbosche with Angela Frater, a widow whom I had met on my previous visit and who is a great friend of Richard Rougier; she is also very knowledgeable about the gardens. After breakfast we went back to her house to try some of the wine from her vineyards, which was absolutely delicious. We entertained her rather modestly at the Vineyard in return.

We made a number of visits to the Waterfront which is a delightful feature of Cape Town with exciting shops, splendid restaurants and superb views. We took ourselves off to Robben Island where Nelson Mandela was imprisoned. I had been before, but Liz had not. It is still a very emotional place. We go to the quarry where the future leaders of South Africa spent nine or ten hours a day, day after day, in the boiling sun. The story goes that, in the little cave where they were allowed a ten-minute break, they composed the future South African constitution. It is very remarkable that they emerged with so little apparent rancour. It is almost impossible now to understand how apartheid could ever have existed.

There was no evidence of racial tension in the South African community. At Newlands, Liz sat next next to Albie Sachs, now a judge of the South African Constitutional Court. She could hardly believe that so relatively recently, as legal adviser to the ANC he had been the brutal target of an assassination attempt by the previous Government in which he lost an arm. Just as surprisingly we met white South African pillars of the old regime of the cricketing community who frankly admitted that they had got everything wrong. But most amazing of all, were the black members of the cricketing community, who welcomed us with open arms as though the D'Oliveira incident had never occurred.

We try going up Cable Mountain but find the queue to be about four hours long and abandon it. Other entertainment is provided by the Lord's Taverners who have a party at the Castle. This is beautifully staged, except that we are in a room 100 yards in length, the food takes hours to get served, there are constant speeches and interruptions, and the evening goes on much too long. However, there are a great number of friends there and cricket talk is always good fun. On another gastronomic evening, we go to Panama Jack's, a fish restaurant down in the docks. It is housed in what one can only describe as a prefab, in a most unpromising area where one wouldn't really want to go, particularly after dark. The fish was outstanding. We were able to choose our own lobsters, one from the west coast and one from the east coast, all beautifully served and not expensive.

We were sad to leave Cape Town, but we had decided that we would go up to Isandhlwana and Rorke's Drift to see the battlefield. This we did, flying to Durban and hiring a car. When Margaret and I had been, we had taken the back road through Zululand, which we had found very intimidating and somewhat frightening. This time we went on the new motorway. Whereas Margaret and I had ended up in a very unattractive downmarket McDonald's, this time Liz and I found lunch at a lovely country club. Here we sat in the garden under a tree, and enjoyed ourselves in the sunshine. We arrived at Fugitive's Drift Lodge, the lodge belonging to the Anglo-Zulu historian, David Rattray. It consists of a central building with eight or ten bungalows, all charmingly but simply furnished in a safari/colonial style. Our bungalow had suffered a bit of a flood the previous week, but it dried out very quickly and we then met

7   Liz at Isandhlwana

for a drink before dinner with our fellow guests. One turned out to be a colleague from the MCC committee and another was a surveyor, who expressed some interest in trying to sell Liz's mother's house!

David Rattray greeted us at dinner and the next morning he took us out to Isandhlwana where, on a very hot day, we walked up to the top of the mound to view the site of the battlefield. We were thankful to be able to sit under the shade of a large tree and we listened enchanted to his description of the battle where approximately 22,000 Zulus defeated a contingent of 1350 British in January 1879. Although I have heard his tapes many times and also his lectures, it is still a remarkable story, which he tells with great imagination and gusto. He manages to bring the whole history of this battle to life. It is a privilege to have heard him narrate the story of these long-ago battles, and give them a resonance for South Africa today. His subsequent horrific murder in January 2007 has deprived the whole country, and, in particular, the Zulu race which he loved so well, of one of its most generous contributors to its future.

The battlefield, itself, is unchanged. Spread across it are numerous white cairns where many of the soldiers are buried. It is not affected at all by commercial activity, except that on the far side there is now an enormous American hotel, which sadly spoils the view. In the afternoon David Rattray's sidekick took us to Rorke's Drift. The story of 150 soldiers defending a supply station against 4000 Zulus is well known, but it was beautifully retold. There was enormous bravery shown and 13 VCs were won including two posthumous awards. The last time I had visited I had thought Rorke's Drift was somewhat less than exciting, but this time it really got to me – as it did to Liz. Altogether, it was a pretty emotional day.

Liz had arranged to go and see an old friend of hers, Colonel Reggie Purbrick, a colonel who had recently commanded a cavalry regiment in Germany. There he had succeeded in taking his tanks across a German asparagus field and destroyed the entire crop. As a result of this, and some other alleged misdemeanours, his services had no longer been required by the British Army. His house was located on the way back towards Durban, and we had been given some vague instructions from an assistant of David Rattray's as to how to find the entrance. We had been told that the house was some fifteen miles along a dirt track. We found the general area without difficulty, but our instructions were wholly inadequate, or we were wholly inadequate in interpreting them, and so we spent about an hour trying to find the entrance to the elusive dirt track. By the time we eventually found it and began to navigate it in our little hire car, it was beginning to get very foggy. Luckily we got to the Colonel's house before it got dark and before we appreciated just what a hazardous and horrendous journey it had been. We arrived very tired, slightly bad-tempered and in need of a drink, only to find that the Colonel didn't seem to be there and that the place was awash with noisy children, who were skylarking on the roof. Not unreasonably, they were totally uninterested in our presence. Eventually the Colonel was also sighted on the roof, where he was organising what appeared to be some sort of ten-gun rocket salvo to celebrate the birthday of one of his sons. He swung down from the roof and greeted us enthusiastically. Order was restored with one bark, spare visitors were dispatched, and we were finally given a large and very welcome drink.

The Colonel was small, and clearly a distinguished soldier for whom peacetime soldiering was not designed. The house and estate were reminiscent of a Scottish Victorian shooting lodge, with colonial embellishments, and overlooked a series of man-designed lakes. He hiked us around the estate the next morning, accompanied by a lolloping dog, which would dart off into the undergrowth from time to time to devour some species of invisible African wildlife. We were then bidden to lunch by the Colonel's wife, Lizzie, from whom he had separated. She lived about thirty miles away. She had been a show jumper and event rider of some distinction, although she, too, had crossed swords with the horse world authorities. We ate and drank very well, and swam and returned somewhat exhausted. Next day the Colonel kindly suggested that he should lead us back out to the main road in his four-wheel drive. The track was narrow and the sandy surface was extremely slippery. Where it wasn't slippery, there were large bumps in the road, and without the presence of the Colonel, I should have packed up and gone back to his house. The hire car was woefully inadequate for the job. After about eight miles he thought it was safe to let us go on our own. It was not much better then, but eventually we made it onto a tarmac road and breathed a sigh of relief. So back we went to Durban, caught the plane to Johannesburg and came back home. It had been an enormously amusing and exhilarating holiday, which we had both much enjoyed.

8

Second Year... Continued

Liz was required, as part of her continuous education, to go to Warwick University and for three days to listen to a series of lectures on serious sex crimes. Most of the presentations were fairly heavy going. However one particular speaker, introducing the new Sexual Offences Act, observed that bestiality with an animal was to remain an offence which would, no doubt, be of interest to those from Humberside. Liz had no idea what had happened at Humberside, and so she asked her next-door neighbour what this was all about. It transpired that a commuter train had been travelling from Humberside, its passengers meanwhile chattering into their mobile phones to their offices, wives and girlfriends. The train then ground to an unscheduled halt by the side of an idyllic Arcadian green pasture, where beasts were gently grazing. While the commuters were idly looking out of the window, they observed a goatherd doing what he obviously did every morning, which was to have sex with his goat. This attracted the full attention of all the commuters, who immediately manned their mobile phones to alert the police and other reportable authorities, as to what was going on. Within a short space of time, sirens could be heard, four-wheel drives with blue flashing lights appeared, and the area was swamped with police who took the luckless goatherd into custody. Next morning the story was in the local paper where there was a picture of the goat, with a black rectangle covering its eyes, and a caption reading 'For legal reasons, the identity of the victim cannot be revealed'.

In February, Liz is invited to the Association of Insolvency Lawyers, which is having a conference in Dublin. She is required to host a number of the sessions and I am invited along as her guest. I had not been to Dublin before and was looking forward to it with great interest. We stayed in a hotel in the centre of the city and had the opportunity of looking at the architecture. Some of it is absolutely delightful, but I found the overall impression of the city somewhat disappointing. Trinity College, I thought, was less exciting than I had anticipated and the city appeared somewhat dowdy. I didn't pretend to understand much about insolvency but Liz conducted her sessions with great self-assurance and the event provoked much discussion. We were also lavishly entertained in Dublin Castle, the scene of many incidents in the past. The IRA were still dragging their heels about giving up their weapons but it was some relief to think that perhaps some of the troubles were now beginning to disappear.

Meanwhile back at Oxford I go to political tutorials with Vernon Bogdanor, the Oxford Professor of Politics and Government. He is immensely knowledgeable, is the author of numerous books and articles, and is highly regarded as a constitutional expert. His tutorials are constantly interrupted by the media who want his views on every subject, with which he deals expeditiously. He is not in any sense overawed by my age, and we have challenging and (what I hope are) intellectual discussions not only about politics but also about the law. He knows a great number of judges and has drafted, as far as I understand, constitutions for a number of countries. It is a privilege to discuss both political and legal matters with him. I find his views about incidents which occurred during my formative years, and of which he has only read, particularly illuminating. He asked me to write an essay about the Attlee administration from 1945 to 1951. He told me that I ought to read a very interesting article about the austerity which existed during that period. I subsequently discovered that the article had been written by an old friend of mine, Michael Sissons, the distinguished literary agent who had been on the MCC committee with me. I pointed out to Vernon that I didn't need to read anybody else's views about austerity, because I had been up at Cambridge in 1948, when food and petrol continued to be rationed and ordinary goods were in short supply. Bread and sweets, in particular, were less available than during the war and ration books remained during my time at Cambridge. Our jam ration was augmented by tins of South African jellies which for some reason did not require coupons. Petrol rationing continued until 1951 and my little scooter, which I used in Cambridge, only survived because my parents generously gave me some of their car coupons. Our whole way of life was conditioned by severe restrictions on what we could eat, drink or buy, but for us undergraduates it was just part of every- day life. I remember the milk ration was a small tumblerful per day. Unhappily, I once managed to drink my room mate's share on the occasion of his parents' first visit to the university. Thereafter, we agreed to part company – not altogether amicably.

Undergraduates were only allowed cars at Cambridge in special circumstances and, in any event, the shortage of petrol was an inhibiting factor. There were frequent fuel crises and life in the winter was a constant battle against the elements. Clothes were in short supply and all the artefacts which now go to make up the average household were non-existent. Telephones were a luxury and there was a long waiting list for installation. There were credit restrictions and holidays abroad were severely limited. Package holidays, as we know them now, scarcely existed and flying was an enormous adventure. Hitchhiking on the continent was the most popular form of holiday, as well as the cheapest, but taking a car abroad was a bureaucratic nightmare, as well as a time-consuming exercise. Driving on the unattractive cobbled roads of France and Belgium was unpleasant and the standard of accommodation on offer on arrival left much to be desired. A lot of it would now be condemned on health grounds.

Vernon Bogdanor invited Liz and me to dine on high table at Brasenose College. This was a delightful experience, and the evening ended with him and Liz singing excerpts from what I was informed were operas by Richard Strauss!

At Easter Liz and I were invited by Tim and Patsy Bergqvist (close neighbours in Buckinghamshire) to go and stay at their quinta (a port vineyard) on the River Douro. They have a lovely comfortable house and are generous and hospitable hosts. Margaret and I had first gone there nearly thirty years ago when we trod the grape. Picnics down the river were one of the great treats of the holiday, and expeditions in Tim's boat were always an adventure. Before the river was dammed, Roger Vernon, an entertaining friend from Bucks and a very experienced sailor, and I had managed to overturn Patsy's dinghy, on a windless day, which had not been very popular. Tim had had to come out in his motor boat and rescue us.

Margaret and I initially went for the vintage in 1977. The pickers started at 6 or 7 o'clock and picked to mid-morning when they had a break. After lunch they worked until about 5 or 6 o'clock. Then a number of them would go into the lagar, the traditional stone vessel in which they would tread the grape, to the strains of an accordion. The house party, after a very good dinner, would wander up and see what was happening. The local boys rather boldly would invite Patsy to dance, and some of the house party would get into the lagar and tread the grapes. The staining on the legs remained there for an appreciable period of time, as did the smell of the grapes. Tasting the vintage on subsequent occasions was a reminder of the fun that we had had. The only fly in the ointment was that, at the end of the holiday, we were all expected either to write a poem or to draw something in the Visitors Book. This had been part of the Bergqvist ritual since well before the war and they had a marvellous collection of poems and drawings.

Liz had never been to Portugal before. The Bergqvists were very kind and welcoming and we enjoyed the visit enormously. Tim had had the idea of buying another piece of land further up the Douro Valley from La Rosa. So we went up on the train from Pinhao, distinguished by its beautiful old blue-tiled decorations on the station walls. The train journey, following the course of the river, offered spectacular views of the vineyards and quintas of other port producers. We took a picnic and viewed the property, which had a tumbledown farmhouse and high-lying, very fertile fields. Here Tim was going to plant a lot more vines, for the production of both port and table wines. Rather unwisely Liz and I decided we would return in the car, and this was a horrendous journey because of the contours of the road. We very much regretted we had not come back by train.

The lagar at La Rosa is now full of modern equipment and, although some wine is still trodden, most of it is done by automatic machinery. Originally, Tim sold his grapes to Sandemans and therefore had no responsibility for the marketing of the port. About ten or twelve years ago, he decided to branch out on his own and to sell his port under the name of Quinta de la Rosa. The marketing of the grapes has, therefore, assumed enormous importance.

His daughter, Sophia, is in charge of marketing and the whole operation is run with great efficiency. They have branched out into table wines as well, which are not only very good in themselves, but are also important for cash flow. At the end of the holiday, we went back on the train to Oporto with much of the journey running alongside the Douro, although there is now a splendid motorway, nearly all the way to Villa Real. It is interesting to see how Portugal, so relatively recently a poor peasant country, has been transformed because of the EU into a modern, prosperous and successful community.

After arriving back from Portugal, we went off almost directly to San Francisco as guests of the Commercial Bar Association (Combar), who were holding their annual meeting there with representatives of the North American Bars. I had been to San Francisco before, with Margaret, when I had done a case in Hong Kong; we had flown home, via the island of Maui, and had spent a week in San Francisco. Liz had never been there before, however. Combar had organised a splendid programme. They had invited lawyers from different parts of the world, so that it was not only educational but also entertaining. There was also a certain amount of networking about mediation and arbitration, in which I enthusiastically engaged. Liz chaired one or two of the sessions. My role was to speak after dinner one evening at a restaurant, across the Golden Gate Bridge, in Sausalito. Luckily few of the guests had heard my very old jokes, and, after a certain amount of drink, they seemed amused by it all and the evening turned out to be a great success. There was a trip out into the Bay to see the bridge and to look at Alcatraz (no longer in use as a prison). When the sessions were over, Liz and I took ourselves off to the harbour area and again went across to Sausalito, where we had a lovely day wandering around looking at shops and eating well.

Some years ago John Witney, who had been on the Independent Broadcasting Authority with Margaret, sent her a brochure about a musical called *The Far Pavilions*, based upon the best-selling romantic novel of the same name, which he and his Really Useful Company were proposing to stage. He invited her to become an angel. Margaret told me to put it in the waste-paper basket, but I was intrigued by it, and, unknown to her, I decided that I would have a punt and did so. Luckily, it was not the entire family savings that I invested, merely a modest sum. About once a year, the Really Useful Company issued a document setting out the progress, or lack of it, in the development of this musical.

Eventually in April 2005 it came to London and we were invited to the first night. I had rather imagined that it would be black tie or bejewelled turbans, and a swank dinner afterwards, reflecting the exotic Indian theme. Alas, it was not to be. The musical had few, if any, memorable tunes. Although the production was lavishly dressed and beautifully designed, the post-show party did not live up to the glamour and we had to hustle to obtain our buffet-eats and a seat. I have the feeling that the show will not last for very long, and that the money invested will not be repaid. But I did not become an angel as a money spinner, but out of amusement. I am not holding my breath.

In May there is the general election. Surprisingly, it would be difficult to discover this from posters or banners in Oxford. Members of the college seem comparatively indifferent to what is going on. There are no loudspeaker vans. There seem to be no public meetings and it is only possible to believe that there is an election going on because of television. In our time in Cambridge we would have been visiting houses, banging on doors and generally taking part. I don't know whether this is the apathy of youth or whether things have changed so much that public opinion polls now control what people think. I have to say I find it sad. There are pamphlets from each of the political parties which are put into our pigeon-holes, including one from a so-called independent expert who recommended voting tactically so as to squeeze the Tory vote. Some independent! One of the odd things that I did discover was that all university students are apparently eligible to vote, including the foreign nationals. How this comes about I do not know. There has been a great deal of criticism of postal voting with all the abuse and corruption that that has generated, but it would seem to be very bizarre if overseas students have a vote in our general election. My cottage in France entitles me, I believe, to vote in their local elections, but certainly not in a general election or in a referendum.

The result of the election was widely predicted, though not the exact figures. Once again Leonard Figg gave us a party to which all our local friends were invited. Leonard had been a senior boy at Charterhouse when I first went and, after serving in the RAF, had a distinguished career in the Foreign Office, ending up as our Ambassador in Dublin. By coincidence, his wife Jane had been a junior girl at Malvern Girls' College with Margaret. We had an entertaining evening, everyone believing that a much-reduced majority for the Government was to the good. Having read a good deal about elections, I forbore to point out that Harold Wilson had managed to run a government, for some period, with a majority of only four and that John Major's last majority had been no more than twenty. In the modern world, governments probably do far better with a small majority than they do with an unyielding mass of MPs, who are sullen and resentful because they have not got a place in government. And because, with a large majority, they know that if they do revolt they are not going to cause any difficulty to the Government, they frequently do so.

I am again asked by Patrick Wright if I will make the speech at the De La Rue dinner and agree to do it. I go and have a splendid lunch with him and Nicholas Brook, the chairman of De La Rue, at Mosiman's, to discuss the sort of thing that I will want to say. When I suggest that I might make some penetrating adverse comments about Europe and, in particular, about the referendum which first France and then Holland have lost, they go sheet-white and suggest that that would be quite inappropriate! Being anti-Europe, I found the result of the referenda enormously encouraging. I have, in fact, read the Constitution, which gives enormous powers to Europe. They include a single Foreign Minister and the ability to overrule national laws. There are a host of other regulations which the European Court, in its wisdom, has the discretion to interpret. From past experience that will be a nightmare.

I therefore had to prepare my speech with some care, because the audience of some 350 included the diplomatic representatives to London from all around the world. I was told by Patrick and Nicholas to be lighthearted and, in view of what happened last year, when the Home Office Minister simply read her official brief, I thought that was a sensible suggestion. But it was a formidable undertaking to address this large body at the Dorchester and to say something that was both intelligent and entertaining and yet did not tread on too many toes. People were kind enough to say that I certainly achieved the latter. My fellow speaker, Sir Peter Middleton, gave a penetrating speech about Treasury Policy, which meant that I felt more comfortable in the comic relief slot.

Meanwhile, Liz has finally settled her divorce. In July, after a certain amount of frisson, she managed to sell her and her former husband's house in South Kensington and is now going to buy a smaller house in London. Whether she will have enough room for all her clothes, we shall have to wait and see!

9

Legal Notes

It has been fascinating to talk to those students at Oxford, who were interested in the law about the rich life I have had, and to try and explain the sort of work I did at the Bar and on the Bench. Not very surprisingly, there was much ignorance about what was involved, what were the qualities required and what were the problems faced. A number who were thinking of coming to the Bar sought my advice about the wisdom of so doing. I tried to explain that newspaper reports of cases gave a somewhat exaggerated picture of what happened in court, and that life at the Bar was much more mundane and less glamorous than popularly portrayed by the media. What was needed was intelligence, hard work, personality, good judgement and a bit of luck. You won't necessarily succeed with these qualities, but without them you have no prospect of a successful career. I therefore tried to explain the problems of the day-to-day life of a barrister.

The qualities which are needed for a judge are different. Many successful barristers do not make good judges and some eminent judges had modest practices at the Bar. Judgement is, of course, all important, but patience and an ability to listen are equally essential. When I reached the age of seventy-five I was no longer eligible, even as a 'retread', to sit in the High Court and try cases. I confess that I missed the intellectual exercise which is involved in making judgements, in deciding points of law, in analysing the evidence of witnesses and in deciding whom to believe and whom not to believe. In the last few years I had done a lot of libel work, involving a jury who decided the facts. It is not, I think, generally appreciated how difficult it often is for a judge, sitting on his own, as I did in the majority of my civil trials, to determine where the truth in a particular case lies. Sometimes there are documents which support one side or the other and, in other cases, the probabilities are so great that it is not difficult to come to a decision. But, in many cases, however, where there are no documents and the probabilities are at least equal on each side and both sets of witnesses seem to be equally honest, there can be very real problems. People who have witnessed events for only a few seconds, or even for a few minutes, tend subsequently to rationalise what they saw and fit it into a pattern of how they think the events unfolded. This is particularly true of quite honest witnesses, who have a firm set in their mind as to what happened and cannot be shaken. Often, the trial of the event which they witnessed takes place a long time after the events themselves and their subsequent recollection often bears no relation to what they said at the time. Anyone who has ever been involved in a motor accident knows exactly how difficult it is properly to reconstruct the events leading up to the crash.

Medical negligence cases were often the most difficult. The result of an operation which has gone wrong has a catastrophic effect, not only on the patient, but on the patient's family, who are now responsible for supporting and maintaining a badly damaged relative. And it is quite understandable that, if something goes wrong in an operation, the relatives will naturally blame the surgeon. The doctors have certainly not helped themselves. The Medical Defence Union, which was, in my day, the main medical insurer, has much to answer for because of its intransigent approach to perfectly legitimate claims. It argues, no doubt, that because there are a lot of claims which have no merit or indeed are a complete try-on, their being tough reduces those types of unwarranted claims.

However, the practice which it adopted in my time of non co-operation, of non-disclosure and of the stringing-out of the litigation process, created an atmosphere of confrontation that was quite unworthy of the medical profession. It was surprising how often medical notes disappeared or had been lost in a move and were therefore no longer available. The profession's declining to accept liability right up to the doors of the court, in cases which should not have been contested in the first place, only too often caused a plaintiff, weary of waiting, to accept a sum far less than the case was worth. It was a very great hardship, and a source of additional misery to a badly injured plaintiff, who may have already waited for four or five years before a doctor or hospital threw in the towel and finally admitted liability. Subsequent alteration to the rules, as a result of the Woolf Reforms to the Civil Procedure Rules, has made this sort of behaviour now much less likely.

Another unattractive aspect of modern litigation is the growth of the compensation culture – 'I have a right to be compensated for almost every ill done to me whether negligent or otherwise.' These types of practices, which have come from the United States of America, with their enormous awards by juries, have started to take over in litigation in the United Kingdom. Such actions used to be fuelled by legal aid, which was often granted without, as far as one could see, any great consideration of the merits. Legal aid has been seriously curtailed, to be replaced by conditional fee arrangements. These enable a claim to be brought without payment by the client, but where the legal adviser gets paid a additional sum for costs in the event that the client wins. This scheme has undoubtedly been a significant additive to the whole compensation culture. Most of this came as something of a shock to many of the students to whom I talked and who were otherwise pretty knowledgeable about current affairs.

One unfortunate result of this compensation culture is that doctors have started to practise defensive medicine. Almost everything they do has to be approved by the client and explained. Risks will not be taken. The idea of league tables for hospitals or surgeons is another one of those manic ideas emanating from Whitehall. The result is that a local hospital will refer any difficult case to a specialist hospital so as to avoid taking the risk of an operation which may not be successful. The specialist hospitals, because they are specialist, will naturally take on the very difficult cases where there is obviously a severe risk of failure. Thus it will appear that Mr A, who is an eminent specialist, has a much worse record than Mr B, from the referral hospital, because Mr B will only deal with cases where there is little or no risk. The doctors have themselves to blame, to a certain extent, by allowing the Health Service to fall into the hands of the civil service and administrators and by not taking charge of the health scheme themselves when it was first set up.

It is important to remember that Whitehall longs to get hold of the professions. It has succeeded in the medical profession and now it is flexing its muscles over the legal profession. Legal aid for young barristers in criminal cases has not been increased for eight years. There is a suggestion that pensions for judges are now to be capped. The Lord Chancellor has devised an elaborate system over who should and should not have silk, to be decided by a worthy body which will have no personal knowledge of any of the applicants. Likewise there is to be a Judicial Appointments Commission to appoint judges at all levels, other than the highest, where much the same will apply. No doubt there is a good deal to be said for not having things done too secretly but the legal profession is a small one, where the ability of those eligible to take silk or become a judge is well known to their contemporaries. At the Bar reputation is all. The idea that the views of lay members are to play some part in these appointments would be laughable if it were not so serious. Even worse is a sifting process apparently to be conducted by civil servants (and without any judicial input), looking at a form with boxes to be filled in. This is a barrier to be surmounted by a candidate before he or she can even get to an interview. Thank goodness we don't choose our military commanders in this bizarre fashion.

I had to point out to my fellow students that one of the difficulties in medical negligence cases was deciding whether the action or lack thereof which had such a catastrophic effect was due to some negligent act or failure on the part of the surgeon, or simply to the risk inherent in any surgery. The distinction between these two situations, which in one case would result in a substantial sum of damages for the plaintiff, and in the other nothing, was often very difficult to determine. Sometimes the views of two equally distinguished experts conflicted and in this case it was never a very easy task for the layman, which is what the judge is, to determine not where the truth lay (because the experts were both honest witnesses) but where the line should be drawn.

All this judicial work was now lost to me, save that I was allowed to sit from time to time outside the country, in particular in Gibraltar. I could also conduct arbitrations and mediations and sit on professional disciplinary tribunals, regulating professions such as chartered accountants or chartered surveyors. Gibraltar is now no longer full of the military. The Navy, since I was there in 1947, seems totally to have vanished. The days when the Mediterranean Fleet anchored in the Bay have long since gone, though shops in Gibraltar still have marvellous pictures of pre-war visits by the Mediterranean Fleet and sometimes by the Home Fleet. The attraction of Gibraltar is that it is a duty-free town. Thus the main street is full of shops selling items of drink and clothing at knock-down prices – a magnet to the sun-worshippers who pile off the visiting cruise liners every day. The apes still occupy the heights and they are a great tourist attraction, as are the casements.

The frisson with Spain has created something of a siege mentality. While I was there on my last visit, Gibraltar held a referendum on links with Spain. By an overwhelming vote, they decided that they were never going to have any accord with Spain. The Spanish, for their part, seem to me to have behaved without very much sense. For thirty years they have been totally intransigent. They frequently close the border without warning; they block telephone calls, and are continuously tiresome about air space. If instead, they had opened the frontiers, made themselves enormously welcome to the young in Gibraltar and invited them to their universities and schools, they would years ago have attracted a new generation who didn't subscribe to the view that England was best. A bit more 'carrot' and less 'stick' would, in my view, have been more sensible. However, it was not to be. The frontier is still subject to delays, there is no direct boat from Gibraltar to Algaceiras, and there are continuing problems about air space. Although occasionally there seems to be some movement, it is of such a slow pace as to be almost imperceptible.

The High Court in Gibraltar has two judges. One is the Chief Justice and the other is a puisne judge. They have the same jurisdiction that High Court judges have in the United Kingdom. My first visit to Gibraltar arose in this way. A well-known Gibraltar citizen, who had been selected for the Olympics, was charged with importing a large quantity of heroin. At his first trial, before the Chief Justice, the jury disagreed. The prosecution then decided that they would have a second bite of the cherry, but were met by an application that to do so would be an abuse of process, by reason of delay. The Chief Justice plainly could not deal with that and so the application was dealt with by the puisne judge. He decided that it was indeed an abuse of process. The prosecution then appealed to the Court of Appeal, who decided that it was not an abuse of process and therefore the trial was to proceed. Accordingly, it was necessary to find a judge other than the Chief Justice or the puisne judge who had made the original order about abuse. I was therefore invited to go out to Gibraltar to try the case.

The case, which was due to last some three weeks, ended well within a fortnight, due to the help of counsel and to some gentle judicial pressure. It resulted in the triumphant acquittal of the defendant. I was well entertained during my stay there by the Chief Justice and by the puisne judge, and also by the Governor and the staff of the Court. And a young member of the Bar, a friend of the Bergqvists who was living in Spain, invited me to have dinner with him in La Linea. I was intrigued to go, because, when I had last been there in 1947, the village had consisted of one shop and one brothel. I had visited one but not the other. It was now an enormously flourishing town and we went to a most agreeable country club for an entertaining dinner. Clive, the Chief Clerk at the Court, arranged for me to go round the casements and to see various parts of Gibraltar. I wandered around the docks where *Virago*, my old ship, had once been, and had a nostalgic week seeking to retrace my movements from fifty years back.

The next time I was invited to sit as a judge, towards the end of my second year at Oxford, was in somewhat different circumstances. The legal profession on Gibraltar is fused and QCs often act as solicitors. In the particular case which I was invited to try, the Speaker of the Assembly (The Gibraltar Parliament), who was a QC, had drafted a will for a lady who had since died. The contents of the will were subsequently challenged by some of the relatives. There were two grounds of challenge. The doctor who signed as a witness, allegedly in the presence of the deceased, subsequently said that, although he had so signed, he had not in fact been present when the deceased herself had signed. If that were right, the will would be invalid. Secondly, there was an allegation that there had been undue influence exerted upon the deceased to leave her money to one of the daughters and not to the others. The question of whether the doctor had been present at the signing of the will depended on a straightforward swearing match between the QC Speaker of the Assembly and the daughter on the one side, and the doctor on the other. The question of whether there had been undue influence involved a whole lot of witnesses on both sides.

It was clear that it would be inappropriate for the Chief Justice or the puisne judge, knowing the parties, to try this case. Somebody from outside, who was not involved locally, needed to be appointed. Thus I came to try the case. It was clearly a matter of some importance because the credibility or otherwise of the Speaker of the Assembly was one of the major issues in the case. The Assembly is a small body, consisting, I believe, of some fifteen members and is the democratically elected chamber. The Speaker exercises a very important role. Furthermore, as he was a Queen's Counsel, any finding against him would be extremely serious. It was not a decision which I would ever have shirked, because it is the job of a judge to evaluate the witnesses and to make a finding about credibility, without fear or favour.

Clive kindly arranged for me to stay at the Elliott Hotel and for the papers to be dispatched. I spent an appreciable amount of time researching the law on validity of wills, with which I have to confess I had not previously been very familiar. Having been sworn in by the Deputy Governor, the Governor being away, I was then poised to try the case. The first morning was spent by counsel, who were both QCs, one from England and one local, asking for time, which I naturally gave them. By lunchtime they had agreed to settle the case, on terms which they declined to vouchsafe to me but which were apparently satisfactory to all the parties. I was thus relieved from the obligation of having to make crucial findings of credibility against one or more of the parties.

I had arranged with Liz that she should come out the following weekend and that we should go and stay in the Andalusian town of Ronda. She duly arrived on the Friday evening. I hired a car in Gibraltar and we set off. I had booked dinner, both for the Friday night and for the Saturday night, at two separate restaurants in Ronda. As we were running a bit behind time, I asked Liz to ring ahead and say that we might be a little late. From the confusion of telephone numbers, she managed (with what she assured me was not her usual efficiency) to alert a restaurant, to which we were booked to go on the Saturday, that we would arrive at about 9.30 that evening, and, at the same time, to cancel the booking which I had made at the restaurant, to which we were meant to be going on the Friday.

The road from Gibraltar to Ronda is now effectively in two parts. A magnificent highway goes all along the coast of the Costa del Sol and then, near Marbella, there is a 45 km-drive up a windy road beautifully tarmaced but narrow and very twisty. I remember the very narrow road that Desmond Lewtas and I had taken when we had stayed in Ronda on leave from the Navy in 1947. Desmond was a store's assistant and very good company, and he much enjoyed good living. We had gone down from Ronda to Malaga on the local bus, a journey then fraught with considerable danger, due both to the precipitous nature of the road and the insouciance of the bus driver. When we arrived at Malaga, then a tiny fishing village, we had sat on a deserted beach which I suspect we could have bought for a few pesetas.

Liz and I eventually arrived at Ronda, which is still very beautiful. We stayed at the Parador which looks out over the Gorge. During the journey we had finally managed to sort out the booking problems and therefore we were able to go straight off to have dinner in an elegant restaurant also overlooking the Gorge, where the staff, after looking somewhat surprised that we had turned up a day earlier than expected, served us courteously and charmingly even though it was well after 10 pm. In Gibraltar everybody had warned us gloomily that 'Ronda is very hot'. But, in the cool of the evening sitting outside with a marvellous view over the Gorge's edge, we dismissed these Cassandras as middle-aged spoilsports and, after a delicious dinner, retired to bed. Next day, we enjoyed the comfort of the Parador's swimming pool after getting up at the crack of dawn to walk all round Ronda. We were anxious not to miss a church or what the guide book characterised as a 'significant' house. One church, the Church of the Martyrs, obviously exploiting its brand, had the most comprehensive and riveting exhibition of torture instruments used, no doubt, in the Inquisition. But they appeared to be in such perfect working order that one had the distinct impression that they had been gainfully employed only the week before. The exhibition included not only a guillotine but also detailed instructions as to how each respective torture apparatus was to be used. I was rather relieved that it was not like the Science Museum in South Kensington, where children are allowed to 'have a go on the machines'. Liz, being of a more bloodthirsty temperament than me, had a distinctly creative and determined gleam in her eye.

We did a bit of shopping, took lots of photographs, and visited the picture-book bull ring which is the oldest bull ring in Spain. It presents not as a real-life place but rather as the Platonic ideal of a backdrop for *Carmen*. But there was no bull fighting until September. I have seen a fight once only, in Mexico, where it seemed to me to be a very exciting, artistic and skilful exhibition. To many people it is an enormously cruel sport, both for the horses and for the bull (and not often enough for the matador), but the Spaniards do not see it in that way. Bull fighters there are accorded a status similar to that which we accord professional footballers. On the Sunday evening, loaded with a certain amount of alcohol, we caught the plane back to England. The olive oil, which we had bought in Ronda in plastic bottles, was confiscated on the ground that it might break and flood the aircraft; the inflammable alcohol in glass bottles was no problem. Sometimes I think officialdom can be very silly.

As I have already said, I was not available to try cases in court except outside the jurisdiction, but I have been able to conduct arbitrations and mediations, both in this country and abroad. Talking to the students at Oxford studying law, it was clear that mediation was not a familiar concept to them or indeed to the general public. Mediation started in America some years ago. The purpose of it is to get the parties together in order to try and solve their dispute with the aid of an independent mediator, thereby avoiding the costs involved in a trial. Put simply like that, mediation obviously has merit. However, it requires the co-operation of both parties. If one party is not prepared to discuss the case, then there is no point having mediation. The saving in costs to the parties of a successful mediation is enormous. Take, for example, a commercial dispute which is going to last three, or even four, months. It will necessarily involve gathering together a vast quantity of documents. A settlement at an early date will result in a substantial saving of the costs of this exercise. Before a trial of any complexity can take place, each party has to satisfy themselves that they have produced all the documents which are relevant not only to their case but to the case of the other side. But this is not the only saving of costs. The principal witnesses need to cast their minds back to the events leading up to the dispute, to record them in witness statements and themselves to read the documents to ensure that they are familiar with them. Taking a busy executive out of his normal company work for several months, in order to organise the documents, and to prepare himself and to prepare others, is not only an enormous burden on the individual concerned but is also very costly to his employers because he is not doing his normal work. There is therefore every incentive to seek to minimise the costs by avoiding having to spend time on preparation or at trial. Even in a successful conclusion to litigation, the winning party does not recover all its costs. Its senior officials may have been made to look somewhat silly in the witness box. Sometimes the victory is no more than pyrrhic. If the parties are to resume commercial relations in the future, they may now find that those relations have been somewhat soured by the hostile cross-examination of their principal witnesses. Thus there is a lot to be said for mediation.

How it works is that a mediator is appointed who is acceptable to both parties or, if there are more than two parties, to all the parties. The mediator will usually have had some training in mediation, either by CEDR (Centre for Effective Dispute Resolution) or by some other organisation. He may be a lawyer or a consultant or, because a number of mediations are about technical matters, he may be an expert in a particular field. His role is to get the parties together and for them to arrive at a solution which is acceptable to them. The temptation for someone like me, brought up as a judge, is that, having read the papers, I may come to some preliminary view as to where the merits lie, and then try and direct the parties to arrive at that solution. That is not the object of the exercise and is to be resisted if possible. It is better for the parties to reach a solution with which they are both happy or at any rate not unhappy.

To that end the mediator spends a lot of time, needing a great deal of patience, in seeing the parties both together and separately, working them towards a solution. The pattern, which is generally followed, is to get all the parties together initially, and for a spokesman from each side to state how they see their case and to do that without interruption. The mediator will then see the parties separately. What is said to him is confidential, and not on any account to be repeated to the other side without consent. One of the functions of the mediator is to try to find out what are the sticking points. Is it a matter of principle, pride, money or something else which is holding up settlement?

He may choose to see one of the parties without their legal representative or the legal representative without the party. Sometimes the legal representatives are the sticking point because they see the matter as more a legal problem than a commercial one. It is important for mediators, if they can, to identify the person or persons on each side who makes the decisions. Before any mediation is commenced, the parties have to indicate that they have the authority to come to an agreement. If they do not do so, any agreement which appears have been reached then has to be ratified. This is time consuming. Sometimes, too, second thoughts prevail and what appeared as an agreement can go off.

Different mediators have different ways of approach. The teaching is that the mediators should not express their view, even if asked, as to what they think the result ought to be. I confess that there have been times when, after a long and wearisome mediation, the parties have asked me for my views. It seemed to me to get the proceedings back on course, that some indication would be helpful to them both. Big mediations can go on for periods of time and be very complex. In some cases, mediators will be chosen for their specialist knowledge, either about engineering, or the construction industry or the oil industry, as the technical details involved will need to be fully understood. A successful mediation is enormously satisfying and the mediator will go away with a feeling of a job well done. The result, or even the fact, of the mediation has to remain, confidential, and certainly must not be talked about by the mediator. Additionally, anything said during the mediation is without prejudice to what will happen at trial if the mediation is unsuccessful.

One mediation which I conducted and which was unsuccessful attracted a good deal of publicity. Because it was fully covered by the press I can talk about it in general terms. The Rugby Union clubs were divided into various divisions. The mediation involved the first and second division clubs. Those in the first division regarded themselves as the elite and were very reluctant to allow anyone from the second division to be promoted at the end of the season and more particularly were totally against the idea that anyone from the first division should be relegated. The reasons were almost entirely commercial. The first division attracts television coverage which provides a very substantial sum to the clubs. The second division, on the other hand, does not. Equally, those who have aspirations to play international rugby believe that to be in a second division club will not enhance their prospects. This is partly because they are unlikely to be seen very often by the selectors, and partly because the quality of the second division is not as good as the first division. There is also the fact that teams in the first division are likely to be paid more than those in the second division, because the first division clubs have the money.

The other factor governing the first division's somewhat intransigent view about relegation was the cost of their stadia. In the first division, it is necessary to build a stadium to a high standard of safety and, more particularly, fully to accommodate those who come to watch. Falling a division is likely to lead to a loss of attendance. I remember this happening to Oxford United in the soccer world, when they moved up a division. They had to build a stadium which was not only new and safer, but larger, to accommodate what was thought would be an increased attendance. However, at the end of the season, when they went back down a division, they were left with something of a white elephant of a stadium.

The other side of the coin was that, if there is no system of promotion or relegation, it means that the clubs towards the bottom of the first division have no particular incentive to do well. And, much more importantly, those who year after year come top or second of the second division have no particular incentive to succeed and have no financial reward for all their efforts. When I did the mediation, Worcester, the top of the second division, was the club most involved and it had a very strong argument for promotion. It had an energetic and thoroughly likable chairman, who faced the universal hostility of the first division clubs. The first division clubs were only willing to concede that promotion and relegation depended on the result of a home and away match between the club at the bottom of the first division and the club at the top of the second division. This was not acceptable to the second division, who saw no reason why, as in other forms of sport such as soccer and cricket, one up and one down, or even two up and two down, should not be normal practice.

I was asked by John Siddall on behalf of the Sports Dispute Panel to mediate this dispute. It involved not only the first division and second division clubs, but also the RFU who naturally had an interest in the matter being resolved. John was immensely helpful and knowledgeable. Initially we met up with the parties before the mediation started. Subsequently we met at a hotel outside Heathrow Airport where for two days we sought to get the warring factions together. Overnight the parties all stayed in the same hotel. On the second morning it looked for a moment as though an evening together over a glass had had some effect, and that the parties might now have reached a sensible solution. But it was not to be. Subsequently, it was agreed that there should be one up and one down, at any rate for a limited period. It is not without a certain irony that Harlequins, who were the most intransigent in opposing this idea of one up and one down, now, for a season, found themselves relegated to the second division. I wonder if their views have now changed?

Other mediations in which I have been engaged naturally have to remain confidential, but there is one in particular which caused me some amusement. I was invited by the Court of Appeal to mediate in a case which they were about to hear. The facts are unimportant. After a day's mediation, I remember that the defendants' offer was not acceptable to the claimant and so the case went to the Court of Appeal. I had formed the view, which I didn't express, that the claimant had a reasonable ground of appeal and that his prospects of success were not reflected in the offer made by the defendants. When the case came to the Court of Appeal, I thought it would be interesting to see how the matter developed. Accordingly, I went and sat at the back of the court while the case was argued. I had notified the members of the court about my interest in the case so that they wouldn't start wondering what I was doing there. I sat and listened to the arguments put forward. Unfortunately, it seemed to me that counsel for the appellant claimant was presenting his case without any skill at all, taking some thoroughly bad points and failing to take the only good point, which I had identified, certainly to myself. In the result the defendant respondent, was not called on, and my judgement, of which only I was aware, was shown to be wrong. I only wish that I had been allowed to argue the case myself!

I am a member of a number of bodies which now do a lot of mediation and arbitration. They are ADR Chambers, the City Disputes Panel, the Sports Disputes Panel, and the Court of Arbitration for Sport (CAS) at Lausanne. The latter is a large organisation which deals with disputes, as the name indicates, about sport. Mostly it is arbitration work although there is some mediation. This arbitration work is of the highest importance to sport. It involves every type of sport dispute. For instance, selection for the Olympic Games may depend on a particular trial race. If the star athlete has a cold on the day of the trial and cannot run, can the National Federation still invite him or her to be one of the team? Is the nature of selection for the team fair? Is a particular athlete eligible to represent that particular country? The answer may also have political implications.

Drug-taking has been one of the banes of athletics and the adoption now of a standard code is much to be welcomed. Decisions about drug-taking, particularly at the Olympic Games, are of the highest importance. At the Games themselves, there are some eleven, I think, members of CAS whose job it is to adjudicate immediately on allegations arising out of the events. Very often, therefore, they have to sit through the night to hear the evidence and decide whether somebody is eligible or otherwise for the gold medal which they had won earlier in the afternoon. The availability of perfectly ordinary medicines, sometimes containing forbidden drugs, adds another difficulty for those who have to make these decisions. The code of practice which has now been laid down about the penalties for the use of drugs is very much to be welcomed. It sets a standard for sport throughout the world.

Members of CAS are very experienced and are of international calibre. We usually meet to arbitrate in Lausanne but can meet elsewhere, depending on the makeup of the panel, and we deal with a wide variety of problems. CAS has now come to be recognised as the leading sports arbitrator. At a recent seminar which I attended in Lausanne there must have been delegates from at least twenty or twenty-five countries from all around the world. Their knowledge and experience is very great and the variety of their sports gives them a wide insight into the problems which CAS faces.

The City Disputes Panel is a more modest organisation but it performs a vital function in dealing with commercial problems in the City, as the name implies. It needs to be better known. In these arbitrations and mediations, I found my experience of employment law as President of the Employment Appeal Tribunal and connection with ACAS of very great assistance. I also sat for a number of years as chairman of several Wages Councils, where we were fixing the wages for those organisations which did not have national agreements with their employees. The way of dealing with them was not unlike a mediation. We would get each party together. The employers would say that they had had a bad year and could not afford any more. The union would say that the cost of living had gone up substantially and that they needed an increase. Then we would see both sides individually and we would try and found out where the common denominator was. I sat with two experienced industrialists, one from each side of the camp, and generally we managed to get the parties to agree on a figure with which they were happy or at least not unhappy. It was a fascinating exercise and most enjoyable.

Arbitration, on the other hand, is a rather different exercise. You either sit on your own or with two others and it is a judicial process but not in the public eye. The reason why people seek arbitration rather than going to the courts is that it is intended, at any rate, to be a speedier, less formal and cheaper form of litigation, although I do sometimes wonder whether it is, in fact, any cheaper. The quality of arbitrators is often very high, containing – sometimes – distinguished retired Law Lords or other lawyers or experts, themselves very experienced in the particular field of activity involved in the arbitration. I certainly get the impression that arbitration and mediation have not only come to stay, but are having a substantial impact on litigation in the High Court.

Another sporting involvement with which I was concerned resulted from the rigging of cricket matches by the South Africans and, although not proved, by others. It will be remembered that Hansie Cronje, the captain of South Africa, was heard telephoning a bookie about throwing matches. Eventually he confessed that he and two others had arranged to throw a Test match. He suffered the appropriate penalty. The International Cricket Council (ICC) was naturally very concerned about this and, under Sir Paul Condon, now Lord Condon, it set up a body to investigate, throughout the world, the various allegations that were circulating.

On the Indian subcontinent betting on sport is endemic. Punters will bet, not only on who will win, but from which end a particular bowler will bowl, or on what the score will be after 10 overs, or on how many runs a particular batsman will make. Paul Condon and his team made an enormously skilful investigation and reported back to the ICC. There were then a number of investigations by the national cricket bodies about the evidence which Paul Condon had found and which pointed towards the Indian subcontinent. A number of inquiries were made by judicial bodies in those countries about the allegations.

The ICC set up a panel headed by Lord Griffiths, a retired Law Lord, to which each country appointed a representative. I was the English representative. Our task was to consider the judgements of the particular judge, to report to the ICC as to whether the inquiry had been properly carried out, and whether any further steps should be taken. Lord Griffiths' position was subsequently taken over by Michael Beloff QC. On these various inquiries I have sat with representatives from various countries including South Africa, Australia, West Indies and India.

In the end, although there was grave suspicion in many cases, the judges often found themselves unable to make a finding that there had in fact been corruption. It was only in a few cases that they did. Because of Paul Condon's work it would now be very surprising if matches were actually thrown. It necessarily requires a number of important members of the side to be actively involved. However, it is impossible to believe that some players do not accept money from bookies for their individual performances. It is simply and easily done, particularly in one-day games. There are hundreds of these games played throughout the year, often of no particular importance. A bet, for instance, will be placed on a particular batsman not making 10. With the game being of little or no importance, and the batsman being secure in his place in the team, if he is offered very substantial sums of money to get himself out before 10, the result is inevitable. It is virtually impossible to detect this. The ease with which the money is earned leaves me in no doubt that such goings-on still occur.

Occasionally some evidence surfaces, indicating that perhaps something has gone awry. When Bangladesh beat Pakistan in one particular World Cup match, eyebrows were raised. However, the judge investigating the result drew no inference from the evidence that Bangladesh one week before the game had apparently been 40–1 against, and on the night before had suddenly became 2–1 on. Cynics might have drawn a different conclusion from the judge's view. While Paul Condon has done a wonderful job, it is much too complacent to believe that the problem of corruption has gone away, never to return. The sums of money involved militate against its disappearance.

I used to be involved in the disciplinary cases in cricket and in *Benchmark* I refer to the cases of Barry Wood and Imran Khan. Now I am occasionally asked to take a view as to whether the actions of the match referee are consistent with the ICC Rules. I recently had to consider the behaviour of a bowler in South Africa. I was able to do this by looking at the videotape of what had occurred and I came to the same conclusion as the match referee. More recently I flew out to Dubai, where the ICC now has its headquarters, to chair a tribunal hearing an appeal concerning the legality of a Pakistani fast bowler's action. He had had to have remedial work on his action which had previously been called into question, and the tribunal had to decide whether his action now complied with the laws. We had expert evidence together with film of the action and we were unanimously of the view that his action was still outside the laws.

The taking of drugs is still a problem, particularly in athletics. There are more and more drugs on the market and it is often difficult for the authorities to keep up with what is going on although they undoubtedly do their best. The facilities for testing have also improved out of all recognition but there is ever present the risk of mistake. I attended a sports seminar recently when Diane Modahl came and talked to us about her experience of being accused of taking drugs, which she subsequently proved to be untrue. She suffered enormously financially, in her reputation and in her athletic prowess, by being falsely accused. She was in fact entirely innocent. Sometimes a person is capable of generating within his or her own body the substance which is suspect. While more sophisticated procedures are now available, it has not always been so in the past. Innocent taking of drugs either from a third person or from a doctor or chemist who is unfamiliar with them is one of the great dangers. It is always difficult to decide whether there have been deliberate attempts to enhance performance or whether it is an innocent exercise. The method of testing, with which I had to deal in Linford Christie's case, has now been very much tightened, and failure to be available for a test is the equivalent of failing a test. Again, such is the pressure to succeed that it would be very surprising if drug-taking did not still go on.

10

Reports

It is now nearly sixty years since I had my last school report, but I remember it well. I had just received a letter from Queens' College Cambridge, where I had sat a scholarship, to be told by them that I had got some award. On the same day I received a school report from my form master which concluded 'Popplewell [in those days pupils were called by their surname] will never, I fear, become a scholar'. At Oxford, at the end of each term, our tutors meet with us and hand over a written report. Each student is given a moment or two to read the report and make any comment on it, and is then given a copy. While the dons are very friendly, they make no concession to age, reputation or experience, and they obviously take great care in the preparation of these reports. I much enjoyed reading them and, although I didn't always agree with what they said, they nevertheless gave quite a good picture of my progress (or lack thereof). It is open to the student to make any comments that he or she wishes, but, in my case, I have always thought that 'least said, soonest mended'. It is rather like pointing out to a judge that he hasn't got it quite right; it is hardly worth the effort.

Some of the reports, however, are worth repeating. The following extracts perhaps suggest that I do not have a natural ability to understand theory, thus:

His natural approach is very much one of the real world and so he needs to focus on developing the skills of philosophical analysis and questioning.

He still finds it quite a challenge to move beyond an every day perception of issues to the simultaneously more precise and more abstract conception required for philosophy.

What I think he needs to do to be successful in political theory questions, is to tackle those questions in a theoretical, rather than positive way.

He needs to be more sharply focussed on the specific philosophical issue addressed, always pushing that bit further than common sense would suggest.

Political theory will never be his natural bent but practice is having an effect.

He is fluent both orally and on paper. [I rather hope that having being in the law for some fifty years I would be!]

He needs to immerse himself more in theoretical literature, even if as I suspect, he is sceptical about the relevance and quality of some of it.

And finally the one I like best:

He also has an unfortunate attachment to common sense and an accompanying desire to close arguments down quickly, where what is needed is a perverse delight in keeping them open and if possible extending them. Philosophers are intellectual trouble makers!

From all this it is clear that I have fairly strong views about a good deal of the theory which is taught at Oxford. Philosophy, of course, is mostly about theoretical problems, but, where politics are concerned, I just have a feeling that what actually happens in politics is of a great deal more interest than the theory behind it. It may be that I have been a judge too *quite* long. One of the dangers of being a judge for as long as I have been is that, having heard an argument, I tend to come to a view comparatively quickly and, in old age, perhaps prolonged argument is less conducive to conclusions.

Anyway, I take these criticisms fairly on the chin and vow that I will do better in the future. One of the problems with philosophy is that each philosopher has his own view about life, which is then rejected some forty years later by the next philosopher, and by yet another philosopher, forty years on. To arrive, therefore, at a satisfactory conclusion about ethics or rights or duties may well depend on which particular philosopher is currently in vogue. It seems to me that the application of common sense to most of the problems raised is not a bad method of approach. However, this is clearly not the way that these matters are taught at Oxford, and, if I am to pass the exams, I must give up my robust, common-sense approach, and fall in with the theoretical literature, in both politics and philosophy.

It reminds me slightly of my first few years at the Bar. Having learnt law at Cambridge, I assumed that I would go to court armed with the latest authority and read great passages from speeches in the House of Lords and thereby win my case. Little did I appreciate that, for the first five, or ten, years of life at the Bar, law reports and law books were of little or no value. The cases depended on the credibility of one's client and the good humour, or otherwise (and usually otherwise), of the judge. Many of those who got first-class degrees in law at Cambridge in my day simply failed to recognise that what was required at the Bar was not only an intellectual ability but good judgement to go with it. The academic world, I suspect, is different. Like all good advocates, I must try to accommodate my approach to the examiners next summer and adjust my arguments accordingly.

The second year at Oxford is sometimes described as the 'cruising year' because, apart from college exams at the beginning of each term, there is, as I've said, no University exam at the end of the second year, as there was at Cambridge. Thus, while lectures and tutorials continue, the pressure is not on and a comparative calm descends on second-year students. It is interesting to compare this summer term at Oxford with a comparable summer term at Cambridge. In the first place, at Cambridge I would be doing an important exam. Secondly I played cricket for most of the summer, which gave little or no time for sociability. I was spending my time reading the books while trying to watch the cricket. At Oxford there is a great deal of sociability, although on nothing like the same scale as happened in my day at Cambridge. There, parties in May Week went on, in effect, for weeks at a time.

At Cambridge, while we were by no means puritan, the standard of behaviour was good, save for the unfortunate occasion in my second year when I am afraid we behaved like hooligans. The occasion was Rag Week when a large body of students gathered in King's Parade and then marched on the police station. There, encouraged by a good deal of drink, students threw a number of thunderflashes after which the mob returned to King's Parade. Here, in anticipation of trouble, there was a policeman guarding each lamp post. The mob took no notice. Each policeman was surrounded. One of the crowd climbed the lamp post and put out the light and this continued all the way down King's Parade. The Senate House windows, which had survived the war, were also attacked and suffered much damage. The mob then returned to their colleges. It was not an evening, even for those of us who were mere bystanders, of which we would claim to be proud.

University cricket, sadly, is now so awful that I have scarcely watched Oxford at all. The university matches follow the modern trend, with all the fielders talking their heads off. Robin Marlar, the incoming MCC President, went down to Oxford and saw this happening. He was appalled and asked the Oxford coach to take some steps to stop it. When that didn't happen, in true Marlar fashion, he marched out onto the pitch and reproved the undergraduates. It is one of the sadnesses of the modern game that the students ape those playing international and national sport. Whenever I watch old films of cricket, I rejoice in the calm way in which wickets were greeted or catches were taken. The very simple courtesies that were customarily exchanged by one side to another, for instance when a batsman got 50 or 100, seem often to be absent from present-day international cricket.

I started the summer watching England play Australia at Lord's on the Saturday and Sunday. England bowled and batted as if they had scarcely ever played any cricket before. On the Sunday, I had a family box. It rained. We spent a miserable day waiting for the execution, as it were, because England were a lot of runs behind with only five wickets in hand. The remaining batsmen surrendered without any difficulty and it was a miserable exhibition, suggesting that the prospects of regaining the Ashes were almost nil. The one-day games and the 20:20 matches had given the public some expectation of a good fight and showed that the Australians were not supermen. But I fear that our recovery of the Ashes is still a long way off.

During the Test match, Roger Knight, the MCC Secretary, entertained a number of friends and some distinguished cricketers in his garden. I sat at a table with Sam Loxton, Neil Harvey and Ray Lindwall's widow and we talked about the 1948 Australian side, which had such a remarkable success. There is much talk of comparing that side with the current Australian side and the general view seems to be that the current side is marginally better. They have had a remarkable period of success, not only keeping the Ashes, but constantly winning against other countries both at home and abroad. This is one of the hallmarks of success. It was a joy to meet up with Neil Harvey, a teenager in 1948 and one of the successes of the side. He was one of the best fielders of all time and still looks young and active. It was marvellous to have spirited cricket talk, particularly as there is deep depression in the England camp and prayers for rain seem to go unanswered.

Another party at Lord's was to celebrate seventy years of the Arabs Cricket Club. This club was founded in 1935 by Jim Swanton and others. Jim himself was a comparatively modest cricketer. He played, I think, for Middlesex twice but without any great success, and was much better known as a commentator and writer. He ran the club with very great panache. Its ethos was to play good cricket in a good spirit and have fun. He selected his own candidates for membership and instilled in them the desire to play well, to play hard and to enjoy the game. The membership included both international, county, university and club players. The standard was always high and woe betide any Arab side which didn't do well. He was a hard taskmaster, but playing for the Arabs was always enormous fun. There were many tours abroad, particularly to the West Indies. On one occasion, his side there did a great deal to restore relations which had been damaged on the international scene. When he died, there was a great debate about whether the club could continue, given Jim's enormous input. Happily, recruitment has been maintained and the club has continued to flourish, albeit with a smaller fixture list. Whether it will always do so is a question for the future. This celebration was an opportunity for the young and old to get together and reminisce about the club and its founder. The party at Lord's started with drinks on the very top of the pavilion which has now been created as a place for a social gathering. A team photograph of the members sitting in the top tier was taken and a very enjoyable evening was had.

One of the difficulties facing cricket clubs now, particularly those which might be described as wandering sides, is to secure players week in, week out. When I was first married, I used to go off on both Saturday and Sunday to play cricket for my local club or various touring sides. Margaret would pack up a picnic and bring some of the children, and then take them home after tea. I would get home late after the match. This is now not possible, for a number of reasons, particularly for members of wandering clubs. The local clubs have first call on their players. If you want to be in the local club's 1st XI, you are required to play every Saturday and perhaps on Sunday as well, because of the league system. Secondly, wives are no longer accommodating in the way that mine was. To be able to play cricket every week or let alone twice a week is simply now not acceptable. A lot of the Arabs, for instance, are playing in their Cricketer Cup side and others are playing for their county 1st or 2nd XI. Thus the whole scene has changed quite abruptly. Additionally, the cost of a day's cricket is now quite staggering. A bat which used to cost £5 in my day is now into three figures. All the equipment, of which there is now a very great deal, is also very expensive. Because the players throw themselves around much more than they did, flannels need constant cleaning. The cost of entertainment also has risen enormously. It is therefore not very surprising that raising sides for itinerant clubs poses a very real problem for match managers.

11

Summer 2005

This will always be remembered as The Ashes Year comparable to Botham's Ashes series in 1983. In the light of what followed, it is difficult to understand how England could have bowled and batted so badly at Lord's. They surrendered without a fight and, apart from the first morning when they bowled Australia out, they never looked like a side which was going to win even one match, let alone the Ashes. They eventually did it by the narrowest of margins and indeed they could have been two down after the first two matches. By and large they managed to outplay and out-think the Australians. The critical moment to my mind was when McGrath managed to twist his ankle before the start of play in the Second Test, which enabled the English openers to flourish as they had never flourished before. It was, also, obvious that the unsung Duncan Fletcher and his fellow coaches had done an enormous amount of homework on the Australian players. The result was that a number of them, who hitherto had had high batting averages, simply failed to do themselves justice. Sorting out an opponent's weakness does not of itself necessarily produce results. It is necessary to be able to bowl accurately so as to exploit those weaknesses. By and large, the English bowlers succeeded in doing this. Apart from his last innings, Hayden was a shadow of his usual self and Gilchrist scarcely made a run. Thus accurate bowling, skilful field placing and homework had their rewards.

It was a delight to see the English batsmen flourishing and scoring at a good run rate. It must be a long time since this happened to an

English side. The one weakness in the side was the wicket keeping of Geraint Jones. I still believe that the best wicket keeper should be chosen, irrespective of his batting ability. There are in fact a good number of other wicket keepers in England who not only keep well but also bat well. It was dreadful to see Jones dropping catches, which, even I, in my amateurish way, would have had no difficulty in catching. Playing with the same slips over five Test matches ought to result in a good understanding between first slip and the wicket keeper, but this did not always happen. The problem is that he simply didn't look like a wicket keeper and his taking of the ball was particularly ragged. He would never have coped with keeping wicket to Shane Warne, for instance, bowling into the rough to a left hander. Although Gilchrist did not have a great series, at least he looked like a wicket keeper. As my son said about Jones, 'He could not even keep bees!'

The problem of wicket keepers and their batting started many years ago when, in the one-day game, the wicket keeper became a first slip with gloves on. It wasn't necessary to stand up to slow bowlers because by and large they didn't exist in one-day cricket. Thus it became commonly accepted that wicket keepers would stand back to medium-pace bowlers to be sure of taking the catches. Thus wicket keeping skills took second place to batting skills. But even when Jones stood back, apart from one or two occasions when he took some good catches, he still didn't distinguish himself. Nor did he look a very capable batsman.

Everyone has his own story of a particular Test match. I was not able to watch any of the other matches in person, though I watched them on television. For the last Test match we were in France. At lunchtime on the final day, we were entertaining my sister-in-law, Helen, Margaret's younger sister, and Tony, her husband, to lunch in Cherbourg. We heard that England were 125 for 5, still with a limited lead and with most of the major batsmen out. We then had an hour's drive to the cottage while we were out of range of a radio. When we did get to the cottage, we found that Pietersen was batting. Another twenty minutes' occupation of the crease would ensure that we retained the Ashes and that's how it happened. The games were played in a happy spirit, although Ponting's complaint about substitutes was ill-conceived and ill-natured. For the young substitute, Pratt, who ran Ponting out, it was a moment to savour, even if his county did not immediately offer him full terms. The relationship between the two teams was epitomised by Flintoff's sympathising with Brett Lee at the end of one of the Tests and with Warne's generous attitude to the England side. If anyone could have retained the Ashes for Australia, it was Shane Warne and it is sad to think

8   At David Sheppard's memorial service at Hove

that we may now not see him on English soil again. We were, I believe, privileged to see a wonderful demonstration of spin bowling and also a great exhibition of character.

Whether England, when they go out to Pakistan, will find success remains to be seen. Until they beat India and/or Pakistan in their own country, they can scarcely claim the crown which the Australians have had for some many years. It is a mark of a great side to be able to play in all sorts of conditions against all sorts of teams. England is a young side, but certainly it needs some young spinners before it can be sure of containing, let alone bowling out, a good side on plumb wickets abroad.

One of the most talented cricketers of my generation, David Sheppard, sadly died in the summer after a long illness and was much mourned. I was lucky enough to play with him in the 1950 and 1951 Cambridge side. David with May, Doggart and Dewes made a truly formidable opening quartet. He was a star performer. If I had to choose one of the four to bat for my life, I would unhesitatingly choose David. He was not as elegant as Peter May or Hubert Doggart, nor quite as determined as John Dewes, but he combined the best qualities of all three of them in a towering presence.

At Cambridge he was a very good close fielder and although subsequently he was somewhat mocked as a dropper of catches, I don't remember him ever doing so when I played with him. It is an astonishing fact that neither he, nor Peter May, ever played in a winning University side. But it is as a man that I shall always remember him. He was an intelligent companion, a compassionate priest, and he probably did more good for the Church than any other person I know. He was a good judge of character, an excellent speaker and totally selfless. He should have been Archbishop of York, if not Archbishop of Canterbury, but his political views did not find favour with Margaret Thatcher. York's loss was certainly Liverpool's gain. I was unable to go to Liverpool Cathedral for his memorial service although David's sister, Mary, had invited me. But I did go, at her invitation, to the Hove Cricket Ground at the beginning of August where a very moving memorial service was held on the field. There was a good attendance by a number of England, Sussex and Cambridge players at the service, conducted by the Bishop of Chichester and others. Moving tributes were paid, followed by a lunch in a marquee, at which David's wife, Grace, spoke with great emotion. It was altogether a memorable occasion, worthy of a distinguished man.

On a different note, the summer saw Hugo and Leo, Ed and Clare's older sons, involved again in the National Children's Orchestra, now a year on from last year, and I went up to Yorkshire with Clare, to hear Leo play. Sadly, being tone deaf, I had no idea whether it was good or not, but Clare said that it was. Hugo's concert was the following week when I was up in Norfolk and so I didn't get to hear him. But they are marvellously lucky to have both the talent, and the encouragement from Clare, to be able to take part in these orchestral performances. Clare has a musical pedigree, because her the grandfather was the well-known composer, Gerald Finzi, her aunt was Jacqueline du Pré, and she herself studied at the Royal College of Music. I assume that this talent does not decrease with time and it is a skill that the children will be able to take with them through the rest of life.

Liz and I then joined Alexander and Sally (third son and daughter-in-law) and their children in Norfolk, at Overy Staithe, where one of the great excitements of the year was the celebration of the 200th anniversary of the Battle of Trafalgar. Initially, I had not wanted to go. But I was persuaded (in my language, bullied), by Liz and Sally. I was wrong and they were right. In the small estuary there were about 300 boats, most of which were under sail. They were dressed overall and flew a white ensign of nineteenth-century design, which they were allowed to fly just for the month of August. Quite smart. The armada was inspected by an Admiral, who was rowed through the fleet, followed by the Bishop of Lynn and accompanying clergy – in full yacht regalia. It was a tremendous sight. Luckily the weather stayed fine. The wind was modest and the whole of the occasion was marked by enormous enthusiasm and excitement. Following this, there was a pig roast on an adjoining field, which rounded off the day quite admirably, despite my original adverse views.

Among our other activities was our annual visit to the musical show on Cromer pier. We joined the Frys (parents of the famous Stephen) and the Sankeys (old sailing friends) for a hilarious evening, having fortified ourselves with several bottles of wine, and ate fish and chips on the pier. I have known the Frys for over forty years. Marianne and Margaret were at Malvern Girls' College together. It was due to them that we bought our cottage in Norfolk. Margaret gave Stephen his first P.G. Woodhouse book and when Stephen had his unfortunate brush with the police, I went and spoke on his behalf. There is much reference to this in his autobiography (*Moab is my Washpot*). We also hid him in our cottage when he came back to England after walking out of a play in the West End. The press were camped out at the Frys' house and Stephen needed somewhere to hide while the drama subsided. Alan and Margaret Sankey are also friends of many years' standing. He was a housemaster at Harrow, now lives in Norfolk and is a highly competent sailor who lets me crew for him.

The jokes at the theatre in Cromer were absolutely awful and must have been fifty years old. The dancing was modest, the singing indifferent, and the scenery extravagant to a glittering degree. The whole performance was so awful that it made a hysterically funny evening. No doubt the alcohol contributed. It is one of the entertaining features of our visit to Norfolk which we wouldn't miss.

On a separate occasion, in the summer, I was put very much on my mettle when we were invited to lunch by Robin Don of Hicks and Don. He is the well-known wine connoisseur. His wife produced the most delicious lunch, and for the main course Robin had chosen two separate clarets for me to taste. Believing me to be something of an expert, he required me to identify them. I did quite well (thanks to Lady Luck) on Left Bank or Right Bank, and indeed on the Communes, but after that I was struggling and his belief in my wine-tasting prowess vanished almost as quickly as the wine itself.

Meanwhile there is academic work to be done. I decided, as one of my exam options, to do a thesis. This involves writing what is, effectively, an essay of some 15,000 words with bibliography and footnotes, and getting the approval, both of my tutor and of the department. Having originally been interested in by-elections, I decided to call my thesis 'The Effect of By-elections on British Politics since 1922'. I chose 1922 because that was when the Newport by-election took place. The result of that by-election is thought to have had some effect on the meeting of the Carlton Club where the Conservative members of the coalition decided to leave Lloyd George's Government. I floated the idea with Lesley Smith, who didn't seem to disapprove, and also with Professor Vernon Bogdanor. At first he thought there might be too much psephology but when I explained to him what was involved, he seemed to agree. He suggested that I should go and see David Butler who is the distinguished psephologist and professor at Nuffield College. This I did. He gave me much encouragement. I therefore armed myself with a whole lot of books during the summer vacation and did a first draft of the thesis. It was a very useful exercise, not only for the thesis itself, but also for revising some of the British politics during that period.

I particularly enjoyed writing the chapter on Dick Taverne's by-election at Lincoln. Dick had arrived at Charterhouse from Holland in 1940 as a rather messy schoolboy and, as I remember, covered in ink. He did not speak very much English but by the time he left Charterhouse he had won a scholarship to Balliol, where he took a first. He came to the Bar and eventually became a QC. He entered politics as a right-wing member of the Labour party. He had serious trouble with his management committee who thought he was too right-wing. Margaret Beckett's husband, together with others, made his life an absolute misery. When he decided to vote in favour of Europe, which the Labour party then opposed (how things have changed), the management committee eventually deselected him. He therefore decided to stand in a by-election as an independent Liberal Democrat. He was a highly intelligent and attractive candidate and easily defeated the Labour candidate as well as the rather eccentric Monday Club candidate, put up by the Conservatives. Paddy Mayhew, later Attorney General, who was then a Conservative candidate and a great friend of Dick's, went up to Lincoln with a number of other lawyers who often lunched together, and canvassed on Dick's behalf. This was an act of great friendship. In the end, Dick not only defeated the Labour candidate, but subsequently held on to the seat. Eventually he joined the SDP but lost his seat and ended up in the House of Lords.

The Orpington by-election of 1962, on which I also wrote, became a legend in electoral history, because of the astonishing defeat of the Conservative candidate. His majority of nearly 15,000 was turned into a Liberal majority of nearly 8000. Margaret and I had by this time left this part of Kent and moved to Buckinghamshire, but the area was well known to us and I was therefore particularly interested in the result. I much enjoyed researching my thesis. It gave me the opportunity not only to examine in detail a number of important political events, but also to seek to pass judgement on the effect of the various by-elections on political life.

Having looked at about a dozen specific by-elections in detail and a number less fully, I came to the firm conclusion that, although they generate a very great deal of excitement at the time, their effect on politics is comparatively limited. Occasionally, as at Orpington, where the Conservative candidate vanished into the night, and later when Gordon Walker, one of Harod Wilson's cabinet colleagues lost his seat for the second time and ended up in the House of Lords, the effect is on the individual. In some cases, the result may have affected Government policy. For instance, it is thought that the result at East Fulham, which was a pacifist result, may have caused rearmament not to proceed with any very great dispatch. Certainly the by-election at St George's Westminster, where Baldwin made his famous speech against the press lords ('power without responsibility, the prerogative of the harlot throughout the ages'), strengthened his position in the Conservative Party and did immense damage to the press.

Occasionally it appears that the result of a by-election may influence the Prime Minister's decision whether or not to call a general election. But there is not much evidence that the loss of a number of by-elections has any very great impact on a subsequent general election. What it does, of course, is to lower morale among Members of Parliament and the party generally, and thereby create a sense of inadequacy in the Government. There are a number of examples of governments losing by-elections a few months before a general election, and then winning the subsequent general election by a substantial margin. Some by-elections, which at the time seemed to cause immense excitement, such as Orpington or those which Roy Jenkins and Shirley Williams won, did not, on analysis, make any lasting impact. Talks of revival are often premature. At one stage, for instance, the SDP was polling something like 50 per cent of the electorate, enough to put them into government. But it was never to be. Doing this research occupied a lot of the summer and I wanted to be ready at the beginning of term to present my first draft to Vernon.

Meanwhile we sailed with Alexander and Sally's children in Norfolk and also with Ed and Clare. We enjoy a great deal of hospitality at friends' houses. We then went with Nigel (my eldest son) and his doctor wife, Ingy, and their children to our cottage in France for a few days. There we were joined successively by the Battens and by my sister-in-law, Helen and her husband, Tony. James and Sue Batten were also friends from Norfolk. He had been a master at Radley and subsequently a distinguished headmaster at King's Taunton. There was a good deal of discussion among my daughters-in-law and Liz about redoing the cottage, because it was said that the kitchen was rather old-fashioned and that the dining room was very dark. For myself, I was very unenthusiastic about the idea, because it is a small country cottage, ideal for holidays, but which is not intended to be smart. We have managed to occupy the cottage quite happily for some eighteen years, without any very real problems. I had to agree that it needed a bit of renovation not only because the carpets and the curtains were the originals but because it had not had any really tender loving care for many years. Indeed the carpets had come from the Battens' house when they moved. How long they had had them, I don't know.

Our next-door neighbour there, Madame Gibe, who is a widow with a boyfriend from Coutances, is very chatty and generally friendly. But she is apt to complain that our hedge overhangs her garden and causes her vegetables not to flourish as they should, or her hens not to lay. Happily we have found an English organisation in Coutances which provides gardening services. They came along and trimmed the hedges to Madame Gibe's satisfaction who then asked us in for a drink of kir and white wine. We reciprocated by offering her and her friend local supermarket champagne and whisky. We also managed to get the gardening organisation to take away a whole lot of duff furniture, which was simply occupying space and looking messy. Whether the grand plans which my daughters-in-law and Liz have in mind will be affordable and whether there is any real point in doing it, we shall have to see. The kitchen itself does need some attention, as I am forced grudgingly to admit, but I suspect we are using a sledgehammer to crack a nut.

The other decision that I made about property was to suggest to Ed and Clare that if they were interested they might like to take over Lime Tree Farm, Chartridge, the home in which Margaret and I raised the children. Liz and I would move out to live locally. They were wonderfully enthusiastic. We had a survey done which showed that it was in quite good condition. I put right various items, which needed to be done immediately. When we had bought the house originally, the builders had re-tiled, re-roofed and re-battened the entire roof, with scaffolding, over a period of a month. It had cost £200. Nowadays, to put up some scaffolding for repairs to the chimney, over two or three days, would cost ten times that amount. With the house surveyed and valued, the financial problems involved then have to be considered. This is my only asset and it has to be equably distributed among all four children. Ed and

Clare, of course, have a house to sell and I shall need to use part of that money towards buying somewhere else for Liz and me to live.

I am anxious that they should not find themselves in difficulty so far as school fees are concerned and it will need some careful planning. There are, I suspect, all sorts of tax problems involved, apart from making sure that everybody has a fair share. I have put the matter in the hands of Nigel's firm to advise us but I very much hope that the project will go ahead. Ed and Clare are immensely keen gardeners and I know how their taking over the house would have pleased Margaret. It is a marvellous place for children to grow up and our children certainly had a happy time. The question of schooling will also have to be sorted out. For Hugo, there is no problem because by that time he will have taken his exam to a public school, but for Leo and Robin it will be more difficult. Clare and Ed have been to look at local schools to see for themselves what is on offer, and have already made some decisions. Lime Tree Farm has always been a happy house although one of my sons, Margaret and my mother all died there. We have managed to get by so far with the help of my nice daily, Brenda, and a gardener, but there will come a time when the garden will get on top of us, and when Brenda, who has been with us for thirty years, finally decides it's time to go. A small cottage in the neighbourhood, within walking distance of the shops and trains and with a small garden, would suit us down to the ground. We don't want to move far away, because making new friends, at my age at any rate, is not very easy.

Meanwhile the party conferences go on. I am not sure whether I am still a paid-up member of the University Labour Party, which I joined at Cambridge, or whether Margaret made me a member of the Conservative Party. But I have always been a floating voter. I watch the fight for the Conservative leadership with some amusement. Kenneth Clarke's view on Europe and mine could not be more opposed but he is a very engaging person. He should have been selected on the last occasion, if not the time before. Now that Europe is not quite the immediate issue that it was, he would certainly have got the party moving. But it was not to be.

It seems very strange that a young man who has been in Parliament only for some four years, who has no ministerial experience and who has made just one very important speech, should be the front-runner in the two-horse race which is now going on. Unfortunately (at least from my perspective), youth now appears to be all the rage. The idea that judgement and experience have any part to play in political life is sadly outdated. We can see the effect of that in the Government's handling of various issues. For instance, the Bar is threatening to strike because of the woeful handling by the Lord Chancellor's Department of criminal legal aid payments to barristers. To freeze, if not to reduce fees, over a period of eight years and expect barristers cheerfully to soldier on is disgraceful. Why a review could not have taken place five or six years ago, I do not know. The Bar has been immensely patient, but bills have to be paid. When I see what it costs for my plumber to come and spend ten minutes fixing the washing machine, and then compare that with a day's pay for a barrister in court, it isn't surprising that the Bar is up in arms.

Meanwhile another ill-thought-out initiative of the Government's is announced. This is the decision to extend drinking hours in licensed premises. On the one hand, the Government seek to crack down on people who drink too much, while, on the other, they are happy to allow pubs to be open all hours, on the basis that it gives the people choice. It will merely result in uncontrolled drinking. The publicans will wash their hands of the problem and those luckless householders who live within shouting distance of a pub will suffer. It will necessitate extra policing and it will result in more violence. Anyone familiar with the criminal consequences of what happens on Saturday nights in towns and cities will recognise that an increase in crime is inevitable. It would be difficult to find a more anti-social piece of legislation.

12

Lord Chief Justices

I am, again, invited to the High Sheriff's service in Christchurch. The High Sheriff, this year, is a fellow Bencher of the Inner Temple and before the service, Tom Bingham, now the senior Law Lord, was invited to give an address to an invited audience, consisting of friends, academics and students. A year or two ago, he had spoken about the 'Alabama Award' with his usual fluency. It was a subject of which I knew only a little from history itself and it was an enormously illuminating address. This time he talked about 'Law and Justice in the Modern World', which kept us all fully engaged for nearly an hour. Sensibly, he invited the students to put questions, which they did with some skill and intelligence, and which he answered very well.

I first met Tom when we were engaged as barristers on opposite sides in an employment dispute in front of a tribunal in London. He was already a star. He had conducted the inquiry into what happened in the oil sanctions drama in what was then Rhodesia. He was clearly destined for high office. I have little or no recollection of the result, but what I do remember was both his skill and his charm, which he continued to exhibit when he went on the Bench. In 1986 he went to the Court of Appeal and in 1992 he became Master of the Rolls. This office is one of the most important in the judicial hierarchy, because the Master of the Rolls is head of the Court of Appeal (Civil Division). Although there can be appeals to the House of Lords and to the European Court of Justice, the vast majority of civil cases of any importance are decided in the

Master of the Rolls' court. Tom Denning, when he was Master of the Rolls, took full advantage of this to stamp his own views on civil litigation.

When Peter Taylor retired from a distinguished tenure of office as Lord Chief Justice, in 1996, there was, as there always is, considerable speculation at the Bar and on the Bench as to who was going to succeed him. Traditionally, the Lord Chief Justice had been an office to which the Attorney General had a reversion and this practice had obtained for most of the twentieth century. The tradition was firmly broken when Lord Goddard, who himself had not been a politician, or at any rate not a politician of any note, retired. The question then arose of whether Reggie Manningham-Buller, who had been Attorney General, should be appointed. He was not. Lord Parker was appointed instead and Manningham-Buller went to the House of Lords. Thus appointments of the Lord Chief Justice since that time have been purely on merit and without any political involvement.

The Lord Chief Justice is the most senior judge in the country and responsible for the administration of the judges themselves. He now presides over the criminal work in the Court of Appeal (Criminal Division). He thus sets the whole tone of criminal law. He has also to be something of a politician, because there is a constant battle between the executive (who want to limit the independence of both the judiciary and of the Bar), and the judiciary and the Bar themselves. I suspect that apart from some sitting as a Recorder and as a High Court judge, Tom's experience of criminal law was almost nil. I should be very surprised if, while at the Bar, he had ever addressed a jury in his life. His appointment, therefore, came as something of a surprise to the profession,which considered that there were other candidates better suited to the task. However, he quickly falsified those opinions and made it clear that an intelligent person with humanity can readily apply himself to any problem, even with which he is unfamiliar, and do it extremely well.

He not only presided over the Court of Appeal (Criminal Division) with great skill, but sought to maintain the independence of the Bar and the judiciary. His ten years of office were regarded as a great success and when he went to be the senior Law Lord in the House of Lords, he left behind a very great reputation. I was reminded of how skilful Tom is when the case challenging the Hunting Bill reached the Judicial Committee of the House of Lords this week. The point of law involved was not about the merits of the Bill itself, about which people have different and strongly divided views, but whether the Parliament Act could properly be invoked in order to force the legislation through the House of Lords. Tom Bingham's speech is a classic, setting out the history and background to the passing of the legislation and its consequences. It must be a 'banker' for students doing the Constitutional Law exams, next spring.

When Tom Bingham became Lord Chief Justice in 1995 he was succeeded as Master of the Rolls by Harry Woolf who himself then succeeded Tom as Lord Chief Justice when Tom went to the Lords. It appeared to be a slight game of 'musical chairs'. Indeed, when the previous Master of the Rolls had retired and there was a valedictory, one bright lawyer observed that the post was now open to any 'Tom, Nick or Harry', referring to Nick Browne-Wilkinson (then a star in the Court of Appeal, who subsequently went to the House of Lords) as well as to Tom and Harry.

Harry Woolf had been a practitioner on the Oxford circuit when I was at the Bar, and like me, he was what was often described as a knock-about practitioner, doing every sort of case and earning a modest living. He was a very engaging opponent, full of common sense and good humour. Some thirty or forty years ago, the expectation of the circuit was probably, that if he took silk, he would end up as a thoroughly sensible county court judge. However, this is not how it turned out. His meteoric rise to the highest office started in 1973, when Patrick Medd, who was also a member of the circuit, ceased to be the common law junior to the Inland Revenue. He was replaced by Harry. The common law junior to the Inland Revenue, as the name suggests, is required to advise the Revenue on tax matters and to conduct their important cases in court. It requires a degree of specialisation, but because the Treasury briefs are always well prepared, the backup for counsel if dealing with something comparatively unfamiliar, is very good. The post is a prestigious one, because it often leads on to other more important posts. This is what happened in Harry's case.

After doing the job for the Inland Revenue for a year or so he was appointed Treasury counsel and therefore responsible for handling the Government's common law work before the courts and advising them. It is not only a highly important and prestigious post, but it requires a great deal of hard work. Cases will often arise, almost over night, in areas with which counsel may be totally unfamiliar. He or she is required to put forward the Government argument and explain difficult regulations at very short notice. Counsel do not do any other work and are effectively standing counsel to the Government. They have to be right. The courts depend on their exposition of the law as being correct, and the post carries a very onerous responsibility.

Customarily, Treasury counsel will do the job for five or seven years and then he or she will be appointed to the High Court Bench. This is what happened to Harry. Thereafter he went to the Court of Appeal and then seamlessly to the House of Lords. He first came to public notice when he conducted the inquiry into the riots at Strangeways prison. From being a Law Lord he followed Tom Bingham as Master of the Rolls and subsequently as Lord Chief Justice. He brought to the latter post a considerable experience of the criminal law, which we had all acquired on circuit. His contribution to English law, for which he will ever be remembered, was the modernisation of the somewhat archaic practices of the English civil law which had obtained for hundreds of years. While not all of the reforms have received universal approval, it was a mammoth task and conducted with great good humour and common sense. A revolution of this sort is not carried out without some bloodshed, but in the end it took place, and will form the basis of civil litigation for decades.

One other important facet of his character was the determination to stand up to the politicians on behalf of the judiciary, and to resist the ever-increasing desire of politicians to interfere with the independence of the judges. This desire was entirely responsible for the lamentable frisson which developed between the executive and the judges. In the end Harry managed to come to some agreement with the Lord Chancellor. His firm stand has been much applauded by his fellow judges.

Another side of his character, which is perhaps best described as general benevolence, came home to me when Margaret was involved in a case in the Divisional Court, over which Harry was presiding. Margaret was then Chairman of the Education Committee at Bucks County Council and was responsible for having to close down a number of schools.

Occasionally, some well-meaning do-gooder sought to take the council to court for not having gone through the proper process. This was a pretty futile exercise, because the council were well advised and had taken every step that needed to be taken. They were shock proof.

However, one of these cases came up before Harry and after a fairly short hearing the County Council emerged victorious. However, no doubt in order not to make the do-gooder feel badly, Harry added 'it may well be that the County Council would like to look at this again' or some such words. They had no meaning in law and were merely a gentle let-down to the do-gooder. However, the County Council took the matter seriously, and I had to use all my persuasive powers on Margaret, to explain to her that this was a throwaway line which had no sanction and could be safely ignored!

Another example of Harry's benevolence was in relation to the Hanratty murder. The case had been the subject of a great deal of controversy both at the time of the trial and ever since. Numerous books and articles had been written by 'investigative' journalists who tended to think that almost every conviction was unjust. There is a great market for these sort of books and articles, because reports of alleged miscarriages of justice, whether accurate or not, command enormous media attention. There is also in any notorious criminal trial the spectre of a conspiracy theory. The case of Hanratty was no different, and spawned a whole spate of books and articles. Eventually, by use of DNA, the prosecution were able to convince the Court of Appeal that Hanratty had, in fact, been properly convicted. That put paid to all the speculative theories which had abounded. Harry, no doubt wishing to let these conspiracy theorists down lightly, added, at the end of his judgement, words to the effect that 'there was no criticism to be attached to those who had engaged in these journalistic activities'. This was despite the fact that, for a great number of years, they had persistently been peddling a theory which turned out to be hopelessly wrong.

Geoffrey Lane, who was Peter Taylor's predecessor as Lord Chief Justice, was much criticised for his views about the 'Birmingham Six'. He died in August 2005 and his obituary did him no favours. He did not get on well with the press. He saw no reason to communicate with them. He took the view that his job as Lord Chief Justice was to lay down the law and to look after his judges. Public relations did not feature in his makeup. He was, for all that, a most distinguished Lord Chief Justice. He had a sound practical knowledge both of criminal and civil work. He had been at Winchester House School, my old prep school, which for some unknown reason he had hated. He had had a fine academic career, served in the Air Force in the war, and commanded an enormous practice at the Bar on the Midland circuit. But his judgement in the first appeal in the 'Birmingham Six' case, which had been sceptically dismissive of the arguments put forward by defence counsel, was much criticised in the light of the errors which subsequently came to be discovered in the scientific evidence.

I first got to know him when I was appointed a judge. He sent for me to explain a number of things. He said to me, 'Oliver, the only problem is that you are much too nice to be a judge but you've got a s**t of a clerk.' I said to him that I thought that was the right way round. On another occasion, I sat with him hearing a criminal appeal. The appellant was making no sort of progress. Geoffrey passed me a note saying, 'There is nothing in this, is there?' and I replied, 'No'. He then wrote, 'I'm going to call on counsel for the Crown to headline his arguments, because I want to see what he is like'. This he then did, saying to counsel, 'Please summarise your arguments quite shortly.' Counsel for the Crown then fluffed around for about twenty minutes. I longed to say to counsel, 'Look, put it very simply, because your prospects of promotion are being considered and every minute you bang on like that is ruining them.' In the end, counsel made such a nonsense of it all that he never did get promoted and he probably never understood the reason why. No system of appearing before a committee can be a substitute for this sort of testing for judicial preferment.

Geoffrey Lane was essentially a defender of the judiciary and saw that as a very important role. His relations with the then Lord Chancellor were not good and it may be that the seeds were then sown for the subsequent in-fighting between the executive and the judiciary. But he was, in my view, a strong, determined Lord Chief Justice and the scribblers did themselves no favours in their less than generous comments after his death.

Peter Taylor, who succeeded Geoffrey Lane, was only Lord Chief Justice for some four years before he sadly had to retire because of cancer, from which he subsequently died. He had an enormous practice on the North-Eastern circuit and his appointment as Chief Justice was universally welcome. He had been a fine rugby player at Cambridge, just missing a blue, and he was also a very distinguished concert pianist in which career he would no doubt have excelled if he had not come to the Bar. He was very much a judge's judge, having been, as it were, at the coal face when at the Bar. He was more adept at public relations than Geoffrey had been and he was recognised as being a thoroughly sensible, down-to-earth judge. When at the Bar he had been in a number of very high-profile cases, including Poulson and Jeremy Thorpe, and, as a judge, he had a very sure touch when presiding over criminal appeals. He was a most entertaining companion, and his death at a comparatively early age was a cause of real sadness.

13

Job Hunting

In October 2005 I have two immediate issues. First, to pass my finals next May. I only wish that my memory were much better and that I were able to retain what I read. Like most people of my age, I find that, after reading something for half an hour, if I have not actually fallen asleep, I have great difficulty in recollecting the detail of what I have read, in the way I used to have to do as a barrister. It's obvious that I cannot cram three years of work into the last half hour before the exam. I shall need to spend some time analysing previous exam papers in order to pick out five or six questions which I am able to answer and just hope I get three of them. I don't have any particular apprehension about the Politics papers. I have four papers to do on this subject, one of which is a thesis, the other three are 'British Politics in the 20th Century', 'International Politics between the two World Wars' and 'Comparative Government'. For some curious reason the paper on the 'Theory of Politics' comes under the heading of Philosophy. The other Philosophy papers are a general paper, a special paper on the later works of Wittgenstein and a paper on ethics.

It is the general paper on philosophers and the special one on Wittgenstein which are going to be the very real problem. Later this term, however, I go for a tutorial to a marvellous tutor at New College, Dr Mulkull, on a one-to-one basis and have the most interesting discussions with him about Wittgenstein. When I read my essay to him, he makes no particular comment. But, during the course of the discussions which follow, where I am convinced that I am displaying my in-depth reading, it becomes abundantly clear that I have only managed to grasp half of what Wittgenstein was saying – and, by then, I am not quite sure which half. My tutor is not only enormously patient, but is also a very good teacher and I come away from the tutorials feeling that I have had a really good discussion. Whether I am on the right track I am still not entirely sure. I was led to believe that Wittgenstein was an amusing man, but all I can say is that I have not yet discovered a joke that I could be sure of getting right in an after-dinner speech. It may be that something has been lost in translation, but I find the language in which his philosophical investigations are expressed is not exactly a model of communication and clarity. I hope that with my tutor's guidance and with the prospect of some lectures next term, I shall begin to understand what it is all about.

Meanwhile I have managed to put my thesis into some sort of shape with the help of Liz, who has taught me how to do footnotes. I have also got over the hurdle of approval of the subject matter from the department and I now have to persuade Vernon Bogdanor of the utility of my chosen subject. One of my lecturers, Dr Hart, who teaches British Politics, has offered to have a look at my thesis and discuss it with me, which I am sure I will find very helpful. An interesting thing about writing the thesis is having the opportunity to examine original documents and diaries. Neville and Austen Chamberlain regularly wrote to their sister long and detailed letters about their political life and thoughts, and the letters provide an insight into their contemporary views, unaffected by subsequent events. It has always been a matter of some astonishment to me that these busy men had time to write these sorts of letters, although perhaps times were more leisurely. Even in the recent past, Dick Crossman, Tony Benn and Alan Clarke managed to record details of their political (and personal) activities at great length. And during the First World War, while still Prime Minister, Asquith was able frequently to write very private letters to Venetia Stanley. More recently Jonathan Aitken, when he was Financial Secretary to the Treasury, conducted what seems to have been a weekly correspondence with the editor of the *Observer* about his trip to Paris, which resulted in his disastrous libel action. No doubt historians of current political figures find that the irresistible temptation to communicate by email provides an even greater swathe of contemporaneous source material to explore but whether they will be as interesting or comprehensive as material written in less fevered times only time will tell.

There is something self-indulgent about listening to lectures on politics about events which are enormously familiar to me. It must be more difficult for the many much younger foreign students reading the same course to know where Baldwin or Neville Chamberlain or Attlee fit into the general picture of British political life or where Czechoslovakia was or what was the significance of the Danzig Corridor. For these students it must be something of a language nightmare to learn that a public school is not public, that the Speaker of the House of Commons has no speaking part and that the Lord Privy Seal is neither a Lord, nor a Privy nor a Seal. And what do they make of the Lord Chancellor's position in the separation of powers? The lecturers do their very best but I sometimes wonder whether the cut and thrust of political life which is enormously familiar to me has the same impact on a younger generation or on those from overseas.

The second issue which I have to address is what I am going to do next June, if and when I get a degree. I have much enjoyed university life but I think I have, as they say, done that. In any event, my level of degree will not be sufficient to enable me to do a master's degree or a doctorate. I have not talked to any of the tutors about this and it may be that I am being somewhat defensive. I have enjoyed doing the research for my thesis and certainly to do some further research into other political work would be very interesting. Whether it would be sufficiently stimulating or fulfilling, I simply don't know.

In November I receive, through my post, a brochure from a number of management consultants who are coming up to Oxford to recruit undergraduates at the end of their time here. I thought it would be amusing to print out my CV and to go along and see, not whether they could actually give me a job working for them, but rather whether they could find me a job working elsewhere, when I come down. To this end, I gave the documents to some surprised young men and suggested that they should pass them on to their chief executives. I then waited to see what would happen. I had replies from about half a dozen organisations, four of whom were friendly but non-receptive, but two said they thought it was all very interesting and they would keep my application in mind. Whether anything will result from this, I have some doubt. I have also been in touch with one or two friends who are head-hunters. They have kindly said that they would put my CV on their websites and let me know. In particular, I wrote to one of the government departments to see whether there were any public appointments for which I would be suited. I got back a helpful package of documents which I filled in. I found sponsors and I shall now sit back and wait to see whether this produces anything.

One of the interesting documents contained in the package was about standards of behaviour in public life. Most of what it said was self-evident. It did no more than confirm how one should behave with regard to conflicts of interest and other seemingly obvious matters. One's first reaction is to assume that such things are common practice and really don't need to be spelt out for those engaged in public life. It is how most judges have behaved ever since I have been involved in the law and I started to reflect that the same does not always appear to obtain among politicians. But recent examples show that such standards are indeed often ignored in public life. Take the case of the minister involved in litigation about the administration of Railtrack, who admitted lying to the judge hearing the case. He further admitted to the judge that he had been lying in the answers which he gave to a Commons committee. However the judge curiously found that, although the minister had in fact been lying he did not actually mean to lie, and so he was able to carry on as minister. Anyone who behaved like that has, in my view, no right to continue in public life.

The world of sports is no different. In football, players constantly 'dive' in order to give the impression that they have been fouled, and if they can achieve this in the penalty area the reward may well be a goal. On a recent occasion, one of the Pakistan Test players was caught on camera, scuffing the pitch with his boot. The purpose of this was to enable their bowlers, when their turn came to bowl, to take advantage of a roughed up wicket. In common parlance that is called cheating. In golf, where the rules are very strict, the player would almost certainly be banned for life from playing. The ICC Rules only provided for him to be banned from playing in the subsequent Test match. He was therefore allowed to continue playing in the current game.

Then it was disclosed that a number of people who had provided substantial donations or loans to their political party had been elevated to the House of Lords. Given that one of the reasons why there was such an attack on the House of Lords was that it was not truly representative, it is perhaps astonishing that effectively buying your way into the House of Lords still appears to continue. In Lloyd George's day it was a public scandal. There is the apocryphal story of the gentleman who handed over a lot of money in order to become a baronet. When he was turned down, he simply enquired how much more money was needed. When Members of Parliament appear to charge for journeys that they have not taken and when MEPs travel steerage, and charge for club class, it does begin to suggest that all is not well in the political world.

The outgoing British ambassador to the United States, Sir Christopher Meyer, has written a book about his time in Washington. He managed, apparently, to secure the approval for its publication by the Cabinet and made severely critical comments about members of the Government with whom he had dealt in the course of his official duties. It seems not to have occurred to him that confidential discussions should remain confidential, certainly while those who took part in them are still in office or alive. If a minister cannot have these sorts of discussions with some degree of confidence that what is said is confidential, how then can government properly be carried out? It is now common practice for ministers to publish their autobiographies as soon as they leave office. I believe a certain reticence in these matters is to be encouraged.

Meanwhile on a wholly different, family note, *The Lion, the Witch and the Wardrobe*, the film adaptation of the C.S. Lewis novel in which my granddaughter, Anna, is starring, is going to have its premiere later in December. The publicity has already started. She was interviewed by a Sunday paper. She was asked about her parents and about me. In relation to me she said, 'I love my grandfather. He's got such bushy eyebrows and he is hilarious.' As the publicity will increase between now and the showing of the film, I expect that there will be a good deal more of this sort of thing. The media find it hard to believe that judges, even retired judges, live in the real world or have relatives that do.

I remember that when Nigel was first playing cricket for Somerset, there was astonishment that the son of a QC (as I then was) should be playing county cricket. To begin with, he was constantly referred to as 'the son of the QC'. Subsequently, as he became better known, I was referred to as 'the father of Nigel Popplewell'. The same occurred when I became a judge. On one occasion, years ago, when I was at Lord's, a young boy came up to me with his autograph book and asked me for my autograph. I patted him on the head rather pompously and said, 'Sonny, you don't want my autograph.' His little face fell and he said, 'Oh, but sir, aren't you Nigel Popplewell's father?'

14

Winter in Oxford

When I first came up to Oxford, I rather imagined that I would meet quite a lot of dons in other colleges, and get invited to dine with them on high table. This has happened on a number of occasions but I have not yet made any lasting friends among the dons. Those whom I have met have been very engaging, entertaining and hospitable, but they have been comparatively few in number. While the life of a don is not quite as it is pictured in C.P. Snow's *Strangers and Brothers*, dons still tend to lead comparatively sheltered lives. Although they no longer have security of tenure, their existence is a comfortable and interesting one. It does not prevent them, however, from expressing some envy about their former pupils, who have gone on to become merchant bankers or something similar in the City. The difference in their respective financial rewards is very marked. I also tend to forget that they are of a different generation and many are the same age as my children.

The Principal of Harris Manchester College, Ralph Waller, kindly invited me to go to a lecture in London on the position of the dons and on the future of the universities (particularly Oxbridge) to be given by the retired Vice-Chancellor of Cambridge. The audience consisted of academics from different universities and polytechnics. The speaker was very much in favour of getting rid of A-levels as a test for entry into Oxbridge and favoured the Baccalaureate. He had some reservations about the American system of SATs, but made no reference to central admissions to the University. The present system gives each college total

9   Oliver and Ralph Waller, Principal at Harris Manchester

control over the entry of their students. This is because the colleges are
very jealous of their own position in the University. They are reluctant
to hand over to any other body the way in which their particular college
is run. Thus, great importance is attached to league tables in order to
attract those who may be thought to be the best students to particular

colleges. Whereas in the old days, a rounded education such as being a games player or a musician or having taken part in theatricals would add something to a student's CV, the colleges now concentrate on admitting those whom they think will best enable the college to rise high in the league tables. Skill in sport is no longer a selling point for an applicant and the effect is only too clearly to be seen in the University matches. Neither Peter May nor Colin Cowdrey would have a chance of getting to Oxbridge under the present system.

I have long thought that central admissions, which would put the choice of student in the hands of the University at large, would be a more equable system. It would work on the basis that if there were a hundred places available in the History Faculty the University would set a general intelligence paper, with special emphasis on historical questions. The University would then take the top hundred in the exams. This would obviate all the drama about interviews. It would stop any bickering about the respective merits of state schools and public schools and would put an end to complaints that little Mary did not present well at interview because her dog had been run over the previous day. Indeed, I gather that for some subjects at Oxford this is how it is now done.

However, the logic of the opposing view has much to commend it. On one occasion John White and I went to have a drink with one of our political lecturers, and we discussed this problem with him. He said, 'Well, in general terms, there is nothing against your proposal, except that, as an admissions tutor, I would want to be sure that a person whom I admitted to my college and whom I was going to tutor, or who was going to be tutored outside my college, and for whom I was responsible, was suitable and intellectually equipped to cope with the challenges of the course.' He emphasised the importance to the maintenance of the individual tutorial and collegiate system for which Oxford and Cambridge are rightly prized, of the ability of individual tutors and colleges to select their candidates. He gave us a recent example of a candidate who had, on paper, reasonable qualifications. The entrance paper had included a question, which ran something like this: 'If the death penalty were to be imposed for parking offences, would that stop people parking illegally?' The candidate had written an essay in which his views were not clear. The tutor therefore had asked him at interview to elaborate on the subject. The candidate said that he thought it was a very good idea to impose a death penalty and that he would certainly support it. This was said in all seriousness. The tutor then asked him what would he do if he had parked illegally and then saw a traffic warden approaching. To this the candidate replied that he would simply shoot the traffic warden. When the tutor asked him whether this view applied to other similar offences, involving the death penalty, the candidate said yes. The tutor had no difficulty in deciding that this young man was a quite unsuitable candidate to be at Oxford, much to the disappointment of his school.

One of the tasks I took on when I retired from the Bench was to be President of the XL Club. This club for the over forties which I mentioned earlier has the same function as the MCC in relation to its 'out' matches: to take cricket to schools and to encourage them in the 'the spirit of cricket'. It also seeks to provide those, who might fairly be described as past their prime, with an opportunity to continue to enjoy the game. It has been the custom over the years, because of the relationship between the MCC and the XL Club, for those connected with the MCC to be invited to be presidents of the XL Club. My two immediate past presidents were Jack Bailey and John Stevenson, both former MCC secretaries. Before that Brian Johnston had been President.

It is not an enormously onerous task. There are half a dozen executive meetings during the year, which are presided over by the Chairman. There are a number of sub-committees but the President's primary job, as said earlier, is to find four speakers for the annual dinner, which is held in October. This has always been a very prestigious occasion. There used to be an attendance of some 600 or 700 at the Hilton. Sadly the numbers have fallen off because the expense of these evenings has gone up, and people find travelling to London less agreeable. We now have dinners for some 350 or 400 and they are held at the Savoy, where we are marvellously well-treated.

On one or two occasions before my time, we paid a speaker to come and speak. I thought this was a mistake and that those who were invited to this prestigious dinner ought to be willing to come and enjoy a dinner without payment. Certainly in my time we didn't pay any speakers. The previous years' speakers are invited to come as guests the following year. I was President of the MCC for two years, and therefore spoke twice. I was invited back the following year but not thereafter, so strictly I am still owed a further dinner!

One of the more agreeable duties of the President is to sit on the committee which arranges and organises the dinner. In the summer, three of us go off to the Savoy to have a tasting for the forthcoming dinner. We do this by having three choices for each course, each of us tasting one and we then share and compare. At the end of it we usually manage to agree on what the dinner shall be. As we also do the same with the wines, it may be understood that by the end of the luncheon, our judgement may be somewhat awry. However, no-one has yet complained.

I now find that I am not able to attend all the meetings which I would like, in particular some of the sub-committee meetings. The District Chairmen organise the affairs of the club in their particular area. They are very important people because they have to look after the match managers who then raise the club sides. On them really depends the whole success of the club. I found that being unable to go to their meetings really cut me off from quite a lot of what was going on in the club. After five years, therefore, I decided that it was time for me to go. Having been persuaded to stay on an extra year, which was a very kind gesture on the part of the committee, I finally went this winter. The Chairman, Jack Hyde-Blake, who had been chairman throughout my time, was also retiring. He had run the club with a marvellous touch of good humour and firmness. At the Annual General Meeting, therefore, there were lots of votes of thanks to him for what he had done. He made a very gracious tribute to my contribution to the club, which was quite undeserved, and then, at the end of the meeting, the Secretary passed me a parcel. I opened it and found that it contained a medallion. I held it up for all to see and thanked everybody for their generous present to me. I then discovered that what the Secretary had in fact passed to me was for me to present to the Chairman. I hadn't expected to be given anything, and there was no reason why I should have been. It was nevertheless a thoroughly embarrassing moment. Anyway, everyone roared with laughter and the moment passed.

Some years before, Margaret had persuaded me that it would be a nice idea if I were to have a sculpture of my head in bronze. I confess I was not enormously enthusiastic but gave in. I had six sittings in my room in the law courts. I was able to read papers for an hour or so and then had to sit still for half an hour. I was careful not to see the progress of the work and at the penultimate sitting Margaret came and pronounced it satisfactory. When it was complete it was taken away to be cast in bronze and was then returned to me. It sat on a plinth in the drawing room of Lime Tree Farm where it aroused mixed comments. The family in particular, while not unduly critical, were much concerned as to whom this treasure was to be left when I died. No-one expressed any sort of enthusiasm to be the recipient of this heirloom. However the problem was solved in a rather unusual way. One lunchtime when there was no-one in the house, the front door was battered off its hinges and the thieves were able to steal a number of possessions including my head. What they were going to do with it was a matter of considerable and disrespectful debate among the family. The police were unable to offer any helpful advice about its recovery. I eventually claimed on my insurers for the cost of the bust and thought no more about it. In June 2008 I had a call from the police asking me whether I was the owner of a bust which they now had under lock and key. It bore the name of the sculptress through whom the police had been able to trace me. The history of it was that a gentleman had bought it at a car boot sale in the belief that it was a bust of Denis Healey. (The eyebrows I suspect!) History does not record what he paid for it. Subsequently he had had doubts about its provenance and had, therefore, as a good citizen, taken it to the police. What, said the police, do you want us to do with it? I got in touch with my insurers who legally had the right to it, or to its value, but they said they were no longer interested. It seemed to me that the honesty of the gentleman who had handed it in to the police should be recognised; though he now knew the bust was not that of Denis Healey, he should be allowed to keep it. I have therefore suggested to the police to hand it over.

At the end of the Michaelmas term, Liz had been invited to Prague to chair an insolvency seminar for a number of Czech judges. Anthony Colman, who is a High Court judge, had been very much involved in the legal affairs of the Czech Republic and he had organised that Liz, together with Richard Snowden (a company law QC) should spend two days instructing lawyers in Prague about recent legal issues relating to insolvency both in England and internationally. I was invited to go along for the ride (at Liz's, and not the taxpayer's, expense) and gratefully accepted. So on a Friday evening we set off to Prague. Saturday and Sunday were to be free, with the meetings on Monday and Tuesday. We arrived late on the Friday night and stayed in a traditional old hotel just below the castle where we woke up to find snow, which made the whole of the city look quite beautiful.

I had last been to Prague in 1964 when I had brought my elderly parents for a holiday. My father had been a student at the turn of the century at the University of Prague. Now aged eighty-four, he was somewhat frail and, on one occasion, when he went searching for his old digs, we lost him for most of a day. In those days Prague was under the Communist regime. While the buildings were attractive, they were in a shabby state of repair. There was nothing to buy in the shops. There was a sense of total gloom over the whole city. We stayed, if I remember, in a dismal hotel called the Hotel Yalta, which had been assigned to foreign visitors by the communists. I suspect that the place was bugged, although we had no secrets to disclose. It was just after the Great Train Robbery and the only English newspaper available in Prague was *The Daily Worker*. The paper had a real problem deciding which was the more important piece of news – was it the £2 million which had been taken out of the capitalist system, or was it the diabolical attack on the engine driver?

We had to make it clear, when we did go into shops, of which there were very few selling anything, that we were English and not German. The Germans were hated even more than the Russians. One couldn't help sympathising with the plight of the Czechs. From 1938 until 1989 they had been continuously occupied first by the Germans, then by the Communists and finally by the Russians. Thus no-one under the age of fifty had enjoyed any sort of freedom until 1989.

The city itself was now, in 2005, a revelation. The old buildings had survived the occupations and there was little room for ghastly modern high-rise architecture. Despite the invasions, there had been no, or no substantial, fighting in the city and little or no damage to the infrastructure. The buildings therefore remained as they had done for 300 or 400 years. The place had now been marvellously cleaned up, and all the buildings were beautifully maintained. The squares were buzzing with families and their children enjoying the pre-Christmas festivities. Wenceslas Square, unhappily, had not survived the impact of Americanisation. This was really the tacky part of the town. Elsewhere, although clearly a tourist hive, the city presented a most attractive façade and it's easy to see why it has become so popular. We found that, disappointingly, a number of the churches were either closed, or entry restricted, because of forthcoming concerts, so that it was difficult to see inside, but they reflected the influence of the Baroque in this part of Europe.

When Anna was filming *The Lion, the Witch and the Wardrobe*, she had stayed in Prague with her family, because of the requirement for at least some 'real' snow. They were therefore able to give us the names of some very agreeable restaurants, which ranged from traditional Czech to surprisingly sophisticated international cuisine. We spent the Saturday and Sunday enthusiastically sightseeing, but on the Monday, Liz had to return to the delights of the European Insolvency Regulation. Luckily I managed to escape most of the lectures, as insolvency had not been my preferred bedside reading during the course of my legal career. Instead I spent my time wandering around Prague and really getting to know it. The premiere of Anna's film was due to take place on the following Wednesday. Liz had been told by Debs (Anna's mother) that it was an occasion for which she could not possibly be overdressed, which, of course, gave Liz total freedom to go on a shopping spree. In a smart shop in the middle of Prague's old square, which looked like the sort of place where Russian oligarchs might take their WAGS to indulge, Liz found a dress and, after much discussion in German about the merits of embroidered sequins (in which I did not participate), she bought it.

On our last night we were entertained by two members of the Embassy at a South American restaurant in the centre of the town. It was amusing to see cut-out promotional figures of Anna, and the rest of the Narnia cast, right outside the restaurant. We learnt a good deal about the Czech economy and about how caringly and efficiently our Embassy staff deal with British stag-night tourists who ring up the Embassy late at night to complain that their hotels have suddenly moved location and to demand a taxi at the taxpayer's expense.

Finally after four days of very agreeable holiday (at least for me) we sped home in order to get ourselves ready for the premiere of Anna's film, which has been much touted in the newspapers. The *Daily Mail* gave it five stars but *The Times* only two. We shall have to wait until after Wednesday to see what the serious critics say about it. The premiere itself was a most extravagant affair. The Albert Hall had been turned into a cinema for the night. Having arrived in good time on a wet and windy evening, we walked down the red carpet – actually blue, no doubt to accentuate the winter theme under a cover of gently falling artificial snowflakes – with press photographers and journalists on one side and an invited audience of teenagers on the other. The stars, including Anna, were being constantly interviewed and photographed by the press, both national and international. We were shepherded into a private room in the Albert Hall for drinks, while the stars continued outside.

I found the film itself somewhat wooden in parts, unlike Liz, who had grown up on C.S. Lewis's books. She knew every word of the script, and was enchanted by the magic of it all. But, even allowing for the fact that grandpaternal pride somewhat blunts the critical faculties, I thought that Anna's part was well done and she and the other children had been well-directed. Tilda Swinton was mesmerisingly scary as the White Witch. After the film was over, we crossed the road into Kensington Gardens, where, in the moonlit shadow of the Albert Memorial, the film company had set up a mock Narnia landscape, which was reputed to have cost over £1 million. Here, once one had struggled through a mock-up wardrobe, with pretend fur coats, champagne flowed like water. There was a banquet. There was dancing and much merriment, a lamp post and more snowflakes. It was an enormously glittering affair, which raised a lot of money for charity as well as publicising the film. There is talk of an Oscar nomination but I am not holding my breath. It was, for Anna, a particularly exciting occasion and subsequently she found herself being invited to various functions and parties as a mini-celebrity. Whether there will be a sequel and whether, if there is, she will want to do it in the light of her scholastic ambitions, time alone will tell.

15

Third Year

Christmas 2005 with its film premiere and also a fine shooting holiday in Scotland was a happy interval amid serious work for the summer exams. My thesis is now in comparatively good order although Vernon thinks it still too much of a narrative. The real difficulty is that I have been trained to set out the facts and then give a judgement. So it is difficult to deal with the impact of a by-election without setting the scene politically in the weeks, or indeed the months, before the by-election takes place. For instance, the impact of the SDP was something that occurred over a period of eighteen months and each by-election fed on the previous one. Without setting out the facts of each occasion, I find it hard to articulate a reasoned conclusion. But perhaps I am still too much the judge and not enough the research student. I am not quite sure how I can improve on what I have already written, but if Vernon remains critical I must necessarily take notice, because his views certainly may count more than mine. He has not, so far, criticised the conclusions to which I have come, although we disagree about the effect of the Carlton Club meeting. Where we differ is that he believes that the result of the Carlton Club meeting was unrelated to the result of the Newport by-election and was inevitable given the views of a number of important junior ministers who much resented Lloyd George. My view was that although there was dissatisfaction with Lloyd George, the tipping point which persuaded the majority to support Bonar Law and not Chamberlain was the victory of the Conservative over both Labour and Liberal. I have listened to

Vernon's view but I have formed my own conclusions. Although I don't agree with his conclusion, I shall, however, sycophantically set out his views in my thesis to indicate that I have read widely!

When we do our exams, or submit our theses, the name of the candidate is not disclosed. We simply have a number. It is, however, impossible not to make reference to the fact that I knew Dick Taverne, the victor of the Lincoln by-election, as a young boy when he first came to Charterhouse. Further, I made reference to correspondence with Paddy Mayhew and also to a conversation with Bill Rogers who was one of the original Limehouse Four. Anyone reading the thesis, therefore, probably won't have much doubt that the author is a fairly mature student. Whether that gives me an advantage or not, I do not know. I suspect not!

So far as revision is concerned, I am comparatively happy about the Politics paper, including Political Theory, but Wittgenstein and the other philosophers are still giving me the odd sleepless night. If all goes well, I anticipate that I will get a 2nd of some sort in the Politics and a 3rd in the Philosophy. Ethics is a subject where chance will play an important part, while Comparative Politics, although a somewhat dreary course, is a subject which I think I can manage. Next term I am going to Professor Caedel's lectures on 'International Politics between the Wars', to which I look forward immensely. It is a subject in which I have always been interested and about which I formed definite views at a comparatively early age. Munich was, for my generation, a dirty word, in which England appeared to have played an ignoble part and where we appeared to have sacrificed the Czechs for our own safety. Now that more documents have become available, it may be possible to revise that view. I shall be interested in learning Professor Caedel's views on the whole issue of appeasement.

I can remember very well, as a child, seeing the newsreels (there was then no television) of Chamberlain coming off the aeroplane at either Heston or Croydon together with Alec Douglas Hume (as he became), one of his officials at the Foreign Office. Chamberlain was waving his bit of paper and telling the world that 'we have peace in our time'. Whether he believed it or not, he certainly gave the impression that he did. The relief of the country as a whole was overwhelming, as evidenced by the cheers which surrounded his progress from the airport to Buckingham Palace. It was a scene firmly imprinted on my mind.

Going to war in Iraq has aroused the same amount of passion that the invasion of Suez did a generation or two ago. The process of reasoning behind the invasion of Iraq has been investigated – at least to some extent – by Lord Hutton and subsequently by Robin Butler. Whatever one's view about weapons of mass destruction, it is abundantly clear now that they did not exist and that the intelligence suggesting that they did was totally flawed. The Attorney General's opinion about the legality is mired in controversy. The Hutton Inquiry, far from reaching a conclusion that satisfied people, simply muddied the waters. Robin Butler's terms of reference were such that he was unable to point the finger at the Government, even if he had been minded so to do. While the fighting is actually taking place, it is natural for the forces to be supported, It is, however, quite clear that, as at Suez, support for the Government was very muted and everything that has happened since seems to demonstrate the folly of the invasion. We simply cannot afford to police the world. Even if we did have the resources to do so, one has to ask what concern is it of ours when Iraq posed no immediate, or indeed any, threat to us or to the rest of the world.

As for the invasion of Afghanistan and the attempt to destroy the Taliban, one needs only to ask why the lessons, which the Russians learnt so painfully and disastrously, have not been learnt by the United States of America and Britain. It has always seemed to me to be a good precept of a country's foreign policy only to meddle in the affairs of other nations when one's own national interest is seriously threatened. Whatever view one might have about Saddam Hussein, he posed only a threat to Israel, and Israel seemed perfectly content to take no part in his removal. The folly of attempting to impose a western solution to Arab problems was one of the lessons we should have learnt from the First World War.

While public demonstrations, certainly in Oxford, have not been on the same scale as one remembers at the time of Suez, nevertheless nationally it seems to me that the outcry has been just as great. Whether it will have any effect on Government, I doubt. A Government at war, with its army in action, is unlikely to be defeated, as was shown by the result of the general election. Whether, if the casualties increase and peace seems no nearer, the Government will suffer, only time will tell.

We see all the family over the Christmas period. We have a lovely time with Nigel and Ingy down in Somerset. Their house and garden are delightful and the countryside of the Quantocks and the Mendips is stunning. 'Miss Alice', as I have always called her, their eldest child, has grown into a fine young woman and will set lots of hearts a buzzing. She has much charm and spent a few days of her Christmas holidays helping Liz sort out old clothes (dating back to the 1970s) and was very much in her element. She is thinking of leaving Taunton School in and going to the sixth form at a boys' school in the autumn, where no doubt she will flourish. Meanwhile Harry, who is a thoroughly sensible boy, is making steady progress both on the games field and in class and has moved up into the Upper School. Thomas or 'Bubble', his younger brother, is more of an extrovert. He too is a good little cricketer and a real competitor, as he demonstrated on the beaches in Normandy, when he declined to bowl either to his mother, his sister or to Liz. He regarded them as unworthy opponents! They are an enormously active family. They all play some musical instrument, some better than others. Ingy is pursuing her medical career and is a member of a GP practice. Nigel meanwhile flourishes as the tax partner in Burgess, Salmon in Bristol and is pretty critical of father's decisions on VAT and Income Tax.

We spent Christmas itself with Andrew and Debs and family, which is always immense fun. Andrew is a successful commercial silk and Debs is a high powered dermatologist at Great Ormond Street hospital. Of Anna much has already been written. Suffice it to say that she survived the excitement of Narnia with great aplomb and kept her feet very firmly on the ground. Lulu is undoubtedly the wit of the Popplewell family. She has a wicked line in repartee over the dinner table (and, I suspect, alas for her teachers, also in the classroom) and an excellent brain, when she chooses to use it. Cinematically, she is currently 'resting', since her moment of glory as Emma Thompson's daughter in *Love Actually*, where she appeared dressed as a lobster. I am not sure that her parents' pride in her undoubted musical and theatrical talents quite extended to applauding her pre-Christmas busking revenues, but I, at least, was impressed at her income generation abilities. Fred, meanwhile, has been achieving much on the games field and at work. He has been keeping wicket for Middlesex Under 9 and Under 10, with a great deal more skill than his grandfather or father, much to their pleasure.

Alexander and Sally decided to move from their London house to the country. They rented another house, while looking for somewhere else to buy, and had the most horrendous experience of returning from Christmas to find that the main drains had backed up and flooded the lower ground floor. Inevitably, the landlord turned out to be a Channel Island registered company, with no transparent shareholder profile, and it was wholly uninterested in the financial consequences of sewage damage to cream linen sofas in Clapham. This nearly gave rise to litigation in which Liz gave valuable advice. Finally, Alex and Sally found a large country house with out-buildings in Berkshire; Sally, no doubt, will exercise her considerable talents in restoring their new home with great taste.

The two older girls, Victoria and Millie, are respectively at Marlborough and Down House. They have both flourished and it is interesting to compare the respective qualities of each school, one co-educational, the other single-sex. To my, in some respects, stuffy generation co-educational boarding schooling would have been regarded as unthinkable – a concept reserved for the dangerously avant-garde. But girls arrived in the 1970s in the sixth form at my old school, Charterhouse, while Alexander was still there. We were somewhat concerned about the possible impact of all this upon the boy's dedication to his studies and his rigorous pursuit of manly sports. But when I asked him whether he had girls in his form, he replied, 'I'm not sure,' and, perhaps falsely, we were reassured. The current judgement on the co-ed/single-sex debate seems, quite sensibly, to be that it just depends on the child and the school concerned and that there are no hard and fast rules. Alexander continues with what was MAM, was subsequently part of Merrill Lynch and now is Blackrock. I don't pretend to understand either the significance of these takeovers or their consequences but he obviously thrives on his work while still finding time to fish and shoot and run marathons. Sally apart from reorganising houses at regular intervals runs a business selling presents at Christmas fairs. They have two other children, Nellie something of a shooting star at her prep school, and Livia, now five, who is very pretty and enormously perky.

Of Ed and Clare's children I have already written something. The idea is that Hugo will sit his scholarship both academic and music to Eton in the spring, and Leo and Robin will go to a local school in Amersham. Ed, meanwhile has moved from Thames Water to Siemens, the German manufacturers, and we are going ahead with our plans for them to take over Lime Tree, as soon as we can finalise the financial arrangements.

16

Summer Term at Oxford

Summer term at Oxford suddenly arrived. The spring term and the Easter holidays were spent revising. I took the view that philosophy was the most important area to which to dedicate my revision efforts, and that politics would by and large take care of itself. I was lucky with all my tutors, both at Harris Manchester and at New College. They had prepared me as best they could for the philosophy, while Lesley Smith persuaded me that political theory was as important as political reality. I was equally lucky to have Vernon Bogdanor teaching me Modern British Politics and Professor Caedel, International Politics. Having lived through most of the events with which they were concerned, I was able to give them some sort of insight into the views of a young man, on matters which were for them only history. I talked to them, for instance, about Munich. As a young man I regarded it as the most terrible humiliation which this country had ever suffered. This view was eventually revised as I began to understand why Chamberlain had been forced to, as we then thought, sell Czechoslovakia out to the Germans. Oxford was very instructive in providing me with a different perspective on events about which I thought that I had formed a decided view at an early age in my life.

In the same way, when discussing post-war events, my views were naturally shaped by the constant threat we faced from the Russians and by the never-ending problems of our balance of payments, both of which continued until a decade or so ago. It is difficult, for anyone much under sixty to understand that our whole life was governed by these two issues and that almost every political decision was influenced both by the threat of Communism and by the imminent risk of bankruptcy of the British economy. I sometimes wonder whether historians who write about post-war events give sufficient attention to these twin problems, which necessarily co-impacted. But for the threat of Communism, neither the expenditure on armaments, nor the costly maintenance of forces abroad, would have been so necessary. Thus the impact on the economy of heavy defence expenditure would have been much alleviated.

The threat of Communism – as witness the Berlin Wall, the Korean war and the Cuban crisis – and the risk posed by Red China were a much greater danger then than that posed now by Iraq or Afghanistan. Such readily explains why it was necessary to maintain disproportionately sized armed forces around the globe. Likewise, until Margaret Thatcher came to power, the constant threat from the unions of industrial action had a devastating effect on the economy. The failure to invest in industry, which enabled the Japanese and the Germans after the war to overtake the British economy, and the inability of management to manage, were two other important factors, and they had an adverse effect on the balance of payments.

The balance of payments problem initially resulted from our spending almost all our capital during the war. The moment the war ended so also did lending through lend-lease and we then had to seek a loan from the United States, on harsh terms. Until Marshall Aid we were a serious debtor. Bill Correlli Barnett has much of interest to say on this subject in *The Verdict of Peace* the final volume of his series of books on the decline of the economy. For my generation the Berlin air lift, the Korean war, Suez, Cuba, Vietnam and the fall of Communism were dramatic moments in our lives which we experienced at first hand. They defined the views of several generations and affected our thinking for decades.

Meanwhile, my thesis has to be submitted on the Friday at the beginning of term. It has to be specially packaged and delivered at the right place. I managed to pack it correctly, and take it around to the department who accept it. They then ring me up and tell me that they are not the people to whom it needs to go, but to some other body. It's all in the regulations, I am told. I find the regulations, identify the relevant one, deliver the thesis and get a receipt. Apparently, it then becomes the property of the University, though I am allowed to quote excerpts, if I want to, which I don't. The view of Liz and the family is that it is much too much of a narrative, and does not draw sufficient conclusions. Not surprisingly, I don't entirely agree with these harsh critics, but no doubt my hubris will be demonstrated by a poor mark. At this point my 'Dragon Speak' – the program which converts what I dictate out loud into words on the screen of my laptop, records the end of the previous sentence as 'a paw mark'. A dog's life perhaps!

I manage to have a certain amount of social life although it is now much more muted. I am invited to go to Phoenix, Arizona to take part in a mediation and arbitration conference on insurance. It seems to me that it should be a good experience which I shall enjoy, and during which I can do a certain amount of networking without seriously interfering with my studies. The organisers are putting us up in a hotel in enormous luxury, but will only pay steerage on the aeroplane. The cost of transferring to business class is uneconomical so I don't. I have to fly by an American airline. The food is fairly awful and we arrive late at Chicago. The result is that I miss my connection to Phoenix and I arrive late for the first evening's entertainment.

I had understood that I was going to speak about terrorism about which I know little more than ordinary members of the public. However, when I read the agenda, I find that I am billed to speak about the effect of the Sarbanes-Oxley Law on the British insurance market and, in particular, on Lloyds. Sarbanes-Oxley takes its name from two members of Congress who introduced a Bill in order to prevent the sort of financial malpractice which had occurred in the Enron companies. It creates an enormous amount of bureaucracy, involving the completion of vast quantities of forms, and bureaucratic mandates about the precautions to be taken by management. It is a typical American reaction to a simple fraud. It will have no effect, in my view, in preventing crime; criminals will simply find other ways of dealing and probably fill in the forms more efficiently than the average honest businessman.

I talk to one of the senior executives of Lloyds to see what effect he thinks it will have on them. His answer is that it will have none. I feel, however, that I cannot just sit there and say that it is all irrelevant to the operation of the London market, so I prepare a very boring summary of how Lloyds operates, why the system went wrong and the steps that have been put in place to put it right. I suspect this will be of little or no interest to the Americans but luckily I have, as a fellow speaker, a solicitor from Freshfields, who will speak about the impact on English insurance. We have, in typical American fashion, three or four telephone conferences across the Atlantic with the other speakers, which are barely audible, are time-consuming and add nothing to our preparation. The conference itself is very well run; we are very well entertained in comfortable surroundings and the sessions are universally good. I manage, when I am not speaking, or when the subject is of lesser interest, to catch up on some work but we have a good social programme, ending in a very engaging dinner which lasts late into the night.

I then set out from Phoenix at lunchtime to get the 9 pm plane from Chicago back to London. The Phoenix plane is delayed and the crew on my plane are not willing to notify Chicago that I am going to be late. The result is that I miss the flight going back to England by about half an hour and am required to stay the night in a rather down-market hotel. Where my luggage has gone, I simply do not know and by this time hardly care. However, as I am booked onto the 9 o'clock morning plane from Chicago, I have a night's sleep and turn up without my luggage, all ready to fly. We go through the usual customs. The absence of luggage causes some ado because nobody in America believes that you travel without luggage. Eventually I get on the plane and, having had a good breakfast, start on doing some more revision. After sitting on the tarmac for an hour, we are told that the plane is not fit to fly, so three or four hundred passengers then emerge back into the terminal building to try and find some other way of getting back to London. It is obviously impossible to get on another plane that morning so I am stuck at the airport with a $10 voucher for lunch and tea. I manage to persuade the powers that be to let me into the first-class lounge on payment and I spend the day there, catching up on my philosophy revision. It is a perfect waste of time and my thoughts on philosophy scarcely do justice to the subject. Finally we fly out late at night and I arrive home forty-eight hours late, with my luggage still somewhere between Phoenix, Chicago and London. As a lighthearted interval before exams, it perhaps was not the greatest idea.

Meanwhile at Oxford, the animal terrorist group have mustered in large numbers outside a building just off Mansfield Road, where it is thought that some animal experiments are going to be carried out. They make a thorough nuisance of themselves, disrupting traffic, shouting abuse and making a tremendous amount of noise, thus seriously disturbing students who are anxiously preparing for their exams. Eventually the University does take some steps to prevent this continuing. The protesters are limited by an order made by Mr Justice Holland, both in number and in volume of protest, and they are also restricted in the areas to which they can go. Some of them are, no doubt, perfectly well meaning, but the attacks on individuals and on families and on employees has been nothing short of disgraceful. It is surprising that the authorities don't treat them as the terrorists that they are. The ringleaders are, I am sure, well known to the police but as with hunt saboteurs little or nothing is done by the authorities to protect the lawful activities which are taking place. Even when these terrorists are arrested, the punishments which they receive seem to be so trivial as to encourage, rather than to discourage, this form of protest taking place.

17

Newspapers and Gripes

Another legal sensation hits the newspapers. This is about the extradition in early 2006 of what are called the 'NatWest Three' or, in American terms, the 'Enron Three'. The large American company, Enron, was the subject of a giant financial fraud. It is alleged that the three NatWest Directors were in some way involved, by reason of various deals with an apparently only marginal relevance to the United States. I have no idea whether they are guilty or not, but the problem which has arisen is that, some years ago, the British Government entered into a treaty with the United States, whereby the United States is entitled to demand the extradition of those it believes to have been guilty of some criminal offence in America. It matters not how tenuous the connection is, and the US prosecuting authorities have to provide nothing more than an allegation.

This is not a reciprocal arrangement. The matter was never considered by Parliament. It was clearly designed to facilitate the exchange of terrorists and was a knee-jerk reaction to the bombings in New York. No-one suggests that the 'NatWest Three' come into that category. They have not been charged or tried in this country, although they asked that they should be, it being alleged that the transaction complained about took place in England. The Senate has not ratified the treaty although this is of considerably less importance than the fact that it is not a reciprocal arrangement. The result is that the Americans, by simply alleging an offence, can require British citizens to be extradited to

America, where they may await trial for two or three years. They may not get bail and they certainly won't be allowed back to this country. Other countries have successfully negotiated an arrangement whereby, if the offence were committed in their country or could be tried in their country, no extradition proceedings would be allowed to take place. Given America's refusal to extradite well-known terrorists belonging to the IRA, it is difficult to see how this Government could have entered into such a one-sided arrangement. But such is the desire of this Government to support the Bush administration that the Americans have only to cock a finger and the Government fall into place.

Apart from revising, which occupies most of my time, I also manage to find time to read the newspapers and am constantly astonished at some of the things that go on in public life and in our courts. A doctor who campaigned to rid Dartmouth of seagulls was charged with an anti-seagull action and convicted of shooting one of them. In fact he had a licence to shoot them but only if they were a danger to public health. Birds nested on the roof of his house at Dartmouth. They were aggressive. They spread disease. They ripped open his bin bags and left droppings everywhere. He had tried all sorts of humane remedies. He tried distress calls and he tried firing blanks. All to no avail. The area where he lived was contaminated with seagull droppings and his property was sometimes inches thick with the stuff. So one day, when a gull dive-bombed his wife as she ate her lunch in the garden, covering her food with droppings, he shot the bird with an air gun and then strung it up in his garden.

He was solemnly prosecuted by the RSPCA. The prosecution alleged that the licence only allowed him to kill a seagull if it presented a danger to public health. The Chief Inspector went on to say, 'Dartmouth is a seaside town and you expect seagulls.' The Magistrates at Totnes, instead of telling the RSPCA that they were wasting everybody's time and money and throwing out the case with a costs order against the RSPCA, convicted the luckless doctor and ordered him to pay the costs. In Totnes, apparently, having your food spattered with bird droppings does not constitute a danger to public health. Sometimes the actions of public officials beggar belief, and perverse verdicts plainly have not vanished from magistrates' courts.

There is a move by ministers to have the proceedings in Family Courts take place in public. This is done in the name of 'transparency' and in order to ensure 'public confidence'. Why knowledge of the financial arrangements between divorcing parties or of the arrangements for the custody of the children should enlarge public confidence is not immediately self-evident. 'Transparency' is meaningless jargon much used by the media, simply to enable the general public to enjoy the tittle-tattle that goes with the details of a ruined married life, and of course enabling newspapers to boost their circulation. 'Transparency' and 'public confidence' are words regularly used to justify intrusion into private matters. 'Security' and 'health and safety' are two further phrases frequently used to justify some idiotic bureaucratic decision.

I wanted to transfer some money from my bank in England to my bank in France where I have an external account. Overdrafts are not allowed there. In order to finance the building operations being carried out to my cottage in France I used to send cheques from England to my bank in France. Unfortunately on some occasions it took so long for the English cheque to be cleared that the French cheque, which I paid to the builders, was presented before my English cheque had been cleared. In order to avoid a similar situation happening again, I rang up my bank in England and asked them to transfer a certain amount of money to my bank in France. To do this, of course, I have to go through the usual process of demonstrating that I am who I say I am, giving my secret details, date of birth, address and so on, information of which only I and the bank have knowledge.

Having gone through this elaborate process successfully, I then asked the bank to send some money to my bank in France. I was told that, unless I either present myself in person or write a letter, I could not do it. I tried to explain that this was going from my bank account in London, to my bank account in France. They still maintained that it could not be done. When I asked why not, I was told it was 'security'. I pointed out that I had already been subject to a security check to prove I was who I said I was and that a letter would have no greater weight — but to no avail. 'Security' is a word which is now used to prevent any information of any sort being given to anybody, even if clearly identified and however limited the information and however unimportant the transaction is. Again when I wanted to find out my National Insurance number which I had lost in the move, I rang up Newcastle and I was told I had to write in and that it could not be given out over the telephone. Again, when I enquired why not, I was told it was 'security'. Yet they are apparently perfectly happy to put the details in a letter to me, without knowing whether I as letter writer am who I say I am. It is bureaucracy at its worst.

Meanwhile the papers are up in arms, both about the way that prisoners are released and generally about how prisoners are dealt with by the prison service. Over the last ten years it has been abundantly clear that the prison population is on the increase. More serious crimes have been committed and therefore more prison sentences are passed. Attempts to persuade the judiciary to reduce sentences have not been very successful. It is difficult for a judge in any particular case to do more. What he is required to do is to pass the minimum sentence appropriate to the offence with which he is dealing. There are tariffs in these matters and courts need to follow them.

It has been obvious for decades that a rising prison population is going to have a serious adverse impact on the limited number of prisons available. It is always said that we have the highest number of prisoners, per head of population, and also that we have a larger prison population than any other country except America. This may well be true. It is however a totally meaningless statistic. It gets repeated parrot fashion by the libertarians without them realising just how meaningless it is. The question which needs to be asked (and isn't) is – compared with other countries – what proportion of people who commit imprisonable offences are actually sent to prison? The statistics relating to the number of prisoners eligible to be sent to prison against those who are actually sent to prison are never produced. At least if they were produced it would be possible to have a more reasoned debate and not just hear the ignorant and facile comments about prison sentencing. In the light of the increase in the prison population, it might be thought that any responsible minister would have put in hand, well ahead of time, arrangements for building an increased number of prisons. They cannot be built at short notice and the short-term remedies like using police cells are not only very expensive, but inadequate. I believe no more than two new prisons have been built in the last ten years and I read somewhere that there is provision for only two new prisons to be built by 2012. No wonder there is a crisis in the prison system.

Likewise the papers are full of how prisoners are behaving. It appears that prisoners have been simply walking out from one open prison. They include twenty murderers and six rapists. In order to be transferred to an open prison, the prison service has to be satisfied that there is little risk of re-offending by the particular prisoner. It is therefore normally suitable for white-collar fraudsters. Of course it may just be that not one of the twenty murderers or the six rapists constitutes any risk to others. A lot of murders are domestic murders and the risk of re-offending may be negligible. However, a rapist who rapes once may well rape again. One immigrant, who was due to be deported, was sent to an open prison. Unsurprisingly, the imminence of immediate deportation caused him to abscond and then vanish. The public is right to be concerned.

At the same time, it appears that the prison service has been paying out substantial sums of money in compensation to prisoners who claim to have suffered some injury while in prison. One prisoner received nearly £3 million because, in the course of attempting suicide, he injured himself. It is little wonder that the general public start to wonder why the victims are so poorly compensated while those who have caused them damage seem to be treated quite differently.

Meanwhile, the Government, having liberalised the licensing hours, even after drawing attention to the amount of drink-related crime, professes surprise that there has been an increase in crime due to drink. To encourage drinking and to at the same time try to curb it by antisocial behaviour orders is a contradiction in terms. In the face of the enormous debt in the country, the Government are constantly preaching the virtues of hard work and shrift. It is, therefore, also somewhat surprising that the Government should now encourage the idea of super casinos. Online betting is now all the rage and the use of credit cards has increased debt for a large number of families. The idea that super casinos will do anything to alleviate the problem is bizarre. It will no doubt bring substantial sums of money to those who run the casinos and to the towns or cities where these casinos are operated. But unfortunately, history shows that large gambling organisations are often controlled by criminal gangs and the opportunity to money launder is too good to miss. Whether safeguards can be put in place to prevent this happening I doubt.

In Oxford, one effect of Mr Justice Holland's injunction against the animal rights protesters is that what he describes as the loud, repetitive and essentially mindless chanting and abuse has come to an end. Alas, the momentary pipedream that we might be excused sitting our exams because of an inability to revise has been blown away. The building in Mansfield Road has been steadily progressing. The animal rights website is, however, used to publish the names of those who have shares in companies supporting research. The purpose of publishing their names on the website is not simply for information, but to enable the activists to trace and track down those people, so that they can be harassed and abused.

The papers report another problem. A security system is necessary in order to check and vet large numbers of people, particularly those involved in any form of public office or in contact with children. It clearly needs to be based on accurate statistics. Unfortunately the criminal records office has been a shambles. Some 2000 or 3000 people were wrongly identified as having a previous conviction of some sort, and this prevented them from obtaining various jobs. Some actually lost their employment and many were subjected to much embarrassment. The Home Office seems unwilling to recognise any obligation in the matter. Sadly public departments rarely admit error or accept responsibility for it.

A series of articles in the newspapers concerns the way in which the police deploy their resources. One example is typical. Tottenham Hotspur were playing a vital match against Arsenal and some members of the Tottenham team went down with food poisoning. It appears that they had had a meal the night before at a distinguished hotel in London. An investigation took place. It required what was described as twenty uniformed policemen, some plain-clothes detectives and members of the Health and Safety organisation to visit the hotel to try and identify what had happened.

In Buckinghamshire we are lucky ever to see a policeman. They are never visible on the streets or in the villages and only appear when they are stopping drivers for speeding. A recent example of over-reaction involved a luckless lady, driving some time after midnight on a quiet suburban road with no other traffic about, who was fined for going at a little over 30 mph in a 30 mph limit. The two officers in the patrol car no doubt earned brownie points for stopping this lady. It reflects something of the league-table mentality, which seems to have affected not merely schools and hospitals, but police forces also. Securing a certain number of convictions gives the appearance that they are being extremely vigilant.

In the same way, local authorities and the police are constantly bringing teachers before the courts. Teachers today have a real struggle to maintain discipline in their classrooms. But woe betide a teacher who even thinks of laying a hand on a child. It is open season for any trouble-maker, or more often, for the trouble-maker's parents, to make allegations against a teacher, which are generally without substance. The Government will not give anonymity to the teacher on the basis that, if it is granted to one group of public employees, it must happen for all. But teachers are at the mercy of often ill-founded allegations which other professionals are not.

The Government, meanwhile, are toying with the idea of harmonising both our laws and our criminal justice system with those in Europe. Having said over many years that this was not something which they would allow, there now seems to have been a change of mind. Understandably, every step should be taken to trace and prosecute terrorists wherever they happen to be. The adoption of a standard system of justice, if that is going to have an effect on defeating terrorism, appears, at first blush, to have merit. But at the moment there are plenty of steps available to countries to extradite terrorists from other countries. Unhappily this does not apply to the IRA terrorists in America where unilaterally the American courts refuse to allow them to be extradited. Nevertheless they expect other countries to extradite those accused of terrorism in America to be fast-tracked back to America.

The idea that there should be harmonisation of our laws with European countries is a lawyer's nightmare. Nothing will persuade me that the criminal justice system in other countries is better than our own system, notwithstanding that from time to time there are miscarriages of justice. That is not the fault of the criminal justice system in particular, but is often due to the failure of witnesses to tell the truth. If there is a failure of the criminal justice system in this country, it is for a different reason. Far too many guilty people are acquitted, either because of the incompetence of the investigation or of the prosecution's presentation, or because juries are frequently perverse in their conclusions. At least the political interference which seems to pertain in France is presently absent from the British system. It has however to be recognised that there is constant pressure by politicians in this country to lay their hands on the judicial system. This will, in time, have a disastrous effect on the administration of justice, as we know it, in this country.

On a more lighthearted note, I read one particular letter in *The Times* with a good deal of amusement. There have been a number of letters about how to dissuade animals from entering private premises, by the use of some form of deterrent. It was suggested that droppings from a tiger were of such a nature. One particular correspondent wrote in to say that when he was a young boy, he enquired why there were empty milk bottles outside his house. He was reassured to be told that it was to keep the elephants out. He wrote to *The Times* to say that, over the past forty years, this ploy had been very effective and his house had been elephant-free.

Today, I also read of a series of resignations at the top of the Health Service, which is very worrying. So, too, is the announcement that the Radcliffe Hospitals at Oxford are cutting some 600 jobs, in order to save £33 million. These are among the premier hospitals in the country. One can't help wondering where all the money which was promised to the NHS has gone. If only the doctors had retained control of the Health Service, instead of allowing it to be a political football controlled by civil servants and managers, would we not all be substantially better served?

I read too of another bright Government idea which is to introduce a house sellers pack, without which no residential property can be sold, from next year. It requires the training of a whole lot of home inspectors, of whom apparently there are not enough. It will naturally add substantially to the costs which are already high, in buying and selling property. The present system, by which the purchaser takes responsibility for ascertaining the state of the premises, puts that responsibility fairly and squarely where it belongs. This is bureaucracy at its worst. The cost of training these inspectors, of whom some 4000 are needed, and the cost of the documentation required, will simply make it more difficult for people to buy and sell property. The idea that purchasers will only rely on reports from these home inspectors is quite unreal. Anyone spending the sort of money which a house now costs will expect a full structural survey and will not rely on the sellers pack. Personal responsibility is something which politicians seem not to understand. The nanny state has to interfere. The present system of *caveat emptor*, with all the requirements of searches, has worked perfectly well for decades and it is difficult to see why any alteration is required.

England's World Cup soccer performances are a fiasco. Pictures of the bus in which the English players are going to celebrate winning the cup are premature. The media start by giving them tremendous hype and then, when they don't succeed, because they are in any event a very modest side, criticise them unmercifully. The antics of the wives and girlfriends supply many pages of pictures but contribute nothing to the success of the team, in fact rather the opposite. Complaints against the referee and against the opposing teams are merely feeble patriotic attempts to conceal the fact that the team totally lacks any sort of talent. Being knocked out at a comparatively early stage does at least mean that we are spared an indigestible diet of monotonous football.

Meanwhile the police inquiry into loans for peerages looks as though it may be stalled by the desire of the Public Administration Committee to hold its own inquiry, before the police inquiries are completed. It is an almost irresistible opportunity for the MPs to get publicity for themselves and enhance their standing with the public. Perish the thought that they would want to pre-empt the police inquiry so as to protect their leaders. I suspect that the police will not be put off by this attempt to gag their inquiry. The importance of it can scarcely be exaggerated. The secrecy with which the loans were made and the conditions attaching to them leave a nasty suspicion that there is something slightly dodgy about the whole process. As one commentator observed, if parties want a loan on commercial terms, there must be a lot of banks only too willing to oblige. It will be interesting to see what the inquiry will reveal. It certainly adds nothing to the dignity of Parliament or politics.

There are more problems with the animal rights activists. They write to all the investors in Glaxo, of whom I am one, threatening to publish details of our shareholdings unless we sell the shares within fourteen days. This is said to be just for information but it has all the hallmarks of a blackmailing exercise. I hope the authorities will do something about it. Sadly the history of these animal rights activists does not encourage any great belief that any steps will be taken to deal with them. However, one good piece of news is that a group, which had dug up the remains of an old lady (an action being used as a bargaining factor against a company which they believed to be involved in research), has been caught and charged. The group disclosed the location of the body with the idea of seeking to reduce the sentence by way of mitigation. The cost of protecting the company's premises apparently ran to some £3 million. There were further threats to dig up another body. I now read that the ringleaders have just been sentenced and they get twelve years apiece. The judge described their behaviour as something of an ongoing holocaust. Whether this will have any effect on other members of the organisation I have some doubt, but at least the right message has been sent out.

Meanwhile the police seem to have failed to distinguish themselves, elsewhere. A sixty-six-year-old grandmother complained about an eleven-year-old boy kicking a ball against a car, whereupon he called her a 'f****** bitch'. When she gave him a good clip around the ear, she was threatened by three other people with a lump of wood. She pulled the hair of a girl who had come into her garden and threw her out. The grandmother was then arrested by the police and locked up all night. There is no mention of the eleven-year-old or the girl being admonished, or the parents being rebuked or punished. Are the police quite incapable of resolving who are the victims and who are the aggressors? There is another story, of a young girl who threw a snow ball at a friend. It missed the friend and happened by chance to hit a passing car in which there was a policeman. He then arrested the girl and locked her up for the night. A whole series of similar incidents are reported and I am asked to go on television with a number of the victims and express views about it. One story concerned a woman whose front door would not open properly. Being disabled, she had difficulty getting in and out of her house; she therefore removed the original door and replaced it with one which was indistinguishable but of different material. However, the council took offence and are pursuing her. We were told about an undergraduate, I think at Oxford, no doubt in drink, who told a mounted policeman that his horse was gay and was promptly arrested. Somehow society has muddled up its priorities and lost all sense of proportion.

18

Final Days

Meanwhile the excitement for the moment is that there is a threat by the AUT (Association of University Teachers) to boycott the exams, either by not setting them or by not marking them. It is difficult to know where the rights and wrongs are. The union want 23 per cent over three years and the employers have offered something like 12 per cent over three years. It's not clear what the actual sums involved are. A good deal of posturing goes on, so that while the local union are advising their members to accept, the national union are taking a different view. Certainly at Oxford no-one could suggest that the dons lead a luxurious life. Those who are employed by the University no doubt do rather better than those who are simply employed by the college. Tutors at college level get paid per capita for tutorials. In comparison with what their students are likely to earn in the City, they are not handsomely paid.

It is sometimes argued that their having long holidays means that they have an easy life. But at Harris Manchester, for instance there is always a good deal going on behind the scenes during the vacations. Interviewing candidates for admission, sorting out the tutorials for the following term, doing some preparation for lectures, conducting research and writing books – it is all part and parcel of a college tutor's remit. Writing is a favourite way of earning money but most works of scholarship, which they usually are, do not command anything like the same sort of rewards as the Harry Potter novels. I suspect that one of the troubles is that the desire of the Government to give a university education to 50 per cent of the student population has spread the money available so widely, that instead of it being concentrated on serious academic scholarship at major universities, it has been wasted on some half-baked courses, where the skills taught could probably better be acquired in well-funded apprenticeships. The result is that the real centres of excellence are starved of resources; elsewhere compared with the big American universities, there is a serious lack of funding.

The students are sympathetic to the union but only to a limited extent, because they realise that if exams are not set, and more importantly are not marked, their future prospects of employment are likely to be seriously damaged. There is some suggestion that work during the term can be measured, but this scarcely applies to the subjects that I am doing and probably not to any work at a university like Oxford. The uncertainty puts a real damper on revising. The mere threat is regarded by most of the students with considerable apprehension. However, I do not believe, whatever is happening at other universities, that Oxford will be seriously affected. There is a suggestion that some law exams should be marked by solicitors' firms or by other legal experts. It would be somewhat ironic if, at the same time that I am doing my PPE exams as a student, I were to be roped in as an examiner to mark the papers of law students. The purpose of a strike at this time, is, of course, to cause the maximum disruption and thereby persuade the employers, namely the University, to come up with an increased offer. It is a tactic not unknown to other unions in industrial disputes.

The other news which continues to generate excitement and dominate the headlines is the honours scandal. Reading the history of Lloyd George's sale of honours and the astonishing story of Maundy Gregory (part of the background to my thesis) reminds me that there is nothing new in this world. No doubt a lot of the peerages from the nineteenth century were as a reward for substantial contributions to the party in power. There have always been eyebrows raised over the nomination of some peers, and the appointment of a committee to vet them was one of the safeguards intended to prevent this happening. Whether it applies to honours bestowed by the Prime Minister when he retires is not entirely clear. Certainly one or two of Harold Wilson's appointments gave rise to considerable criticism.

The police are still at loggerheads with the Commons Committee and want to interview a number of vital witnesses. They do not want a lot of self-important MPs muddying the waters. It rather looks as though this is an investigation which will run and run and run. The loop-hole that the parties have discovered, namely to accept a loan rather than an outright donation, seems to me to be chicanery of the worst sort. The idea that these people might have any responsibility for the administration of justice is too awful to contemplate. Curiously the press, while reporting the story in some detail, have so far adopted a very uncritical attitude to the whole affair. Given the press's rather holier than thou approach to public affairs, it is rather surprising that the broadsheets, if not the tabloids, have been so remarkably silent.

Meanwhile, on a happier note, at Easter the annual Boat Race takes place. This time a canny Oxford coach installed some sort of pump in the Oxford boat while his Cambridge counterpart did not. Because of the conditions, the effect was immediately obvious. As soon as the boats struck rough water, which they did within a short period after the start, Cambridge began shipping water. They then spent the rest of the race gallantly, but hopelessly, pursuing Oxford with their hull low in the water and the boat full of additional weight. It was really no contest. It was all rather sad because Cambridge were said to be a very good crew and to lose because of the lack of a simple piece of equipment after training for six months must have been devastating.

It is also rather sad that the Boat Race is used by some experienced rowing internationals to enhance an already substantial rowing CV. It applies to both universities. It is pot-hunting of the worst sort. The effect is to deprive undergraduate oarsmen with skills of opportunity to achieve a little glory. If the pot-hunters want more trophies, let them have their own race, separate from the University Boat Race. But that is how it has been for some while and no doubt will so continue.

Preparations for the exams start in real earnest. I have done my thesis so that is out of the way. Now I must concentrate on the Philosophy. I get hold of the papers for the previous five years and try and analyse what questions are likely to be asked. By and large there are twelve or so questions in each paper and three need to be answered. It is therefore a question of making an intelligent guess as to what is likely to come up. Bill Mander is giving us some lectures this term and, as he is in charge of the examination, we may get some clue. I suspect however that that is too much to expect and not an approach seriously to be relied upon! My exams start towards the end of May. I have one a day on average, although I do have to face Ethics and the Theory of Politics both on the same day. I then have two or three days without exams, before I do Wittgenstein, which is convenient. My last exam is on Bank Holiday Monday, at the beginning of June.

Different departments have exams on different days. The result is that, from the very beginning of term, hundreds of third-year students are walking around with their white tie and gowns, and sporting carnations. Some students have back-to-back exams for ten days. Others don't start their exams until we have finished. We still have to wear the idiotic costume which the students, by an almost overwhelming vote, decided to continue. I don't know whether it's because the girls like dressing up, but I find it exceedingly tiresome. How much to work and how much to play is a delicate balance. Liz and I go to Scotland for some racing and stay with her old friends, Richard and Vicky Vernon, and this gets me off to a good start to the term. We also have a day at Lord's with the family and with friends.

And then somehow it doesn't seem very long before I start my first exam. Because I find my detailed memory retention lasts about half an hour, the time spent immediately before the exam is enormously valuable. Comparative Government is the first exam. I do that without any great problem. The same is true of Ethics and the Theory of Politics. But when it comes to the Philosophy exam, which is the central exam, I have a complete wobbly. I had worked very hard in preparation for it and reckoned that I was as well equipped as I would ever be. However the first question, one for which I had in fact carefully prepared, caused me to have a total blank. The result was that the rest of the paper, for which I wasn't so well prepared, was woefully done.

I am normally very good at exams but this was a total disaster. I have never been in a situation before where I froze. It was a very unnerving experience. When I returned to my room, I didn't dare look at any of the books to see what a total mess I had made of the paper. John had also done the paper and it was very discouraging to be told by him that if you fail one exam you simply don't get a degree. I spent the weekend, therefore, in total gloom, just wishing that I had done myself justice. Later, after it was all over, the children and Liz told me that they had all been very concerned when I had sounded so downcast and subdued over the telephone. It was like being an adolescent again, with over-concerned parents who are trying not to interfere.

The next exam was British Politics. Vernon had adjured John and me not to show off the totality of our knowledge, but rather to answer the question which was asked, and no more. I was so determined to show that I really did know something that I went off at a canter and wrote pages and pages. I was enormously familiar with the subject about which I was writing, some of which I had acquired from doing my thesis on by-elections. I hoped that the examiner, who read my thesis on by-elections, didn't also read my answers to some of the questions on British Politics! Whether the examiner will be impressed or will take the view, as Vernon did of some of my essays, that I hadn't answered the question asked, I don't know. Anyway I felt very much better at the end of it, having been able to use my knowledge to some purpose. The evil Wittgenstein paper followed three days later and was not quite as awful as I thought it would be. A weekend intervened before I had my last exam, which was International Relations. This was, I hoped, going to be my best subject and I think I managed to acquit myself sufficiently well.

I suspect that I will get a 2:2 in the Politics part of the paper and a 3rd in the Philosophy. Whether that will take me into the 2:2 bracket, or will result in a 3rd overall, is the critical issue. My chief anxiety now is whether, on account of perhaps failing Philosophy, I have ploughed the whole thing, which would be absolutely terrible, particularly with all the ghastly attendant publicity. There is an amusing little snippet in one of the papers from a fellow examinee. He complained that he had been sitting behind me in the British Politics paper and that it was very unfair, because I had lived through most of the period with which the questions were concerned, whereas he hadn't! This did something to lighten the trauma of the exams.

There is nothing now to do except await the examiners' verdict. Luckily moving house, or the prospect of moving house, engages me. Everybody wants to know how I got on and whether I know the result. How I will explain to the family, if I do fail, I do not know and it would be a sad conclusion to my academic career. I feel particularly sorry for Bill Mander, who has done his very best to teach me philosophy and whom I feel I have let down very badly.

Meanwhile college life goes on because there is still another ten days of term to go. It is all a bit *pianissimo* at Harris Manchester, because other people are still doing exams. There are various drinks parties for the leavers but I have to spend the time moving things out of Lime Tree in preparation for our house move. The result is that I miss a good deal of fun at the college with everybody celebrating the end of term. Fortunately, I was able to arrange that my exam results should not be published. I did not wish to be the subject of more media interest, particularly because I am terrified of the result! Nobody seems to know when the results will be announced. So it is about three weeks later that I first learn that I have got a 2:2 when Vernon sends me an email. My first reaction is of considerable relief. I get hold of my marks. It is clear from them that the Philosophy paper was the least successful and that it brought down the general marks. Looking at the figures, I got the equivalent of a 2:1 in Politics and a 2:2 or a 3rd in the Philosophy papers so, while I am delighted with the end result, I have the inevitable feeling of regret that I didn't do better!

19

Houses

Margaret and I had bought Lime Tree Farm, Chartridge in 1960 for what then seemed the enormous sum of £6000. It was an eighteenth-century building at the front with a Jacobean cottage at the back. At that stage it had a number of barns but, sadly, they were in a derelict state and they had to come down. If we had had enough money to convert them into a play room or a garage it would have been immensely valuable. The property had some three acres of land, including a grass tennis court which we converted into a hard court and an orchard which we turned into a football field for the children. It was a marvellous place for bringing up the boys. But they had all left home long ago, and now seemed to me to be a good opportunity to hand it over to any of the children who were interested, and for Liz and me to find a smaller place to live in the country.

Ed and Clare were enormously enthusiastic at the prospect of taking over the family home, and so it was arranged that in July they would move from their house at Swindon and Liz and I would find a cottage in the area. We were keen not to move too far because many of our friends lived close by and also it would be convenient to be not too far from Lime Tree. We settled on the financial arrangements with the help of our advisers and 3 July was set for the date of the move. At Lime Tree this involved getting rid of enormous quantities of perfectly useless articles which had simply accumulated over the years. The attic itself was full of great quantities of rubbish which had to be put into a skip, not to mention the dead flora and fauna. In the space of about a week, we managed to fill three or four skips. The removal from Lime Tree was something of an organisational nightmare, not only because the house had been occupied for some forty-five years, but also because Margaret and I had squirrelled away great quantities of ornaments and documents which had to be sorted out.

When Liz and I had started to look for somewhere to live she had had the idea of a big Georgian house. I had the idea of a modest country cottage. I started by taking her to look at a minuscule cottage which, to my delight, had a wine cellar. Even I had to admit that it was almost impossible to descend into it, even when sober, without falling down or hitting your head. This viewing proved not to be a great success. My enthusiasm for the wine cellar was derided by Liz's comment that the house lacked any other feature whatsoever – redeeming, architectural or otherwise. After this we saw some faintly agreeable houses in the area but none to our liking, until Liz found, on the internet, a cottage at Quainton, north-west of Aylesbury. I went to look at it first, and was much taken with it, but this time withheld from expressing my views until Liz had had the opportunity herself to look at it. It was a charming thatched cottage, which as an amalgamation of three smaller cottages, had three separate staircases. We both fell in love with it, despite the condition of the electric wiring and the fact that one needed to have the proportions of a dwarf to manage the transfer from dining room to sitting room. We negotiated with the owner and arrived at what to him was no doubt a satisfactory price.

This had all coincided with the lead-up to exams; my attention therefore was not wholly focused on the removal. The move itself was not easy, because the vendors of the cottage at Quainton postponed the completion date for three or four days. This put our removal men into a great state and caused consternation with Ed and Clare, who thought that they were never going to see the back of us. However, in the end we managed to clear out what, as we thought, were the contents of Lime Tree, ready to move to Quainton.

Elsewhere we also had problems. Our small cottage in Normandy had been bought in 1987 and over the years we had spent many happy holidays there. Gradually, however, it had got somewhat run down – the daughters-in-law and Liz would no doubt describe its condition rather differently. One or two of the holiday tenants complained, in fairly

10 Liz at Château de Pirou, Normandy

vociferous terms, in the type of emails that one just doesn't want to open, that the cottage was not up to the standard which they had expected. One couple found, when they arrived, that the house had not been cleaned since the previous summer. They naturally walked out. It turned out that the local cleaning lady, whom I had engaged, had either misunderstood the instructions which I had given in what I (at least) considered my rather good conversational French, or had simply not bothered to show up. In the summer I therefore engaged some local English agents, who came to look at the cottage. After their initial muted, but shocked, reaction ('So charming, but…'), they advised me that if the cottage were to be let it would need not only a complete face-lift but also some structural alteration. My daughters-in-law and Liz were triumphant. Together they drew up some rough plans which we discussed with the agents.

We then got in touch with our builder in France, who some years ago had added an additional bathroom onto the house. He drew up some detailed plans and, armed with them, in the autumn, we decided to go to France with Clare, to meet the agent and the builder and to sort out what needed to be done. When the builder showed no signs of arriving, we became very apprehensive that he had forgotten, which would have frustrated the whole object of going to France. However, once he turned

11 Liz waiting for lunch after a morning's skiing

up, an hour late, we discussed the various plans with him. We particularly urged upon him the necessity for getting the work done in good time, in order that all the expenses could be paid for out of letting.

There then flowed from our side constant emails, telephone calls and letters to the builder, enquiring when work was going to be started and when it was going to be finished. French business seems to be conducted on the basis that provided you don't answer any enquiries, all will be well.

12 Oliver with Andrew, Debs and Liz at St Anton

We found it all enormously frustrating because the months gradually went by and an occasional reply that 'work would start soon' did not create much confidence on our side. I found it particularly frustrating because in any event I was not overwhelmingly enthusiastic about the whole venture. It seemed to involve knocking down walls and replacing the kitchen altogether, as well as some pretty fundamental re-carpeting, painting and re-designing. However, my daughters-in-law and Liz were firmly of the view that it needed to be done, that it would enhance the value of the house, that it would therefore be worth letting and that it would, more importantly, provide a much better holiday house for the family. Throughout the summer we rang the agents, we rang the builder, and we emailed, sent text messages, and generally encouraged the builder to get on with the work. We told him that we would be arriving at the beginning of August to prod him into activity. We discovered subsequently that this was a terrible mistake. He had assumed that he needed to do nothing until we arrived and that we would then make decisions about various matters which had not appeared in the original design.

In the end, we arranged to go out at the end of August, alerting the builder to that fact. We arrived late on a Friday night, after a very tiresome journey on Brittany Ferries, to find that there was no hot water, there were no cooking facilities, that the electricity in the dining room was non-existent; power also seemed totally absent from the kitchen. The prospect of eating cold meals for a fortnight really made me incandescent. Neither the washing machine nor the washing-up machine were working. We retired to bed in a state of some disarray. Next morning, Bank Holiday Saturday, we managed to persuade the builder to come to the premises. We got the hot water switched on, and some of the electricity. Matters began to take better shape. Liz managed to organise cooking facilities. She ordered a fridge and got the washing-up and washing machines working. Thus, although the house was very much a building site, at least we were able to live in part of it.

We then left for four or five days to stay with the Burbages at Arcachon in Bordeaux. This holiday nearly ended in disaster. Staying with the Burbages were Charles and Cindy Gray. Charles had been counsel for Jonathan Aitken, and we had also met them both in South

13 Sailing in the Arcachon Bassin

Africa. He was now a High Court judge. We had an enormously engaging two or three days, swimming, sailing, eating and drinking. One morning, it was decided that we would all go out and have a swim on the far side of the Bassin. There were notices on the beach saying that the area was not patrolled but the Burbages had swum there before, without problems. So we plunged into the surf and the stronger swimmers went out beyond the bar. The tide was on the turn. Liz and I had not gone beyond the bar and eventually we decided that we would come back in because we could feel the current getting really quite strong. When we turned around we saw that Charles and David were following us, but there was no sign of the girls. David shouted to Liz that his wife, Sandra, was in trouble beyond the bar and gave Liz his mobile phone which luckily was tuned to the number for the SOS. Liz had no trouble alerting the authorities but her difficulty was that she didn't know which beach we were on, or what directions to give. Luckily there was a French lady there who spoke quite good English, and she was immediately able to tell the authorities where we were.

Meanwhile Cindy had, perhaps rather foolishly but very bravely dived back into the surf to keep Sandra company. Within a short period of time, vehicles arrived with two husky young men armed with life lines. They plunged into the water, went beyond the bar and attached themselves to Sandra and Cindy. However because of the current they were unable to swim with them back to the shore. Luckily, a helicopter had been alerted. There were apparently two helicopters, but one was either out of service or elsewhere. However, after what seemed like an eternity, the other helicopter arrived and hovered above the two girls. Meanwhile, a motorboat had come out from the shore and was also circling around the girls. The helicopter lowered a line, the girls were lifted up into the helicopter and then winched down gently onto the beach.

This all happened within about twenty or thirty yards of the shore where a fisherman was quietly fishing, wholly unaware, until the helicopter arrived, of the drama that was unfolding around him. The girls were none the worse for their ordeal although one of them said she had wished she had been wearing something more substantial than a bikini when she was lowered from the helicopter. However, it was a very frightening experience. When we apologised to the life savers for getting them to turn out, they said that that was their job and that they preferred rescuing somebody to sitting at their base. They also told us that during the summer there had been about 100 calls for them to attend to from swimmers in distress along that part of the coastline. We never did hear whether they were all successful or not. Luckily, I am not a very good swimmer and so I had decided not to go beyond the bar. But, I had found getting in against the current, in any event, very difficult – as did Liz, and she is really quite a strong swimmer. I think on reflection that we were very unwise to do what we did. Indeed there would have been a major disaster if there had been nobody on the beach to tell us where we were or how to alert the authorities.

We hoped that when we returned to our cottage in Normandy it would be less of a building site. Sadly this proved to be a somewhat optimistic view. When we return, wires still stick out of walls, which remain unplastered and unpainted. We continued to 'camp'. How long they will take, we shall see. I suspect it will be another two or three months. Meanwhile we are actually living in the house. This has the advantage that we can supervise and see that things are getting done. On the other hand, trying to live in a house which is part of a building site does have its own problems. The work that has been done so far has been a considerable improvement. Whether the end result will justify what is going to be quite a large expenditure, effort and general angst, I am doubtful. However, the family seem very much in favour. It is their house, and no doubt they will benefit from the improvement.

Meanwhile, the move to Quainton is also something of a nightmare. The rooms of the cottage are comparatively small and we have hundreds of packing cases. I take a great deal of wine out of the cellar at Lime Tree in the expectation that I shall be able to find somewhere at Quainton to store it all. Although there is a large garage and a big hut into which a deep freeze is to go, there really is nowhere particularly convenient to house all the wine. The result is that the luckless removal people, having brought over a large number of cases of wine, have to take them all back to Lime Tree. Ed is comparatively happy at housing the wine, but I doubt whether he will be happy for any length of time.

It was clear before we moved in that a number of improvements needed to be made. These would not only enhance the value of the house, but make life a bit easier. The previous owners had got planning permission for a conservatory and this we plan to build. We are also going to enlarge the kitchen which is comparatively small. Likewise the dining room needs more space and some of the bedrooms require attention.

There are also, this being partly a sixteenth- and partly a seventeenth-century cottage, a number of low beams and one doorway which is very low and something of a hazard. Through Christopher Prideaux, we managed to find a very nice architect, Janet Frost, who comes and advises us on what needs to be done. For instance, the three staircases need some sort of rationalisation. Liz's dressing room is next door to the bedroom, but in order to get to it, it is necessary to go down one set of stairs, through the sitting room and the drawing room, and then up into her dressing room. Because this is a Grade II listed building, I have some doubt as to whether it will be possible, from a planning point of view, to knock down a wall and put in a door to connect them. However, while we were away in France, Janet and the County Planning Officer met up, and it looks as if this will be allowed.

As Liz's house in London is also having work done to it, we find ourselves in a situation of not being able to have a fixed home for a while. The work in her house will be over, we hope, by the end of September and if we have to go and live in London, so be it. One particular problem in all these moves is that trying to find anything is an absolute nightmare. We also discover that whereas at Lime Tree we had a great number of mantelpieces on which to place our large collection of ornaments, the same does not apply in the cottage. However, we are absolutely delighted with the cottage, and turning it into a really comfortable place in which to live will be well worth all the effort and inconvenience. The addition of a conservatory will also have the great advantage of housing furniture, which seems to have arrived from all quarters. Liz's mother had a flat in London and when she died she left a considerable quantity to Liz, who also had a certain amount of furniture from the division of property in Scotland. Most of the furniture from Lime Tree also came with us. Thus, once we get the conservatory built, this problem will take care of itself.

Meanwhile, all the building complications are starting to sort themselves out. Liz's house, after some anxiety about dry rot in one of the windows, is now completed, and we shared a party with Alexander and Sally for some of their friends and some of our friends to celebrate that fact. It is well furnished, beautifully decorated, very comfortable and is a joy to live in.

Meanwhile at Lime Tree, Ed and Clare have been doing wonderful things. The area where derelict barns used to be has been converted into hard standing for cars and the trees on the roadside removed. They have re-designed the garden, and the house, now the subject of tender loving care, is very attractive. The vegetable garden has been transformed. The children are going to put lime trees in an avenue, from the house down towards the tennis court and, altogether, the place has taken on a fine new look. We could not be more pleased.

In France too there has actually been progress. We went over for a weekend in December to see what was happening and although on the face of it nothing much seems to be being done, it is clear that there have been marked improvements. We have had to put in another drain, a *fosse d'eau*, because the *fosse septique* was receiving not only what it was designed for but also bath water and ordinary washing-up water. The result was that it was getting overworked and necessitated being emptied much too frequently. Likewise the builders have put up a pipe across the front of the drive to prevent the flooding which occurs from time to time. New curtains, well chosen by Liz, have been hung and with luck, the carpets will be laid very shortly. The boiler now works, and perhaps the end is in sight. We have spoken to the agents and it will not be too long before they can come in, take some photographs, advertise it and let it. The garden, which has had the *fosse d'eau* going through it, still looks a bit like a building site and needs reseeding but Alistair who runs a gardening service in Coutances and is related to our English agents, has got that in hand.

The news about the cottage in Quainton is good. Janet has obviously done her stuff with the planning people and it looks as though all our ideas are being accepted by the Planning Officer. Janet hopes to get specifications out fairly soon but it is obviously going to be a long process. To that end we are going to have to move out for two or three months (which turned out eventually to be 10 months!) and this presented quite a challenge initially. However, the Bergqvists who live about seven or eight miles away have just converted a barn which they are going to let commercially. It is unfurnished and we have negotiated with them to go and live there while the building works at Quainton take place. It is a very happy arrangement because we shall be not very far from Quainton. Janet will to some extent be supervising the works but there are always one hundred and one things that need to be dealt with, and we shall be only a short distance away.

Likewise, being next door to the Bergqvists will be enormous fun. Their barn has been most beautifully converted and will house even the vast volume of clothes which Liz will no doubt be taking with her. The idea of packing up all our things again is something of a nightmare, but it has to be done and it may enable us actually to find a lot of things which are in packing cases and whose whereabouts we have not yet discovered. Thus hopefully by the spring (though more likely by the summer) we shall have our various properties in good shape and be able to enjoy them fully. We had been squatting somewhat at Quainton since we arrived, knowing that we were going to have to move out shortly. We have not been able to entertain people as we would like, or indeed as many as we would like. However, both the cottage in France and the cottage at Quainton will be transformed, and I am now satisfied that what seems to have been, and will continue to be, a vast expense is going to be very well worth while.

20

Reflections on Oxford

When I applied to Oxford to read PPE, I think I really had two ideas in mind. One was to continue my education and to keep my mind active. Secondly, because I was then on my own, I wanted to be involved in college life, to meet people and to have an agreeable social life. That latter object became less important after I had met Liz, but nevertheless, it was one of the benefits I received from my three years at Oxford. The education was very good. My tutors both in Harris Manchester and elsewhere were not only enormously clever but also very good teachers. It was a real pleasure to be engaged in intelligent discussion and sometimes in argument with them. They all had the great ability to give explanations and also to criticise constructively.

However, time has not healed the anger I still feel about the conduct of the Economics department. The first cause of angst was at having to do the idiotic IT/Statistics paper, which wasted nearly two months of my life when I had many better and more useful things to occupy my mind. Secondly, the way in which we were ambushed, as I believe, by the constantly changing mathematics syllabus in the Economics paper reflected no great credit on the department. Economics is a subject in which I was very interested, particularly macro-economics, and to which I had looked forward with great anticipation. It was not the fault of Mark Rogers, our Economics tutor in college. He gave John and me an enormously sound training in Economics; he made a difficult subject comparatively simple to understand and guided our faltering footsteps with immense skill. I only wish we had been able to continue learning about balance of payments, inflation, unemployment, interest rates, world trade and other matters of immense importance in the modern world. Sadly the department made it almost impossible for me or John to continue. Given John's banking background it was a particular blow.

I found the Philosophy not entirely easy and, as my reports showed, it became fairly clear at an early stage that I am not a natural philosopher. I found that some of the philosophers seemed to live in a little world of their own and that in a great number of cases they were simply tilting at semantic windmills. Even in subjects such as ethics and morals which have much to offer intellectually, there seemed to be such a divide, not only among the various philosophers themselves, but also between the theoretical and practical views, as to make any reasoned conclusion almost impossible to arrive at. I suspect that a pragmatic approach is not the way to deal with Philosophy. But my tutors, Bill Mander in particular, were enormously encouraging, and certainly provided me with a good deal of material on which to exercise my thought processes.

It was, however, for Politics that I had the greatest affection. I found political theory and comparative government of very great interest. One of our more interesting exercises had been to draft a constitution in respect of one or two hypothetical countries. Having spent some of my life at the Bar, drafting policies, I realised just how difficult it is to do and how easy it is to criticise those who have done it. Naturally the constitution of any particular country depends to a large extent on the background to its creation and to the nature of the citizenship which make up the country. Should you have one or should you have two legislative bodies, should they be elected or selected and, if so, how? Should there be a president and if so what should the presidential powers be? Should it be a federal or unitary state? Who has the power to make laws? All these are matters of enormous interest and topical. The present argument about the constitution of the House of Lords is but a continuation of a debate which has raged in other countries for decades. When one looks at the constitution of the United States, now over 200 years old, one cannot help but admire the felicity of the language and the breadth of scholarship with which it was framed. That it has stood the test of time, almost unamended, is a remarkable tribute to those who drafted this memorable document.

It was a pleasure, too, to study in some depth the political history through which I have lived. Having the opportunity to look at documents and distinguished publications, in detail and from a more detached perspective, was one of the great joys of studying the history of

Sir Oliver Popplewell

From this long established university college of higher education, dedicated to truth, liberty and goodness, we salute you for the contribution you have made to the life of our time by your words and deeds, we desire to thank you, and to honour you and ourselves, and to celebrate the bonds of affection and respect between us, by appointing you to be an

Honorary Fellow
of Harris Manchester College
in the University of Oxford

30th October 2006

Revd Dr Ralph Waller, MA, BD, MTh, PhD

16 Certificate appointing Oliver an Honorary Fellow of Harris Manchester College

International Relations and British Politics since 1900. To be able now to understand, for instance, Stalin's and Hitler's motivation, which necessarily affected the lives of my generation, has been a revelation. To witness British politics as it developed in the twentieth century was one of the more exciting features of my education. It was fun too to do my thesis on by-elections, and to surprise myself by concluding how limited their impact was on the political scene.

I was, as I have already indicated, enormously lucky in my tutors. Most of the lectures, though by no means all, were of a high standard. I also enjoyed going to some of the outside lectures, particularly those on American history. Thus, while on reflection, I am somewhat disappointed at not getting a 2:1, I nevertheless learnt so much that the original idea of adding to my education was amply fulfilled. Oxford enriched the whole fabric of my life and I count myself truly fortunate to have had the opportunity to spend three happy years there.

Of Harris Manchester itself, I can only speak with enormous enthusiasm and affection. It is a small college, with its own distinct ethos and with a strong sense of service both to its own and to the greater community outside its walls. Ralph Waller, the Principal, is a man of great charisma and drive, who is determined to enhance the standing of the college. He has created a happy, thriving and active community in the college and is keen to increase the standard of scholarship among its students. That he will succeed I have no doubt at all. At one time he had the idea that I might be a sort of roving ambassador for the college, promoting its image both in the University and outside, but that proved, for various reasons, not to be a viable proposition. However, I am generally tasked with the idea of promoting the college and all its activities wherever I go. The college were gracious enough to invite Liz and me to be Honorary Fellows of the college. This was a very great honour and one which we both much appreciated, particularly as Liz was not a student there. But it epitomises Ralph Waller's determination to put Harris Manchester high on the academic map. It will enable us not only to continue to enjoy the friendship of other members of the Senior Common Room, but also to feel part and parcel of an exciting community.

If there is one disappointment about my time at Oxford, it is in my failure to have really lasting friends among either the dons or my fellow undergraduates. I suspect that age plays its part, because most of the

and pomposity, judicial cant, time at
one's cottage in France, shooting, etc etc

dons are one generation younger, if not, two. There are, of course, notable exceptions to this situation, such as my tutors in college, Vernon Bogdanor, Professor Caedel, Robin Butler and Michael Beloff, whose company we hope to continue to enjoy. John White, who was my constant companion throughout our three years, where we moved like Mutt and Jeff as the two old stagers in the college, will always remain a friend. I am much indebted to him for guiding me through the regulations, for getting me to lectures on time, and for ending up with the same degree as I did!

The question of top-up fees continues to dominate not only undergraduate life but university governance. Whereas my generation of Oxford undergraduates had to pay some £25,000, in a very short time that figure has now gone up to some £33,000. To be saddled with this debt at the start of life is a millstone around the neck. Whatever the arguments about relative numbers of admissions from state schools or from public schools, Harris Manchester contained a real and healthy cross-section of students. When I was at Cambridge, it was easy to identify students at Trinity or Magdalene who were not only very wealthy but who also took little trouble to conceal the fact. The same certainly didn't apply at Harris Manchester.

It would be difficult to make any distinction, save for age, between my fellow undergraduates at Harris Manchester and my fellow undergraduates at Queens' Cambridge. I believe that those at Cambridge were more politically inclined, but both sets were anxious about the future: those at Cambridge because of the political uncertainty which the Russian threat and the balance of payments created, and those at Oxford because of the difficulty of finding employment. But I suspect that the prototype of an undergraduate has scarcely changed over the years. I first met Margaret at Cambridge when she was at Newnham and we got engaged there. I remember that, when her mother, who had been at Newnham in 1924, came up to visit us, we told her with great excitement what we had been doing, as if we were doing it for the first time. She smiled quietly and observed that her fellow students had done much same when they were up. We told our children the same. I am sure our children will tell their children the same. 'Plus ça change, plus c'est la même chose.'

Meanwhile on a wider front, the Vice-Chancellor has been trying to persuade congregation to allow some independent business people to be part of the governance of the University. The proposal so far has not been approved and there is, I believe, to be a postal vote. It is difficult, because of the rhetoric involved on both sides, to understand what is the best policy. The dons themselves are very busy people and I suspect that not many of them have much business experience. The heads of colleges seem to spend their time not on education but on money-raising. But colleges have the ability to tap into business expertise from outside Oxford. Sadly the benevolence which obtains in the top American universities seems absent from the elite universities here and it is not easy to see how the present system can continue without a major shake-up. The idea of getting more research students from overseas is a short-term one and must in the end be damaging to academic excellence in this country.

What then of the future? Aside from considering various academic options over the last two or three years I have talked to a number of head-hunters and put my name down on various websites. I have filled in a great number of CVs. I have talked to a television company about producing a series of programmes about the law. I have written a good number of articles both for newspapers, periodicals and done book reviews. Likewise I have allowed myself to be interviewed by the media about almost any subject, particularly some connected with the law where they wanted an immediate response.

In an ideal world I would like to have some sort of non-executive directorship, which would involve two or three days a week with an interesting company or companies and allowing me to exercise judgement and contribute some constructive criticism. Unfortunately, notwithstanding the passing of the Age Discrimination Act, I fear that these sort of opportunities are very limited. Retired judges are regarded as something out of the ark, and while I still can and do conduct arbitrations and mediations this is by no means a full-time occupation. Somehow sitting around, doing nothing very much, is not part of Popplewell philosophy.

21

Australia

Cricket meanwhile is not far from my thoughts. Looking again at the DVD of the Ashes series in 2005, I was reminded of just how close the result was. A dropped catch, a missed stumping, a poor lbw decision or a run-out could well have changed the result. McGrath's injury at the beginning of the Second Test was undoubtedly an enormously important factor in England's recovery. The narrowness of the margin of victory has not damped speculation that the team, now to go to Australia, is likely to hold onto the Ashes. Illingworth and Gatting both came away from Australia with victories, but it is an unusual result. I tend to think that we have got somewhat carried away in the belief that we shall do it.

The conditions under which the touring team to Australia play are now quite different from those which existed when I was younger. In those halcyon days, the side set off by boat some time in October without wives and returned in March or April, having spent the best part of six months abroad. The immediate advantage of that arrangement was that the team, when they arrived in Australia, were bonded as a team. They were able to play a great number of state and other matches, both before the First Test and between the other Tests. The team which has recently been selected is going to India to play a totally inconsequential tournament and is then coming home again, before finally flying out to Australia. Before they play the first test in Brisbane, therefore, they will have had only about a fortnight in the country and two pretty elementary games.

Both the light and the pace of the wickets are quite different in Australia. It used to be the graveyard of left-handed spinners, apart from J.C. White in the 1930s. Bob Berry never looked like taking a wicket and off-spinners, who used to flourish on uncovered wickets in England, very rarely made any sort of impact in Australia. The bounce is much sharper than in England and bowlers from abroad take some time to learn where best to pitch the ball. While nets are no doubt useful, practice in the middle is vitally important. Equally, if a batsman has a bad Test match, he needs to be able to play against one of the states to recover his skills. The proposed itinerary seems to me to be perfectly ridiculous. The contest in India is no more than a money-raising exercise. It would have been much better to have sent an A team. They would have benefited from the experience and the Test team would not have been subjected to a meaningless exercise.

The absence of Simon Jones and Michael Vaughan will necessarily make a substantial difference. Michael Vaughan's captaincy was quiet and efficient and much underrated. Simon Jones always seemed to produce wickets when it was necessary and his accuracy will be very much missed. The picture of injuries is not a very happy one. Flintoff still seems to be in the wars and no-one can be quite sure whether Trescothick's mental state will enable him to stay the course. The selection of Cook is undoubtedly a good one and he will, I think, make a lot of runs in Australia. Collingwood is an interesting cricketer. He is a 'bits and pieces' player, rather like Barry Wood used to be, but whether he is good enough either as a bowler or a batsman must be in some doubt. His fielding will add immeasurably to the quality of the English side. The continued selection of Geraint Jones remains a puzzle. It isn't that he cannot bat at all. He does occasionally score runs. It is just that he is not a proper wicket keeper. Happily Read is also included in the party so perhaps, at last, England will have someone behind the stumps who can actually keep wicket.

Liz has never been to Australia and she and I are going to have three weeks there. We shall start in Melbourne, go on to Sydney and then end up on Lizard Island. We propose to break the journey on the way out by having two nights in Singapore. There is always a debate as to whether it's worthwhile breaking the journey and having a rest, but Liz has never been to Singapore and it is a good opportunity to see something of the city. We manage to get tickets for the Melbourne Test but those for Sydney are very much more difficult. Melbourne has recently rebuilt its ground and there is now an enormous stadium which will hold something over 100,000 people. We are kindly invited into the Members' Room from which to watch the game. At Sydney we are in the New South Wales box for one day, but then are sitting with the public elsewhere. Liz has organised all the hotels and made all the travel arrangements on the internet. When I used to do all the travel arrangements, it seemed to take weeks and weeks communicating with travel agents, whereas now it is all done comparatively simply on the internet, with small bits of paper acting as tickets. Everything is controlled by computer.

I try to persuade Liz that she doesn't need four suitcases and a trunk to go to Australia, and that taking summer clothes is all that is required. In any event we shall not be taking part in too many fashion parades. We leave the week before Christmas and fog descends on London Heathrow. As a result the whole airport comes to a grinding halt. When we arrive there we find that hundreds if not thousands of passengers have been camping out there for a number of days because the domestic flights and those to Europe have been very severely curtailed and the Christmas rush is on. Happily, our plane is delayed for no more than two hours. When I went out as President of the MCC, I was travelling business class and got upgraded to First Class but no such luck this time.

In Singapore, we have arranged to stay in the Fullerton Hotel, which is the old Post Office, and we arrive there late in the evening. There is much debate as to whether we should have stayed at Raffles or not. I have been to Raffles, and while it is an agreeable place to have a drink, it is a bit 'OTT'. The Fullerton is much praised in the books and accordingly we decide on it. We have a really comfortable room overlooking part of the river and after a quick meal in the restaurant in the hotel, we retire to bed. There is no jetlag and next morning, having had breakfast, we take a short river trip and then go and do some shopping. The weather is warm but not too hot, and we manage to suss out the intricacies of the underground system, which here, as in Hong Kong, is superb. Everything is immaculately clean, and everything runs to time. It is all very efficient but somewhat sanitised.

We make our way to Orchard Street where, among the other shops, we manage to find Jim Thompson, the well-known manufacturer of Thai silk. Here Liz is in her element and I volunteer to give her some to have made up into a dress. She is delighted and ends up with swatches of turquoise, electric blue and aquamarine silk.

Singapore is a vital city. It is bustling with people and shopping is obviously the order of the day. We go to China Town in order to see whether we can find some jade, but none of it is very attractive, and without having a specialist knowledge, it is difficult to determine whether what we are being shown is worthwhile. Liz also thinks that she might want a crocodile handbag and we go into a rather downmarket shop where one bag is offered. Business is plainly going very poorly because the shopkeeper marks it down from 2000 odd to about 850 Singapore dollars and every time Liz says it's not what she wants, it comes down by another 100. Eventually we get to rock bottom, but Liz cannot make up her mind and we therefore go away and in fact never return. Liz afterwards said it looked as though the crocodile in question had been rather a sad and shabby one which put her off the whole idea. Suddenly the crocodile has a storybook life of its own and bags are off the agenda.

We eat Chinese on the banks of the river. We also go for dinner, to what turns out accidentally to be an Italian restaurant overlooking the water, where again we have a delicious meal. Like all tourists we have a drink at Raffles and try the local cocktail, which is not only expensive, but very unpleasant. We try to visit the law courts but they are shut. We had thought of making contact with the Chief Justice in order to exchange pleasantries. Happily we didn't, not only because he was not there but because it would have taken up too much time on a very short visit. It is a fine city, with a combination of attractive modern buildings and old houses where law and order is very much the operative word and cleanliness and efficiency is part and parcel of life. Forty-eight hours is enough to get a feel of the city.

Meanwhile we read of the horror stories at Heathrow over the Christmas period with fog still causing chaos. We catch the night flight to Melbourne (a comparatively short journey) in some comfort and arrive at the Park Hyatt. England, by this time, has lost the Ashes. It has been a melancholy performance. It was epitomised by the first ball that Harmison bowled at Brisbane, which went straight to second slip. England lost that game easily. In the second match, at Adelaide, it looked for a moment, when England had made over 500 that England were back in the game, but Australia fought back. In our second innings we collapsed leaving Australia to win easily, by six wickets. At Perth, Australia made over 500 in their second innings and England were unable to bat out the last day with the result that we lost the game and the Ashes by a considerable distance. Altogether it has been woeful. Thus, when we arrived in Melbourne it was without any very great expectation of success in the two remaining matches. On the first morning that we were there, we fell in with Jonathan Agnew who was rightly full of gloom about England's prospects. It is difficult to see how things can in fact improve.

On Christmas Eve we decided not to go to the Cathedral because of the difficulty of getting back afterwards but find a local Lutheran Church where we go for midnight mass. Surprisingly it turns out to be very much like Little Walsingham in that it is very High Church. There are a great number of prelates, marching and counter-marching, with incense being wafted at regular intervals, much genuflecting, and chanting Ave Marias. But it was a welcoming service and a fine introduction to Christmas Day. Spending Christmas in a country, where it is summer is slightly unreal, but we managed to capture the spirit of the occasion!

On Christmas Day we team up with James and Sarah Sassoon. They are old friends of Liz's. James Sassoon is a distinguished member of the Treasury team. They have come out with their children and their son is working for Channel 9. They have arranged for us all to go down to Portsea, where we are to spend Christmas Day at a hotel on the beach. To that end, the Sassoons arrive at our hotel in a very scruffy hired white van. They are then told to go and park round the back, it being thought, no doubt, that a tradesman's van ought not to appear outside a smart hotel. We pick up James's brother and friend and motor for about an hour and a half down to the coast. It is bitterly cold, but we find the hotel easily and have an enormously good Christmas lunch on a balcony overlooking the sea. After a good deal of drink, Liz and I and the Sassoon children venture into the water, which is near to freezing, but we feel much the better for it. That evening the Sassoons have taken a private room in a smart restaurant and we sit down with others of their friends and have a marvellous Chinese meal.

On Boxing Day morning we were due to go to the Lord's Taverners' breakfast which is a feature of Australian Test cricket. Some time back, I had had to speak at a similar occasion at Sydney. The other speaker on that occasion had been an Australian Test cricketer, who had, unfortunately, had a previous brush with the law; in his speech he said that it was very nice to meet a judge who didn't sentence him to two years' imprisonment. I thought that the Boxing Day breakfast was being held at the Melbourne Cricket Ground (MCG) and we therefore took a taxi down there. There seemed to be a number of breakfasts going on but none of them appeared to have any connection with the Lord's Taverners. It was then suggested that it was being held at the Hilton. Accordingly, we signalled a taxi and asked him to take us there.

One of the failings of Australian taxi drivers is that they have no idea of the local geography. We are so used, in London, to taxi drivers knowing exactly where to go that it is difficult to understand why the same does not apply in Australia. It is partly because most of them are immigrants with limited English, and partly because they do not seem to have to pass any sort of test. This particular driver didn't know where the Hilton was and suggested that we got into another taxi, which we did. This second taxi driver told us that the Hilton was within eyesight, about 100 yards up the road. Full of bad temper, I rushed Liz up to the Hilton only to find that the breakfast was not in fact at the Hilton, but was at some conference centre next door to the MCG. We therefore got another cab. By this time we were really quite late and, when we eventually got to the conference centre, we found another Taverner wandering around trying to get in. Finally we managed to see our hosts. We had missed most of the speeches, but there was enough breakfast for us to have and the remainder of the speeches were extremely funny.

We then walked to the MCG where we were greeted in the most hospitable manner by a number of old Australian friends including John and Rosie Lil, whom we had met before, both in Australia and in England. John had been heavily involved with the MCG and was very much in the driving seat. We were also entertained by a retired Australian judge, whom I had first met at a conference in Lausanne on Sports Law. We had very good seats in the Committee Room, straight behind the bowler's arm. England again batted poorly. The first four or five made some runs, but thereafter none of the others contributed anything. Hayden and Langer managed to play out time. We went home before the end of the game and watched the last few overs on television.

It was plain that Hayden was low on two separate occasions, the ball going to hit middle stump, about halfway up. This was unfortunate because he was then only just into double figures and he went on eventually to score 159. Australia at one stage next day were something like 60 for 5 but Hayden and Symonds pulled them around and they reached a massive score. Strauss got another bad decision. Normally these decisions work their way out and both sides suffer equally over time but it always seems to be the side which is on the defensive which suffers most from bad decisions. Australia probably got the rough end of the call when they were in England in 2005, so there is no reason to complain. But how different the result would have been if Hayden had been given out on either occasion. Reid replaced Jones as wicket keeper and it was very encouraging to see him at one stage standing up to Hoggard. He made no more runs than Jones, but at least he looked like a wicket keeper. At one stage it seemed as though England might make a decent score but it was not to be. The familiar pattern of numbers 6 to 11 contributing nothing, resulted in the match being over in three days.

David Batts, one of the Secretaries at Lord's, had organised an evening at the MCG for members of the MCC; we had an entertaining dinner and a quiz show, with distinguished international cricketers answering questions about the game. No-one was very optimistic about the future of English cricket, and there was a good deal of criticism of the way the tour had been organised. The idea of arriving in Australia and almost immediately playing Test cricket, it was agreed, was self-evidently stupid, as was the decision to go on a tour to India to take part in a purposeless round-robin contest. Then to go back to England before going out to Australia simply compounded the problem. It has to be said that this was a very good Australian side, which bowled, batted and fielded with considerable skill, were well led and had a discipline similar to that which England had in 2005. Above all, in Warne, they had probably the greatest bowler of all time.

Flintoff's captaincy came in for a good deal of criticism. To my mind that was very unfair, because he was carrying the burden of the batting and the bowling, and captaincy is not a skill which is acquired over night. Indeed, a number of captains never achieve it. It is legitimate, however, to complain that very little pressure was ever put on the Australian batsmen, either by having close fielders round the bat when a new player first came in or by varying the field placing to upset the rhythm of the opposition.

The greatest moment of the match was of course Warne taking his 700th wicket. It was a moment to savour and it was an achievement which is scarcely likely to be bettered. Muralitharan no doubt will achieve the same number in due course but in circumstances where some of his wickets have been obtained against a number of fairly moderate sides and where his action, notwithstanding official approval, is still subject to some questioning. Given Warne's absence from cricket from time to time because of injuries, and also because of his suspension for drug-taking, it is a particularly remarkable achievement. He has always played with considerable verve and enthusiasm. He was enormously generous in spirit when Australia lost the Ashes in 2005, to which his dropping of a vital catch at the Oval may have contributed. He has been nothing less than a wholehearted sporting cricketer and we shall not look on his like again.

It was also McGrath's last match at Melbourne. He has been an immense force in Australian cricket and his absence from the Second Test in England probably contributed to England winning the Ashes. However, his personality has been such that he has not endeared himself either to cricketers or to the public, and his ill-tempered sledging has not been worthy of a fine cricketer. Curiously there was never the thrill of anticipation when he started to bowl, as there was when Lillee and Thompson were in harness or, before them, Lindwall and Miller.

We had booked to leave Melbourne after the third day of the Test match so its premature conclusion, then, did not interfere with our travel arrangements. We managed to visit the art gallery which had a fine collection of pictures. We ate exceedingly well, both Italian and Chinese, and were entertained to dinner by Leila and George Embleton and to drinks by friends of Alexander and Sally, out in smart suburbs. We had known Leila when she and her first husband Ken lived in the Thames Valley. Ken Spence had played scrum-half for Scotland and their son had been at Radley with Andrew. She had now remarried, after Ken's death, and taken herself off more or less permanently to Australia. We much enjoyed our trip to Melbourne, a delightful city, of which we managed to see a good deal.

We then set off for Sydney where we arrived after a short flight. As we got on the plane, we were handed a sheet from the airline, telling us what to do if our luggage went missing. This was not a very promising start. When we got to Sydney we waited at the carousel for about an hour, without any official information, only to be told that the baggage had not been put on our plane at Melbourne, but would be delivered to our hotels later. Lack of communication is endemic in all airlines and this was a supreme example. They knew at Sydney, when our plane landed, that our luggage was not on board. Nevertheless they allowed two or three hundred people to stand idly about for an hour or so, getting more and more bad-tempered, waiting in the heat for non-existent baggage. No-one seemed to be in charge or able to take responsibility and thus we arrived at our hotel in slightly frayed mood.

However, Liz had booked a superb room in the Intercontinental Hotel, with a view straight out into Sydney Harbour and overlooking the Opera House. We were also able to take advantage of the top-floor restaurant which had an even better view than that from our room. On the second day of our arrival, we decided to go out to the Hunter Valley where an excellent coach trip took us to a game reserve. Here we saw kangaroos, possums, emus and a koala bear. From there we went into the Hunter Valley itself, where we had several wine tastings of different Australian wines, together with knowledgeable explanations and a well-organised lunch. The countryside looked quite beautiful, although the absence of rain had caused serious drought in this part of Australia.

Next day we decided that we would go and see Palm Beach, which is a small peninsular up the coast from Sydney. To this end we flew by seaplane, which was enormously exciting, flying over the coast at a comparatively low level and seeing beautiful beaches. When we arrived we were met by a car from the hotel, where we were having lunch. This was all part of the package and we had a superb meal overlooking the sea. Australian cuisine somewhat to my surprise, is excellent, and we certainly did ourselves well. The next day we went by ferry to Manley, about fifteen miles up the coast, where we took our swimming things and sat on the beach. The surf was magnificent and we were shepherded into safe zones but because we took neither hat nor full covering, at the end of the day we were red and somewhat sore. The ferries up the river are a feature of Sydney life and a very agreeable way of seeing something of the coastline.

Unfortunately, we were too late to get tickets for the Opera at the Opera House, but we went down to the docks and had a number of meals there. New Year's Eve in Sydney is one of the great events of the world. The fireworks which start at 9 o'clock in the evening are quite magnificent. The whole of Sydney turns out to watch. People start taking up viewing positions from 8 o'clock in the morning. Yachts come in two or three days earlier and moor just below the bridge, in order to get a good vantage point for the fireworks.

The MCC had organised a boat trip for their touring party to which we got ourselves attached. We found ourselves on a comfortable boat where we sat down to a good dinner, spoilt only by two crooners who could not sing. Thanks to their terrible noise we could not hear ourselves think or what the next-door neighbour was saying. Eventually they stopped and, on this balmy evening, we cruised up and down the harbour waiting for the fireworks. There were a great number of boats in the harbour and eventually the fireworks started. There were various points from which they were being lit, and to see them in reality was one of the great excitements of the holiday. The only problem was that at the end of the evening the boat had to return to the quay, and with a lot of other boats also queuing up to get alongside, we seemed to be hanging about for hours. We finally disembarked at about 3 am, by which time the whole of Sydney were returning on foot to their homes. All the roads around the harbour had been closed off because of the fireworks. We tried to persuade the MCC bus driver to take us back to the hotel but he would not. As a result, we found ourselves about a mile or so from the hotel, struggling to get through the mass of spectators, all going in the opposite direction. Eventually we found our way back to the hotel, somewhat exhausted, but exhilarated by the events of the evening.

Next day we got to the Sydney Cricket Ground (SCG) in good time and were well entertained in the Members' Room, where we had a splendid view. In Melbourne Liz had bought an earpiece, which could be tuned either to Channel 9 or to Channel 1. She was thus able to tell me exactly what was happening on the pitch, without my having to explain it. She had brought it with her to Sydney where she was able to do the same. Both at Melbourne and at Sydney we had met a whole lot of international cricketers and at lunch there was a lighthearted competition to select best teams from the old players present. There was a jocular suggestion at our table that I might get the wicket keeping place, but Rodney Marsh was reckoned to be a stronger contender. The cricket, sadly, was no better from England's point of view and it was another disappointing day.

The next day, we were no longer in great comfort but sitting at the far end of the ground among the general public. Here we had a good view, but no serious facility for food or drink except for sandwiches at lunchtime. We were told by our Australian friends, who were members of the SCG, that they had had to get to the ground at 4 am in order to get a seat. That began to explain why the MCC had had so much difficulty in getting tickets for us. We were therefore much less critical of the general organisation. We watched two days' cricket, which was just as well, because England collapsed again on the third day. The end of the Ashes series was therefore nothing less than a disaster.

We had a delightful evening with Diana and Ken Hanley who had an attractive house at Cremone. He is a judge in the Court of Appeal. We had met him when he was doing research in the Inner Temple and he had kindly invited us to visit him when we were in Sydney. He had gathered together a number of other lawyers, including Roger Gyles, now a judge, who had come over with an Australian Bar cricket side about thirty years ago. They had come for a cricket tour to last a month and had arranged to spend a couple of hours en route doing some IT training. (This was in order to enable them to write off the expenses of the cricket tour as a legitimate tax deduction.) They played against the English Bar at Radley, and then they had all come back to Lime Tree where they had spent the evening with us. They were now therefore amused to hear that we had passed Lime Tree on to my son. They had had happy memories of wandering around our house, which had been built some hundreds of years before Captain Cook arrived.

We now set off to go to Lizard Island. Because we were coming back to Sydney for a night on our way home, we managed to leave most of our luggage in the hotel in Sydney, flew to Cairns, and then transferred to a small plane containing only four passengers. This journey to Lizard Island took about an hour and we flew over the Barrier Reef, which was dazzlingly impressive from the air. The island itself is comparatively small. It has the one hotel, which houses some forty guests. No children are allowed to stay at the hotel and it is luxury of a high quality. The weather turned beautifully warm. This time we sensibly wore hats and protective clothing. The beaches of which there are many are covered in white sand. There were motorboats available for the guests and the next day we chugged around to a nearby bay where we spent the day in the sunshine, swimming and, in Liz's case, snorkelling. There were also some catamarans, but the wind was so slight that there really was little pleasure in sailing.

Liz wanted to go out to see the Barrier Reef itself and so one morning she went off for a half-day expedition. I do not like snorkelling. When, on my previous visit, I had been out to the reef, the weather then had been so rough that I had felt sick all the way going out and all the way coming back. This time I decided that I would sit in the sunshine on the beach, read a book and quaff a gentle bottle of wine. Liz very much enjoyed visiting the Barrier Reef. She was able to have a really close view of the coral and the wonderful variety of colourful fish.

We spent the remaining three or four days enjoying the peace and quiet of the island, the sunshine and the luxury of it all. The island amply justified its name as there were a number of huge but apparently friendly lizards, sniffling round the gardens of the hotel. Finally, it was time to start off for home, so we flew from Cairns to Sydney where we spent the night at the Intercontinental again. We then had a marvellous lunch at the Iceberg restaurant on Bondi Beach. The beach itself, contrary to popular view, is rather downmarket, but the restaurant itself was very attractive with a staggering view. It had a swimming pool on the rocks, which was washed directly by the sea and propelled by the wind, which was hugely exciting to swim in.

All too soon we had to fly to Singapore, and after changing planes, back to London. It was altogether a very successful holiday and we looked and felt well, although it took us four or five days to recover from jet lag.

22

Academia

At Oxford, I was constantly being asked what I was going to do with my degree and whether I would pursue further academic studies. My tutors were full of encouragement that I should do so, but when I looked at the syllabus for a master's degrees or doctorate in Politics or in International Relations at Oxford, there seemed to be a great deal of theory and not much else. I was exceedingly doubtful whether it would be of any interest to me. I was also concerned that my degree in PPE would not be sufficient to get me admission to any of the courses. The prospectus was also full of gloom about the number of people applying in relation to the limited number of places. In the end I decided that Oxford was not the place for further studies. There was a suggestion that I might go on a private venture and engage some of the tutors who had been teaching me during the years, but this did not seem a very worthwhile exercise, even if it were possible.

I then wondered whether there were other universities where I had a better chance and London University seemed to be the ideal place. It would not involve serious travelling. I would not have to live in college and I could use my flat as a workplace. Accordingly, I got the prospectus from the LSE and found that there was indeed a course in International Relations, which lasted a year. The course involved writing a thesis, and the subjects included the Spanish Civil War and the events leading up to Munich. Both these subjects had been of great interest to me, not only at the time but since. Additionally, Anthony Beevor, who had written two splendid books about Stalingrad and about the fall of Berlin, had recently republished his book about the Spanish Civil War, so it was very much a hot topic. Hugh Thomas, who had been up at Queens' College shortly after me, was the author of a distinguished book about Spain and this too I had read at the time. Thus the idea of this particular course became rather inviting.

The Munich crisis, rather like Suez some twenty years later, had divided the nation and opinions on both sides scarcely ever met. Both at the time and immediately subsequently I thought, as did many others, that the country had betrayed a strong ally for short-term gains and that we had lost not only prestige but some sort of honour. Subsequent reading, which I did for politics at Oxford and for my thesis on by-elections, led me to believe that this was a rather knee-jerk reaction. Looking at the matter as a whole, there probably was very little that Chamberlain could have done about it. The Russians seemed reluctant to get involved, the Americans were full of platitudes but no action, the French were in their usual political crisis and Britain was financially and militarily weak. Thus, what appeared at the time as a weak surrender may well have been justified in practical terms.

Chamberlain seemed genuinely to believe that this was Hitler's last demand in Europe. There is an argument for the view that having a year between Munich in September 1938 and the outbreak of war in September 1939 was in fact a major factor in enabling us to defeat Germany because we were able to improve our military strength. Both our radar defences and the quality and quantity of our fighters built up during that period enabled us to win the vital Battle of Britain. Additionally, the attitude of the Dominions, which had been less than wholehearted in 1938, was, after the German invasion of Prague in 1939, almost unanimously supportive of our decision to go to war in September 1939. These were both very important factors in our survival. Whether they were the reasons at the time for not supporting the Czechs is still a matter of heated debate.

Full of enthusiasm therefore, for the idea of this particular course, I applied to LSE and received a number of forms and the prospectus. The first chilling response was that there were likely to be something like 300 applicants, all postgraduate, both from the UK and from abroad, and that the number of places available was something of the order of thirty. The next problem was that the application had to be done online. My IT skills are almost non-existent. To make matters worse, every line had to be completed and to make any mistake was likely to result in the form being returned. It was necessary to get two referees and to get hold of the documents relating to my previous degrees. Because there was no interviewing process, it was also necessary to fill in two or three pages stating why I wanted to do this course at the LSE and informing the college generally about my background.

Vernon Bogdanor and Lesley Smith kindly said that they would act as referees. A complicated system ensued in which they sent their references to me; I was not allowed to open them but sent them on to the LSE. Much more difficult was filling in the form online. For instance, under date of birth, the earliest date available on the form was '1940'. To put in '1927' would have invalidated the whole process because the computer was simply not geared for any date before then. Liz was absolutely splendid in sorting all this out, and a number of telephone calls between her and the office finally resulted in my being allowed to insert 1927. I suspect that the computer (which, I believe, is housed somewhere in the United States) went into a complete sulk.

Getting hold of the documents relating to my previous degrees was also a difficult exercise. The exact date when I had matriculated was required. Getting the documents from Oxford posed no real problem, but my degrees at Cambridge were housed in some archive, and they needed to be retrieved. I was unable to give the particular dates of matriculation, other than in the most general terms and it took some time before these documents became available.

Filling in the form about why I wanted to be there was a test of intelligence. Did I want to stress my age, in the sense that the subjects were familiar to me, having lived through them, or was that likely to be counter-productive in that a place was more likely to be given to a younger person, whose opportunities for further education might be thought to be more pressing? Liz's expertise in this field was of immense value and between us we concocted a workman-like CV which included the contribution I thought I could make to various discussions. The documents were checked and rechecked and finally sent off in December.

The LSE were very efficient and kept candidates fully informed about the progress of their application. But the results were not going to be made known until after Christmas and so the matter was left very much in abeyance while we went off to Australia. My feeling was that I had made as good a fist in the application as I could, and that anyone who could cope with the various problems raised by the application form jolly well deserved to get a place!

A few days after we returned from Australia, I received a large package from the LSE. I opened it with some anxiety to find that I had indeed been accepted and I was required to fill in a form saying that I was willing to accept the offer. Thus, at the end of September 2007, I shall go to the LSE and do a year's course in International Relations, to which I look forward immensely. I have in mind not only to write a thesis on the Munich crisis but perhaps to develop that subsequently into a book. Vernon tells me that although there is a great deal of literature on the subject, definitive books are hard to come by. When I went to see Lester Crook (my editor) about a book on Munich, he seemed very interested in the possibility of publishing something, so that's another idea for the future. Whether I have the research ability to do that sort of book, I simply do not know. It will involve looking at a number of documents in the original German, Russian and Czech.

The archives at Churchill College, Cambridge contain Churchill's papers as well as a whole collection of other politicians' and civil servants' papers. It is a veritable Aladdin's cave of fascinating documents. Alan Packwood, the Director of the Archives, invited me to visit the college in the summer and arranged that I may go and use the library and the archives as I want. This I do and am taken round by Andrew Riley, his deputy. I spend two days going through a number of original documents and I stay overnight in the college. It is, as might be expected, very well organised and it is a great thrill to lay one's hands on the realities of politics. The volume of material is quite astonishing and there are little vignettes to be discovered in some forgotten minute from a civil servant to his minister or in a letter from one minister to another. I am surprised when I read Beevor's books about Stalingrad and the fall of Berlin to find that he managed to write them with very little assistance from researchers. How I will cope is a problem for the future. I have spoken to Vernon who has given me a list of books to start my reading and I shall enjoy the period between now and September in doing a certain amount of research. I regard myself as extraordinarily lucky to be taken on by the LSE because of the very limited number of places. Perhaps old age does have some advantage.

23

TV Adventure

There was an exciting interlude before my LSE studies started in the autumn of 2007 when I had a telephone call from a TV production company called Hat Trick, well known for producing *Have I got News for You*. What they were intending to do was to produce a television court drama over a period of days, with celebrities as the jurors. Lucy Buck, the assistant producer, enquired whether I would be interested in taking the part of the judge. She explained in broad terms that members of the Bar were to play the part of barristers, that the characters in the film would be actors and that, as mentioned, the jury would consist of celebrities. One of the selling-points was going to be that the discussions of the celebrities, acting as jurors, would be recorded and be part of the programme to show just how members of a jury react to a particular court case. Would I be interested? I rang back to say that I would, but made the proviso that I was not going to take part in some *Judge John Deed* sort of production, in which the judge apparently sleeps regularly with counsel, and generally behaves in a most unprofessional way. I was asked to suggest the names of counsel, which I did, and it was then arranged that I would meet up with the producer. No doubt they wanted to see whether I was the right person to play the part of the judge and I wanted to discuss with them the nature of the programme. I was provided with a provisional script, which was of a very good story. At this stage there was simply an outline with the various characters identified. The only immediate criticism I had was of some of the language used, such as 'the witness will now take the stand', which is an Americanism and never used in English Courts. Nor did I approve of the recalling of prosecution witnesses by defence counsel, at regular intervals; this seemed to me not to accord with proper legal procedure.

I then met with the executive producer, Jed Mercurio, who had written the story. He outlined to me the nature of the programme. For the court room scene there was to be no actual script but an outline of the story was to be provided to each actor so that the evidence would appear more spontaneous. The actors and actresses were to be unknown, in order not to detract from the jurors. The jurors were to consist of a dozen celebrities whose names were not revealed at that time. The purpose of the celebrities was to attract viewers to the programme. They were to be televised in their discussions, both during breaks in the trial and at the end of each day, and that would be an important part of the programme when it was shown. It was intended that there should be five separate programmes of an hour or an hour and a half each, on successive nights, some time later in the summer.

I was immensely impressed with the idea of the programme. Jed seemed to me to have produced an interesting story and to have got the right sort of approach. I did point out that having prosecution witnesses being called by the defence was not something that could be part of a proper court scene; nor could witnesses be treated as hostile simply in order to give a bit of excitement to the story. They seemed pleased that I should take the part of the judge. My clerk in Chambers, Debs Anderson, negotiated my fee. I think she had rather grander ideas than I had, because she was used to negotiating on behalf of the very successful QCs in my Chambers. I suggested that she should speak to Anna's agent who had much more idea of the level of fees charged for this sort of programme. She told Debs the sort of fees which the TV people were likely to pay, and in the end, Debs negotiated a perfectly fair fee for me.

Thus the scene was set for me to take part. I was required to have a medical so I went to see a doctor in Sloane Square who specialises in vetting actors and actresses. After managing to pass, I went off to Hammersmith where Hat Trick have their premises. When I got there, I found that counsel were busy taking witnesses through their evidence. The purpose of this was for the juniors to cross-examine the witnesses, so as to give them an idea of what it would be like when they were actually in the witness box. More particularly it meant that the leaders themselves, who would in fact be doing the cross-examination in open court, did not have to reveal the sort of questions they were going to ask. Thus the witnesses' answers would come out more spontaneously in court. They had already had two or three days in rehearsal. They had helped Jed to shape the production into a more manageable legal framework, and on the Saturday and Sunday, immediately before shooting started, we all assembled at a studio in Wembley where we had full rehearsals. There was a mock-up jury to give the idea of how it would be, because the celebrities were not to be allowed to appear until the Monday, when shooting was due to start.

During the weekend rehearsal, the witnesses were taken through some of their paces again, to give them a feel of the procedure. It was necessary also for the cameras, of which there were a great many, to be properly positioned. Unfortunately the chair in which I was to sit was placed so that I was about two foot below the parapet in front of me. It therefore had to be raised by inserting a platform under my chair. Every time I went to sit down or got up, I was terrified that I was going to trip up and fall flat on my face. On the Sunday we all dressed up. I had borrowed Liz's red gown and black cap and gloves, and, with my old wig, I felt comfortable in familiar clothes. There was constant discussion about the script because changes were being made at frequent intervals. The studio was equipped with a room full of TV screens so that the producer could decide which particular shot at which particular moment was appropriate. The barristers and I had in front of us a very small screen on which the producer could give instructions to us as we went along, but out of sight of the cameras. Thus, I would receive an instruction that this was a convenient moment to adjourn or counsel would be instructed to ask a particular question, or to refrain from pursuing a particular topic.

The trial was a trial for murder and so naturally there were expert witnesses, pathologists, DNA experts, fingerprint experts and firearms specialists. These parts were played by ordinary actors who had had to learn the particular expertise of their discipline. This they did with consummate skill. Because notionally the filming started at 9 o'clock in the morning, a car was sent to pick me up. From Quainton this meant a 6.30 start. At the studio there is a canteen where I can get a good breakfast. I have a splendid dressing room, with lots of bright lights, which compares favourably with some of the dressing rooms I have seen when visiting friends acting in the West End. The organisation is enormously efficient. There seem to be hundreds of people working in the studio, but everybody has an important job to do. The film set has been improved since we started rehearsing. I can now see over the top of the desk. Counsel each have their own desk and microphones, instead of a central table, and a coat of arms has been put up behind my chair to give an impression of the Royal Courts.

On Monday morning we are all summoned to make-up, to ensure that we are properly dressed and that our noses don't shine. The jury of celebrities are wheeled in and we are off. I only recognise one or two of the celebrities but I am told that they will be well known to viewers. I start by giving them my usual spiel, telling them what the case is about and about the times which we sit and warning them not to talk to anybody outside the case or let anyone talk to them about it. Then counsel start opening. Richard Lissack, QC and Mark Trafford are for the Prosecution and Nick Purnell, QC and James Leonard are defending. A young girl called Laura Haddock is playing the part of Gemma Laing who is the accused, charged with murder. She is clearly going to be the star of the show. One of the other stars is Deborah Cornelius, who plays the part of the grieving widow. These are all unknown actors and actresses and first impressions are that they are remarkably good. The first morning goes off without much of a hitch. Witnesses come and go. We get instructions from above as to when there is to be an adjournment, because there will be problems if we have an adjournment before the cameras are ready.

During the course of the day Jed comes to me complaining that some of the jury are not concentrating. I don't find this very surprising as we have had a long session, without an adjournment. I am required to read a slight riot act to two of the jurors, which I do. Jed is very concerned on the first day, when he watches the discussions in the jury room, that they don't seem to be paying full attention to what is going on. I have to explain to Jed that this is how juries normally behave and it doesn't surprise me in the slightest. Also understandably, juries do not seem to understand that in an adversarial system not every point in which they might be interested is going to be raised, and that the opposing parties fight their case on their own terms. The result is that – contrary to an inquisitorial approach – not every point is dealt with, in evidence. The jury come back with a whole lot of questions, which shows that they don't seem to understand the distinction. It may be my fault or the fault of the system that this misunderstanding arises. However, the producers insist that we answer every question that the jury ask and to that end further evidence is produced from time to time. One further complication arises, because two of the jury have been spotted, having a social evening together. Personally I can see nothing wrong with this, but I have to tell them that they should not discuss the case in the absence of the others. It would be difficult to imagine two jurors having a social evening without discussing the case. I suspect that the producer does not want to have any discussions by the jury which are not recorded on camera.

The jury continue to raise streams of questions. At Jed's prompting, I have to tell them that unfortunately their interventions are somewhat counter-productive and that a lot of the questions they are asking, have only marginal relevance to the issues which they have to decide. I suspect that they want to try and show to a wider audience that they are taking a full part in the production. A slight crisis also arises because one of the so-called experts doesn't appreciate that an answer which she gives is the wrong answer and steps have to be taken, by producing further evidence, to put her back on course. Additionally, Nick Purnell observes, during the course of his cross-examination, that there is something on the revolver which shouldn't be there. This again causes some consternation with the producer. The result is that further evidence has to be called. The jury, by the second day, as the tale unfolds, have clearly begun to get the hang of the evidence and are more readily following what is happening. The producer now seems more satisfied.

The witnesses are really very impressive in their acting ability, and particularly, in their ability to absorb the detail of the case. Because the producers have the jury deliberations at each interval on tape, they report to us how the jury's thinking is going and suggest questions for counsel to ask, in order to deal with the jury's anxieties. Meanwhile, Liz makes a fleeting visit because she is in court herself and Debs, my clerk, comes for a morning, which she thoroughly enjoys. The preparation for the production has been painstaking in the extreme and there are a whole series of videos which are exhibits in the case, which contribute to making it a cracking good story.

Eventually we get to the stage when the accused goes in the witness box. She is absolutely splendid. I believe she will have a great acting career ahead of her. I cannot reveal the twists and turns of the plot but there are many. They give rise to a legal problem as to whether not only murder but manslaughter needs to be left to the jury. This occupies a lengthy and intense discussion, not only with the producers, but with the top ITV brass, who have arrived to see what is going on. Eventually a serious crisis is resolved by the lawyers and the production team, coming to an agreement.

I sum up to the jury, for which I am allowed twenty minutes or so. They are very concerned with what being 'sure' means and I have to give them some further direction about that. They go out to consider their verdict on the Thursday evening. Overnight they have not agreed and Jed comes to see me, as he is not sure they are approaching their function in quite the right frame of mind. I am therefore urged to go into the jury room to tell them how they should approach the matter. This is, of course, totally unconventional, but the producer thinks it is important, which it probably is. I am greeted like a hero by them and we have an entertaining discussion. This eventually proves fruitful and they finally come back with a verdict. Suddenly that's the end of the drama. We all take a tender farewell of each other and arrange to meet at a wrap party on the following Monday.

It has been an enormously interesting and worthwhile exercise. The producers have been very good in putting together a programme which is as close to reality as is possible. The presence of the celebrity jurors is there to sell the programme which I am sure they will. Everyone is very complimentary about our performances. It will be particularly fascinating not only to see ourselves on the programme but also to listen to the jury's discussions about the trial and how they reached their verdict. The feedback about jury trials in real cases is so limited that one never has any idea, except by rumour, as to how juries go about their business.

As it happens I was not a great supporter of the jury system. In my career, both at the Bar and on the Bench, I can think only of two cases in which juries have convicted where I have been very unhappy. But in at least 30 per cent or 40 per cent of the cases, there have been acquittals which I can only describe as perverse. Sometimes it is due to inefficient prosecution or to inadequate police evidence, but the number of cases where serious villains have been acquitted, in the face of overwhelming evidence, is a serious blot on the criminal justice system.

The wrap party, which is held in Soho, is a very lively affair. The cast are there, as well as camera men, supporters and some members of the jury to whom it is fascinating to talk about their views. Liz and I go off and have dinner halfway through, at a local restaurant, and then return to what continues to be a very lovely evening. We then say goodbye, vow eternal friendship and wish everybody enormous luck.

When the jury came back on one occasion, after we had finished filming, I said to them by way of a joke that they might like to notify their agents that there was a judge available to take part in further television or filming. Whether anything will come out of this I do not know. And whether the production will be as good as everybody believes, we shall have to wait and see. It would be great fun to do something of a similar nature again, because appearing on television or in a film is a very heady experience. Everybody seems to enjoy it. It is not unlike being involved in a long case at the Bar, which generates a sort of corporate spirit among those involved and which will remain as a happy memory of shared experiences for many years to come. No doubt we shall all meet up again at a later date to reminisce about our activities.

The five of us lawyers get together for a dinner in London where the producer and a lady who is responsible for organising the ITV schedules tell us that they are pleased with what they have so far but that no date has been fixed for its screening. They have promised us a copy of the DVD when it becomes available so we shall have the opportunity to see ourselves privately before it hits the small screen. Meanwhile we must wait patiently until that happens. A month or so later, in the spring, we are invited to see the first two cuts of the film at a private party in Holland Park. There, after a superb dinner, we watch the results of our efforts and are enormously impressed with the way the material has been so skilfully woven together to give a most realistic picture of a murder trial. Shots of the jury's discussions, much of which we hadn't previously seen, are not only immensely instructive as to how a jury reacts but highly entertaining. Given that the jury is made up of celebrities, it is perhaps not very surprising if some of them tend to behave like prima donnas. But, alas, alas, all this hard work and dedication has come to nothing. Silence from ITV means that 'star of screen' I shall never be, and that somewhere on the cutting room floor lies a career in tatters. Pride goes before a fall. Perhaps a DVD will be the only record of a great acting performance!

24

Reflections

In May 2007 we spend a weekend in Scotland during the local elections which end in something like chaos. Because of the complexities of the ballot papers, and the introduction of unsupervised postal voting, some 140,000 votes are invalid and goodness knows what chicanery has occurred in collecting the postal votes. It is a good example of leaving things alone unless there is serious need for change. It makes us look like a Third World banana republic. In the old days there had to be a good reason for having a postal vote and voting was the simple exercise of putting a cross on a ballot paper at a polling station. Apart from in Northern Ireland ('vote early and vote often'), there was little complaint about the present system and no suggestion of vote rigging. Now that agents go and collect ballot papers, it is no surprise that dishonesty has surfaced. The astonishing thing is that anyone should be surprised that it happens. Whether there will a number of election petitions, who knows, but if I were a voter whose vote was judged invalid, I should be kicking up a great stink. It is of great importance in Scotland, because the SNP presently have one more seat than Labour and will try to form a government.

Meanwhile in England, Labour do badly, and the Conservatives quite well. The legacy of Blair plays some part. Dustbin collection, now a major factor in our overhyped environmental world, is a strong local issue. Why councils think families with small children can cope with a two-week collection beggars description. People would mind less if council officials were not so bossy about waste. Lack of money from central government and the nanny state are to blame.

Blair has finally announced that he is going. He will of course be remembered for Iraq but for me, as I expect for others, it is the disappointment of opportunities lost and the triumph of spin over substance. It is easy now to forget the excitement of 'education, education, education' and to compare it with the dire evidence of failure of many state schools. And attempts at social engineering at universities has happily been rejected, in spite of the lamentable intervention by Brown on one memorable occasion. Is the NHS better, given the billions which have been poured into it? Crime has risen inexorably, to which the Government's response is to suggest reducing the tariff for burglars. I fear too that the introduction of a Minister of Justice who will be in charge of the judges will spell the end of judicial independence. What ambitious politician, probably a failed lawyer, will be able to resist for long the opportunity to tell the judges what to do? The Lord Chancellor may have worn any number of hats but the judges' position was safe in his hands. But it's the spin and the grubbiness of much that was done that will remain as the chief legacy of this administration. The words 'The Dome', 'Ecclestone', 'peerages', 'WMD', 'asylum seekers' and 'Campbell' sum up a great deal of how history will record the events of the Blair Government. Meanwhile I must turn to my books and prepare myself for my master's degree at LSE on International Relations in October 2007. There history has already given its verdict.

Life at LSE could not be more different from Oxford. I am doing three subjects which tend to overlap but are essentially about international relations from 1914 until Vietnam. So much of the period through which I have lived is now taught as History. There are no lectures but we have seminars every week in which one of the students does a presentation and then we all contribute to the following discussion. Because most of the students are from overseas (I interpose, cynically, that they can be charged more than English students), there are a wide variety of differing views. Professor Stevenson is in charge of us. He is a very impressive teacher, allows everyone to have their say, and points out the inadequacies of some of our answers with charm and sympathy. For a number of the students life is not very easy. One Chinese girl confessed that she took an hour to read ten pages of a particular book and was in tears. I wondered how she had managed to be accepted. Another Chinese student electrified us in a discussion about Vietnam by revealing that his grandfather (or was it his great grandfather?) had been an active member of the Viet Cong and describing their activities. And when the subject of Palestine came to be discussed, which generated a lot of heat among the class, I upset a number of them by giving them my experience of what it had really been like there when I was in the Navy. One agreeable American student told me that he had taken *Benchmark* out of the LSE library and had been much entertained by it. The other dons, like those at Oxford, rightly paid no regard to reputation or status and once again, I received a number of criticisms about answering the question. One don in particular seemed to confuse style with substance and I was reproved for spelling Pearl Harbour in the English fashion and not Pearl Harbor in the American.

I decided not to do my dissertation on the whole subject of Munich and confine it to the responsibility of the French, which had Professor Stevenson's blessing. It was a useful exercise as a template for a book I want to write on the whole subject. In 2008, I managed to get the equivalent of a 2:1 in my master's degree and decided that enough was enough. A doctorate would involve four years' work and I would rather potter away at Munich. But the LSE was a most agreeable experience and I like to think that I contributed as much as I received.

In August 2007 I reach the age of eighty, still in comparative control of my marbles. Gladstone, in equally difficult and anxious days, was Prime Minister again at that age. Now that there is an Age Discrimination Act, perhaps we shall return to the days when experience and judgement are regarded as assets and the cult of ignorant youth is no longer accorded prime position in our society. To celebrate, Liz organises a wonderful party for me and all my family at Cliveden, where we spend two nights in spoiling luxury. The clan that gathers there together consists of the four boys, their wives, thirteen grandchildren, two grannies and my sister-in-law and husband. We go on a riverboat for one evening, organised by the children, with pop music of my generation. Next day there is tennis, squash and swimming for some, while others go to the health spa and have beauty treatments – but not me, as no need.

I received a splendid collection of presents, most thoughtfully chosen, and enjoyed a montage of old family pictures, collected from many and varied sources. We sat down, some twenty-seven, to a superb dinner in Cliveden's French dining room, again all organised superbly by Liz. Nigel made a most entertaining speech, in rhyming couplets but the highlight of the occasion was that I asked Liz to marry me and she accepted. The children and grandchildren were greatly excited and, as they have been over the past four years, delighted to welcome her as part of the family.

For me, of course, it is the most wonderful present that I could have. How this young, beautiful, intelligent High Court judge could want to be attached to me for the rest of our lives (in my case perhaps for not so very long) is difficult to believe but there is no accounting for taste. I regard myself as a very lucky man. The announcement of the engagement in *The Times* gave rise to a small problem. Liz emailed them the notice 'Sir Oliver Popplewell and Dame Elizabeth Gloster are engaged to be married'. We thought the usual notice 'the engagement is announced between' and the details of parents and their addresses rather pompous. The next day we were told by *The Times* that there had to be a slight amendment. My reaction, to the suggestion of some amendment, was to enquire who it was I was now to be engaged to. The problem was that it was 'policy' to have the formal notice and that the editor would have to be consulted if we insisted on any amendment. So the editor, who no doubt was busy deciding on the leading article for the following day, was required to adjudicate on this monumentally trivial problem. He decided in our favour. Thus we now look forward to many years of happy married life.

25

Marriage

The next excitement in our lives was to celebrate my eightieth birthday with my friends. We had thought of having a dinner in a marquee at Lime Tree, which would have been nostalgic and an opportunity for daughter-in-law Clare to show off her lovely garden. But on reflection we decided against it. The dinner would be in the evening and no-one would see the garden – and what if it rained? Secondly, the logistics of finding accommodation for many of our friends coming from all parts of the country was an insuperable nightmare. So we decided to have the party in the Long Room at Lord's, where all the catering would be well organised and we should have no anxiety about the evening's success. The room itself is the most elegant place for a party with a fine view of the ground and of the media centre. The pictures on the wall reflect cricket icons and matches over the decades, if not the centuries. Some years ago the Long Room was handsomely redecorated. The Arts and Library Committee reorganised our wonderful collection of cricket pictures and memorabilia, creating an exhibition unrivalled anywhere. Dream on, Melbourne Cricket Club.

Liz had organised magnificent, skyscraper-like flower decorations on the tables, Andrew made a friendly witty speech, and the score-board was lit up with the words 'Lucky old Pop – time for a second new ball'. This was the least vulgar of a number of increasingly wicked suggestions which the family (i.e. Nigel) had thought up, but, for those with the right sense of humour, it provided a certain amount of amusement. And it is always exciting to see one's name in lights.

One party over, we then had to turn our attention to the wedding itself. We fixed the day as 15 March to suit Liz's judicial programme. It also coincided with the Easter vacation at the LSE. People constantly reminded us that this was in Lent and that the Ides of March might not be a very propitious day for a wedding, but we ignored the soothsayers of doom and went ahead. We were both very keen to get married in the Temple Church and so we approached Robin Griffiths Jones, the Master of the Temple, to see if the church were available and whether he would be able to conduct the service. He could not have been more generous-spirited. Liz had been divorced but if we had a civil ceremony first at a registry office, he would be only too happy to have a full service of Blessing for us in church.

The Inner Temple was licensed as a registry office for civil weddings, so that posed no problem. But obtaining the State's sanction to marry, involved struggling with yards of red tape. First we both had to go to the Aylesbury Registry Office, armed with various documents to prove (in triplicate) that we were who we said we were, and that we were not about to enter into a bigamous marriage. By the time they had taken us through the full routine and I had given my date of birth at least four times, and had to guess at that of my intended bride, one felt it might have been quicker to have organised a full Nuptial Mass in the Sistine Chapel, with the Pope officiating. But the most special thing about this experience was the three Jack Vettriano prints on the wall. We were told by the two charming lady registrars, bursting with politically correct pride, that they had replaced the previous, olden-days picture of a romanticised bride and groom with these prints, in order to reflect each of the three different relationships which they had to 'regularise' by the civil ceremony of marriage or civil partnership. The man and the woman dancing seemed fairly obvious, but one was slightly puzzled by the message that the picture of three girls in party frocks was meant to convey, and still more so by the picture of a clutch of manifestly heterosexual men smoking cigarettes on a beach. It was perhaps not kind of Liz at this stage to ask whether the prints were compliant with the council's anti-smoking policy.

After getting the banns published, it was necessary for me go to Islington Town Hall to see the registrar who has jurisdiction over the

Inner Temple. We arranged for the civil service to take place at 12 noon followed by a family lunch in the Inner Temple, with the church service at 2.30. The only hiccup in the arrangements was that we had hoped to have the reception in the Inner Temple but, because there was to be a children's Easter Egg Hunt on the Sunday, they needed the Hall on the Saturday for preparation. Liz, who is also a member of Lincoln's Inn, solved that problem by booking Lincoln's Inn Hall.

I was responsible for organising the honeymoon, which had to be done secretly because Liz did not want to know where we going. My first thoughts were to go to St Petersburg and Vienna, neither of which Liz had visited. On second thoughts, neither seemed a very good bet in the middle of March, although the idea of going to two different places still appealed. It seemed to me that we should go first somewhere for comfort and culture and after that to find sunshine and enjoy a bit of sightseeing. We did not want to go to the Caribbean: we did not want to spend twenty-four hours flying one way and twenty-four hours flying back; nor did we want to sit on a beach all day. One of the problems was that Liz never travels without an appreciable amount of luggage (all very necessary, I am sure), but without her knowing whether to take a fur coat or smart beachwear, the chances were that there would be a surplus suitcase or two. In the end, she simply made an intelligent guess (or two or three), but we still seemed to travel with quite a number of suitcases.

The next problem was the question of bridesmaids and pages. I have thirteen grandchildren – seven girls and six boys. They range from age four to nineteen. And were any of them, and if so who, to play some music at the wedding, to sing a solo or to read a lesson? Happily the matter was readily solved. Three of Alexander's children, Millie, Nellie and Livia, were to be bridesmaids with Robin, Ed's youngest, as a page. Leo, Ed's second son, was to sing a solo. Lulu, Andrew's second daughter, was to play the piano before the beginning of the service, while her brother Fred was to read one of the lessons.

We had a number of discussions with Robin Griffiths Jones and with James Vivian, who is in charge of the music at the Temple Church, and agreed the hymns, Leo's solo, and the anthem to be sung by the Temple Singers. Liz asked our old friend Tim Bergqvist to give her away and I asked Richard Davis, whom I had first met at Winchester House School in 1937, to be my best man. We sent out well over four hundred invitations (at our age we have a great number of friends) and had acceptances from about three hundred and fifty.

On one weekend we went for the day to Calais where we not only bought quantities of champagne, but had an exceedingly good lunch on the quayside. Both Inner Temple and Lincoln's Inn were generous about charging corkage and helpful about all the arrangements. Liz had many happy hours trying on various outfits to which I was not privy, but she did organise me to have a new waist-coat to go with my morning suit, in which I had first been married over fifty years ago.

Liz had a hen party at Boodles, kindly hosted by Tim Bergqvist, which seems to have been a riotous occasion, while I had a much more sober stag night at the Garrick. Alexander took Nigel and me out to breakfast at the Wolseley on the morning of the wedding while the girls were busy making themselves ready. My niece, Nicola, came over from the States for the wedding and we also had friends from South Africa, Bermuda,

15 Wedding day in Inner Temple

Slovenia, Switzerland, Germany, France, Wales, Ireland, and a large contingent from Scotland.

The civil service was movingly conducted by the efficient registrar and her assistant. We had to reaffirm that we were not going through a bigamous exercise but it was all done with considerable dignity. Liz looked stunning in French blue with a matching Jackie Kennedy pill-box hat and managed a quiet weep in the middle of the service, all due to happiness and emotion. We then had a drink or two and a large lunch. Liz went off to change again after a series of photographs and the bridegroom's party then proceeded to the church. The *Daily Mail* couldn't, of course, miss an opportunity to be troublesome, by sending along a photographer, uninvited to what was essentially a private function, on private property. He was, I believe, magnificently seen off by Robin.

At the dress rehearsal, Liz had had the foresight to put on her Jimmy Choo wedding shoes, with high heels, to see how they would feel, but she got the heel caught in the grating in the nave leading up to the altar. As there were half a dozen such gratings, it was necessary, both going up the aisle and coming down, to take a somewhat circuitous route. Tim managed to get her up the aisle (on time!), slaloming the grates, to the tune of 'Immortal, Invisible', after Lulu had played 'Somewhere over the Rainbow' most beautifully. We thought afterwards that 'Nothing like a dame' would perhaps have been more appropriate, given Liz's judicial nomenclature. The bridesmaids and page looked adorable and (contrary to grandpaternal expectation) behaved immaculately, even though, unknown to us all, Livia was sickening for chicken pox and broke out in a horrific rash the following Saturday. After the marriage vows, we sang 'Lord of all Hopefulness' and then Vicky Vernon read the first lesson from St John with much feeling.

This was followed by twelve-year-old Leo singing Handel's 'Where e'er you walk', which he did with such composure and aplomb as to move many of the congregation to tears. It was the performance of a lifetime. Poor Fred, who was to read the second lesson, was struck down by flu but bravely came to the service. In his place, Anna did the reading – a passage from Shakespeare's *Julius Caesar* with professional skill. This was followed by an anthem from the Temple Singers and the robust singing of the 'Battle Hymn of the Republic', with a descant composed especially for the occasion by James Vivian. Robin

16 Wedding day in Temple Church

conducted what was a joyous, old-fashioned service with much dignity and good humour. Sadly some of our friends from Bucks got caught up in road works, traffic jams and a demonstration march, and they missed the service.

The reception at Lincoln's Inn was superbly arranged by the staff there, with the Great Hall decked out with huge flower arrangements in white and blue. There were so many friends that it was impossible to talk to them all. Suddenly I was making a speech of short duration and Richard proposed our health and that of the bridesmaids. We had insisted that we were to have none of 'I remember Oliver as a small boy when he....'. Far too revealing for comfort. I did, however, have one appropriate story which Anthony Jefferson had told me some months before. A young clergyman conducting a wedding service forgot the name of the groom. Extemporising wildly, he turned to the groom and said, 'In whose name do you present yourself at this wedding?' The groom had not prepared himself at the rehearsal for this question and, in much confusion, replied, 'In the name of the Father, Son and Holy Ghost.'

Then it was time to cut the cake and we were changing to go away. Liz's wedding dress was sensational but she looked even more terrific in her shocking pink silk coat, Cossack boots and sable hat, as we went away. She still didn't know where we were going either that night or on the honeymoon. I had observed jokingly in my speech that we had had to cancel a Saga holiday to the Isle of Wight because she was too young to qualify for the discount. There was also mischievous talk of a coach trip to Bridlington!

When we passed Victoria Coach Station in the car she breathed a sigh of relief and did the same when we passed Heathrow because that meant we were not flying long distance overnight, nor staying at an airport hotel. Eventually, we arrived at the Vineyard Hotel near Newbury, which I had picked out of *Decanter Magazine* as having a good cellar. In fact, it turned out to be a two-star Michelin Hotel and we had a sensational dinner which did full justice to those stars. The owner came to our table and, when he learnt that we were on our honeymoon, sent up a bottle of champagne to our room. Next morning we set off for Heathrow. Liz still didn't know where we were going. Was it Helsinki? Rome? Perhaps even Zagreb? They all appeared on the departure screen. I had wandered off to buy some books, leaving Liz for a brief moment, on her own. She became very worried because the flight to Moscow had been called, and she was, by now, certain we were going there. Where was I? Panic was soon over and we went to one of the gates for passengers going either to Berlin or Madrid. Soon the secret was out and to Madrid we went.

We stayed at a small, comfortable hotel, in an old palace, with literary connections. Our bedroom had a large balcony, on which was a sunken jacuzzi. We tried it out and decided it needed some bath gel. By mistake, I poured some shampoo in instead, with the result that the foam poured over the sides of the jacuzzi and threatened to flood the room below. We had two visits to the Thyssen collection, now much enlarged by pictures belonging to the Baron's wife, including a splendid collection of Impressionists and seventeenth-century Dutch pictures. It is rather a sad story, because the collection could have had a permanent home in London if the British authorities had been more forthcoming. The Prado, by contrast, has (for my taste at any rate) too many indifferent pictures, so that finding those that I wanted to see and enjoy was a time-consuming process. But Liz had never visited it before and was impressed by the sheer splendour of it all. We ate extremely well with one or two exceptions, though, after a while, even suckling pig loses its novelty. We sorted out the underground. We visited the Royal Palace and had lunch in the beautiful Plaza Mayor. We took a coach out to El Escorial, Philip II's palace, built at the height of his powers and finished shortly before the Armada. The library, at one time containing some 40,000 books and manuscripts, is enormously impressive. There are rather austere royal apartments and chapterhouses for the monastery's monks. Somewhat ghoulish are the Pantheons where Charles V and other royals are laid to rest. Remarkably, the bus journey, which took over an hour, cost something like four euros each.

I had promised Liz an afternoon of retail therapy at my expense. She had studied the guide book and knew exactly where she was going to go and what she was going to buy. We decided to go to Toledo on the Thursday and shop on the Friday. We were then told, but only on the Thursday, that, perhaps not surprisingly, shops were shut on Good Friday. So we decided to stay in Madrid and shop, only to be told that the shops were also shut on Maundy Thursday. So, alas, no retail therapy at all. Liz has a suspicion that I did it deliberately but I plead not guilty.

We still went to Toledo but our trip got off to a bad start. We decided to go by train only to discover that because it was a holiday, all the tickets had been pre-sold. There was nothing for it but to take a cab which we did. Toledo was swarming with people. The Alcazar was shut for repairs and the Cathedral could only be visited if you belonged to a coach party. No amount of stamping our little feet produced a change of heart by the guardians at the gate. But we did see the pilgrimage procession leaving the Cathedral, surrounded by vast numbers of worshippers and TV cameras. We wandered gently through the narrow and very crowded lanes, admiring the locally made knives of all sizes and shapes for which Toledo is famous. But I had to draw the line at Liz's enthusiasm to buy a cross-bow to take back to England for my most warlike of grandchildren, Bubble. A delicious lunch outdoors in the sunshine added to our pleasures as did some marzipan biscuits. We found a bus to take us back and had a cheerful and inexpensive journey home.

We had enjoyed our week in Madrid. The weather was warm and sunny, we had seen lots of interesting pictures, admired the grandeur and charm of the City and eaten exceedingly well. It was now time to move on. Liz didn't know where our next port of call was to be and, until we went to the gate for Marrakech at Madrid Airport, still had no idea.

Shortly after I had booked our trip to Marrakech, it so happened that Jill Husselby, a friend from my days in Birmingham, rang up and asked if we would like to join them for a few days in Marrakech, where they had taken a villa with friends. This was about three weeks before we were due to go there. Liz was enormously enthusiastic but I had to make deprecating noises about a few days being not long enough, promising that one day I would certainly take her there. Luckily she did not pick up the scent but it had been a tricky moment.

I had booked for us to stay at the Sofitel. However, when we arrived at the airport I could not remember the hotel's name and had only the telephone number, so Liz had to ring up on her mobile and find out who they were and whether we were indeed booked in. The Marmounia is Marrakech's most famous hotel because of its association with Churchill, but when I had stayed there before I thought it rather over the top; in any case it was now going through a major reconstruction and closed. The Sofitel, though equally large, was French run, had staff who exuded charm and courtesy and provided us with much comfort for a week. We did all the tourist things, wandered round the Medina, visited all the souks, bought spices and soaps, drank mint tea and lounged in the pool. In between, we both did some work, me revising for exams later in the summer and Liz catching up on a judgement.

After managing to visit most of the sights in the Medina we hired a car to go out to Essaouira which is a three-hour drive to the coast. It was a very boring but quite lazy drive, through sprawling suburbia at the beginning, and then through endless charmless villages and unkempt landscape. As we neared Essaouira I became increasingly impatient with slow moving traffic. The Moroccans drive on the basis that other drivers will always give way, so overtaking and being overtaken is a nightmare. When I finally hooted at a taxi, occupying the centre of the road and started to overtake, I received an arm signal indicating some form of dissent. When we reached the next stretch of road, I was confronted by two policemen with a hand-held radar gun who stopped us. He asked for my papers and informed me I had been doing 95 km per hour when the limit was 80. He then asked me for my occupation. I thought 'retired' sounded better than 'student'. But then he wanted to know what I had done before I had retired. When I told him that I had been a judge, I expected a homily on how I, as a judge (even retired) of all people, should know better than to break the law. Instead he was charm itself. In perfect English he wished us a happy holiday and we went cheerfully on our way. Would the speed cops in England have behaved so courteously to an eighty year-old Moroccan judge even if they could understand the language?

We found a splendid place for lunch on the beach in the sunshine and then had an exhilarating swim in the sea. We wandered round the old town only to discover that I had lost my French credit card on the beach. This I needed, because I had arranged to stock up my account with euros before going on honeymoon and I wasn't sure that my other cards would bear the cost of the hotel bills and other expenses. So we decided to return to our hotel and sort that out. We were still an hour out of Marrakech when darkness fell, and negotiating thrusting buses, unlit cyclists, donkeys and frenetic taxis was something of a nightmare. Liz was superb in finding the way back to the hotel. On reflection, it would have been better to have arranged to spend a night in Essaioura. It would have enabled us to see more of the attractive town and to have avoided the hazards of too much driving particularly in the dark. We also thought of driving out to the mountains, where I had been before, but there really wasn't time and we should have had to spend nights away. Perhaps another time.

We ate very well in lovely restaurants, mostly in riads, which are old palaces, in the Medina. To reach them involved taking a taxi and then being escorted through narrow lanes by a watchman, carrying a lantern, until we arrived at the beautifully designed, but unmarked door, of the restaurant. French, Italian and Moroccan menus were entrancing. Liz brought back spices from the souk and a book on Moroccan cooking in the confident expectation that I would create some marvellous tajine suitable for consumption in Bucks. Then it was time to return home, Liz to start a five-month criminal trial and, for me, revision and the preparation of a dissertation.

When I look back over the last few years, I marvel at how lucky I have been to enjoy three exciting years at Oxford where I had the opportunity of meeting so many interesting and intelligent people, not only among the dons (who were stars) but also among my fellow undergraduates. Don't let anyone denigrate the modern generation or suggest that Oxford was in some way class-conscious. It was certainly elitist in the quality of education. I hope it will continue to be elitist in that sense, by choosing students who, intellectually, can contribute to the Oxford ethos, from whatever background or country they came. And, dare I say, in this politically correct society in which we live, that the admission of a few more distinguished sportsmen (particularly cricketers like May and Cowdrey) would do wonders for the prestige of the University.

Finally, and most importantly, throughout these years I have been so lucky to have beautiful and intelligent Liz as my constant companion, sharing in all these happy events.

> There is a tide in the affairs of men,
> Which taken at the flood, leads on to fortune;
> Omitted, all the voyage of their life
> Is bound in shallows and in miseries.
> On such a full sea are we now afloat;
> And we must take the current when it serves,
> Or lose our ventures.

Julius Caesar. Act 4. Scene 3. 216

INDEX